D0907061

Studies of the New Testament and its world

EDITED BY JOHN RICHES

The Purpose of Luke — Acts

by

ROBERT MADDOX

edited by

JOHN RICHES

T. & T. CLARK
36 GEORGE STREET
EDINBURGH

Printed with permission of Vandenhoek and Ruprecht, Göttingen. Originally published in Forschungen zur Religion und Literatur des Atlen und Neuen Testaments

Printed by Billing & Sons, Worcester,
bound by Hunter & Foulis, Edinburgh
for
T. & T. Clark Ltd, Edinburgh

ISBN 0 567 09312 3

First printed 1982
Reprinted 1985

Contents

Foreword

Most of the work on this book was done during a period of study-leave granted by the United Theological College in Sydney, and spent at the Protestant Theological Faculty of the University of Munich in 1978. My stay in Germany was made possible by a research-fellowship provided by the Alexander von Humboldt Foundation, of Bonn. My warmest thanks are due to the Foundation and its officers, not only for this financial support but also for their hospitality on a number of occasions and their continuing helpfulness. The Foundation has also provided a subsidy for the publication of this book.

Next I wish to thank my academic host in Munich, Professor Ferdinand Hahn, for his generous personal assistance, encouragement and friendship. He found time to read the whole manuscript in its various stages, and to spend many hours discussing various parts of it with me. He also provided me with excellent facilities for getting the work done.

I acknowledge with gratitude the liberality of the New Testament editor of FRLANT, Professor Wolfgang Schrage, and the publisher, Dr Arndt Ruprecht, in finding a place for a foreigner's contribution in a venerable German series. Professor Schrage has also kindly given me a number of suggestions, which I have gladly incorporated into the book.

Without the untiring enthusiasm and hard work of my wife, who has compiled the bibliography and indexes, the final completion of the manuscript for printing might well have been indefinitely delayed. For their competent work in typing the manuscript I thank Brigitte Huber of the University of Munich, Betty Dunne of Sydney University, Gwen Morris of Macquarie University, and Anne Cameron of UTC.

Robert Maddox,
United Theological College,
Enfield, NSW, Australia.

Pentecost, 1980.

1. The Unity and Structure of Luke–Acts and the Question of 'Purpose'

1 The Question of 'Purpose'

How much 'purpose' did Luke need, when setting out to write his work? And what advantage shall we expect to derive, supposing we are able to define what that purpose was?

One of the great pioneers of modern Lucan studies, H. J. Cadbury, explicitly played down the significance of the first question. He saw Luke's motive as provided mostly by his material, his personality and his opportunity: like many another gifted writer, he simply felt within himself the urge to self-expression on a subject that interested him.[1] All the same, Cadbury proceeded to suggest what seemed to him the chief purposes reflected by Luke–Acts: the demonstration of 'divine intervention' as 'one of the credentials of the Christian movement'; and the demonstration of 'the legitimacy of Christianity from both the Jewish and the Gentile point of view'. The latter point is then developed at some length, concentrating on the specific argument that Luke aimed to establish the political innocence of Christianity with respect to the Roman empire.[2]

Cadbury was by no means the first to raise the question of Luke's purpose. It was actively canvassed in the nineteenth century, and has again been vigorously discussed over the last twenty-five years.[3] I begin with him simply in order to show that even a scholar who was sceptical about the significance of the question nevertheless pursued it and expressed a judgement on it. Since Cadbury's work was written, we have become aware, especially through the development of the form-critical and redaction-critical approaches to the books of the New Testament, of two factors which make the question of Luke's purpose seem much more important than Cadbury allowed. First, we must take proper account of the influence exerted by the on-going life of the church on the writing of the New Testament books, especially the gospels. Although each book is ultimately the product of a single author, with his own distinctive aim and plan, we find it more natural today to say, with C. K. Barrett, that 'the Church in Luke's day had reached a point at which a variety of considerations . . . called for the sort of book Luke wrote'[4] than to mention only motives of individual authorship. Second, the main thrust of studies on the gospels over the last quarter-century has been to establish the fact that the gospels, all four of them, are deliberate works of theology, in which even quite small details of wording may often be seen to have theological significance.[5] A student of the gospels today could hardly say, with

Cadbury, that '(Luke's) changes in Mark . . . are compatible with such quite minor purposes as the improvement of style'.[6]

Here, then, are some initial clues as to what we are looking for in inquiring into the purpose of Luke–Acts. We may presume that Luke lived within some particular situation in the life of the church, and that a significant part of his purpose was to contribute to objectives, or help to meet challenges, that were important to the whole church, or more particularly to those church-circles within which Luke lived, in his own day. One major task of our investigation must therefore be to uncover, so far as possible, what Luke's circumstances were. Since the information available from outside is slight and of disputable value, we are forced to rely, virtually completely, on what can be detected from the work itself.[7]

Moreover, the large and fruitful work that has been done in recent years on Luke's theology suggests that Luke's purpose had a dimension which can properly be called theological.[8] That is, it is unlikely to be enough simply to look into questions of ecclesiastical politics, whether by that we mean the relationship of groups within the church, or the relationship of the Christians as a whole to specific groups outside. And while it is true, as a number of recent interpreters have emphasized, that some of Luke's concerns may be described as 'pastoral',[9] this must not be taken to mean that Luke has an eye only to practical matters, and is uninterested in questions of fundamental principle.

On the other hand, the present study does not undertake to give a complete description of Lucan theology.[10] There are several large topics, important in themselves, on which little will be said in the following pages: for example, Christology, soteriology, ethics, and even pneumatology. As several scholars have recognized, the really burning theological issues for Luke, and therefore those which are likely to point us to his situation and his purpose in writing his work, are ecclesiology and eschatology.[11] Luke appears to be raising with some urgency such questions as, Who are the Christians? Where do they come from, historically and culturally speaking? What is their vocation? What justification do they have for their existence as a self-conscious, distinctive group? And what is their historical situation, not merely in relation to their immediate cultural environment (Judaism and the Roman empire), but in relation to God's whole dealings with the world?

To inquire into Luke's purpose in writing is, essentially, to ask why Luke raised such questions, what he meant by them, and what sort of answers he gave to them. If we can explain this, with some degree of precision, the first and most obvious benefit will be that valuable light will be shed on the meaning of Luke and Acts, not only in their totality but in many of their details. Furthermore, however, any positive results we can obtain will be indirectly a contribution to understanding the history of the church in the first century. Between the death of Paul in the early 60's and the writing of Revelation and 1 Clement in the mid-90's AD we have a famous dark patch of early Christian history. Within this period, as most scholars agree, the four gospels and Acts were written, and though none of them describes it, they may nevertheless provide some hints of contemporary events and developments. Luke–Acts, being by far the longest of these works, may well be looked to to provide some such hints. Finally, any solid discoveries we can make about Luke's purpose will help to inform and discipline our use of Luke–Acts for the practical needs and interests of the church in our own time.

2 The Unity of Luke–Acts

By phrasing the subject of our inquiry as 'the purpose of Luke–Acts', we imply that the two volumes are indeed a single work, which therefore can be regarded as sharing a common purpose. The claim that this is so was insisted on, in a number of publications, by H. J. Cadbury, to whom we owe the coining of the double title 'Luke–Acts'.[12] Today most workers in this field accept it as proven; and one recent, major review of the history of Lucan studies actually concludes that 'the primary gain of the recent criticism of Luke–Acts has been the recognition that the Gospel according to Luke and the Book of Acts are really two volumes of one work, which must be considered together'.[13] Yet the point is from time to time denied;[14] and therefore, so that our further inquiry may be placed on a secure foundation, we must consider briefly what is at stake here.

There are three levels at which the literary relationship of Luke and Acts has been viewed. First, they have a unity in the sense of both having been written by the same author. This conclusion is overwhelmingly probable, on grounds of language, theology, and the ancient tradition about authorship. The last serious attempt to argue otherwise, as far as I know, was in 1933.[15] We may therefore take this first level of relationship as established. On the other hand, a minority opinion has been put forward occasionally, that Luke–Acts was originally a single volume, which was later divided by an editor, perhaps in connexion with its acceptance into the New Testament Canon, the first part being cut off to be matched with the other three 'gospels'.[16] On the latter point, E. Haenchen made the decisive criticism, that acceptance into the Canon was not a decision made on a specific occasion by a committee, which could order a revised edition of an existing book and call all earlier copies out of circulation: there is no evidence for the existence of the alleged single volume, and no convincing occasion for its division and supersession has yet been suggested.[17] Moreover, the theory requires an appeal to hypothetical literary reconstructions on which there can be little agreement; and there is in the first place no compelling need for the theory. It is much more probable that the two volumes were originally composed much as we now have them, each beginning with a dedicatory preface addressed to Theophilus, and overlapping through the repeated narration of the Ascension.

We have, therefore, two volumes by the same author, sharing certain features in common, such as the address to Theophilus and the fact that one continues the story begun in the other. Is the connexion any closer than that? The possibilities seem to be three: (1) Luke planned the whole work as a unity, though in two volumes; (2) Luke wrote a work in the genre 'gospel', in which his scope, materials and aim were largely determined by the work of his predecessors (Luke 1:1–4), and only subsequently decided to add another volume (Acts 1:1); (3) Acts was written first, the dedicatory sentence, harking back to the Gospel as the 'previous volume', being a later addition.[18]

Only if the first of these is true can we speak confidently of 'the purpose of Luke–Acts'. It is indeed conceivable that, even if the author planned his two volumes at different times, without any immediate connexion, he was nevertheless pursuing the same program: but in that case we would have to be all the more careful about interpreting themes that seem to recur in both volumes: we would have to bear constantly in mind the possibility that the author's intention was different in each case.

Argument on this point has hinged mainly on three questions: (1) Does the preface in Luke 1:1–4 introduce both volumes, or only the Gospel? (2) What relative dates of composition are likely for the two volumes? Are there good reasons for thinking that they were composed some time apart? (3) Is there a discernible difference of outlook between them on any major topics?

Concerning the preface, two points call for attention here. First, it was emphasized by H. J. Cadbury that the opening verse of Acts is naturally taken as a recapitulatory preface of just such a kind as was frequently used in the Graeco-Roman world for the second or subsequent volume of a multi-volume work.[19] Probably the closest illustrative parallel to the case of Luke–Acts, in both style and date, is the pair of prefaces to the two volumes of Josephus' *Against Apion*.[20] We have therefore amply adequate evidence that if Luke intended the preface Luke 1:1–4 to look forward to the whole work, with a brief resumption in Acts 1:1, he was using a literary convention of his time. The objection to this view raised by H. Conzelmann, E. Haenchen and H. W. Bartsch is surprising, and certainly inadequately argued by all three, in view of the evidence in its favour.[21] The existence of this convention for multi-volume works is, however, still not conclusive evidence that Luke planned the whole two volumes as a unity from the beginning. For prefaces of that kind were also used for single-volume works, and Luke may conceivably have added volume two subsequently, without its having been part of the original plan. Therefore we must turn to the second point. Cadbury's lexicographical study of Luke 1:1–4 showed that παρακολουθεῖν in v.3 cannot refer to historical research but must mean either 'to keep informed about current events' or 'to participate' in them.[22] This conclusion has never been refuted;[23] but many commentators have refused to accept it for this context, because Luke says explicitly in v.2 that information had been handed down to him by those who 'from the beginning were eye-witnesses and became servants of the Word'. Luke thus marks himself as belonging to a later time, and cannot have been a participant in all things from the beginning. Cadbury also showed, however, that ἄνωθεν often means 'for some time past' and not necessarily 'from the beginning'.[24] Cadbury's own explanation of the relation between v.2 and 3 was rather confused, and no doubt this is why his lexicographical conclusions have been so widely disregarded. But the correct solution was pointed out shortly afterwards by J. H. Ropes, building on Cadbury's work.[25] The 'we'-sections of Acts, whatever their historical basis, cannot reasonably be taken otherwise than as a claim by the author to have participated personally in at least part of the mission and later career of Paul. V.3 therefore, when taken as strict lexicography requires, cannot apply to the Gospel of Luke, but can very well refer to part of the story of Acts; v.2, on the other hand, certainly refers to the Gospel, and no doubt to the earlier sections of Acts.

Thus the preface, taken with its recapitulatory counterpart in Acts 1:1, gives us two good reasons for understanding Luke–Acts as a unified work in two volumes. But we can confirm this conclusion from the body of the work also. We can leave aside for this purpose such a major theme as the role of the Apostles as witnesses, which is important in both volumes, for that may represent an ecclesiological conviction of the author's but not necessarily be an indication of structural unity between the two books.[26] More significant is the fact that the mission of Jesus begins with a scene in which the rejection of the message of salvation by the Jews and its acceptance by the Gentiles is anticipated, and the mission of Paul ends with a scene in which this is declared to be an established fact (Luke 4:16–30; Acts 28:17–28). This looks like a deliberate, structural element. It has often been observed that Luke omits certain details from Mark in his parallel passage in the Gospel, in order then to pick them up in a similar passage in Acts: of these the most important is the transference from Jesus to Stephen of the charge of claiming that Jesus would destroy the Temple (Mark 14:56–59/Acts 6:11–14), but there are also smaller details such as in Mark 5:40/Acts 9:40 and in Mark 14:2/Acts 12:4. This phenomenon suggested to H. G. Russell 'that Acts might actually have been written before Luke, for an author would be even more likely to omit what he had already used than what he was merely planning to use'.[27] This would be quite a good argument if the examples were more extensive and numerous: just such a case may be found within the Gospel of Luke, where Luke omits Mark 14:3–9 in view of the similar story already used at Luke 7:36–50. But in fact the only significant example is the charge used in the trial of Stephen, and this could be explained equally well on either theory of the order of composition. The same could be said about Luke 21:12–19 and 27: the description of the coming sufferings of the disciples may either anticipate or reflect the narrative of Acts, and the single cloud may either anticipate or reflect the narrative of the Ascension in Acts 1:9–11. Most important of all is the fact that Luke 24:47–49 explicitly looks forward to Acts and especially to Acts 1–2, and this has the effect that without Acts to follow the ending of Luke would be something of an anti-climax.

We may therefore conclude with confidence that the Gospel of Luke was written with Acts very much in mind: it was never intended to stand independently of its companion-volume. By far the simpler explanation of this is that the two-volume work was planned as a unity from the beginning. Whether there is any force in the alternative suggestion, that Acts was written first and that it was the Gospel which was something of an afterthought, will depend largely on our judgement concerning the date of composition, to which we shall come below. For the time being we can note that this theory suffers the disadvantage that it was for the Gospel rather than for Acts that Luke had literary precedent: it is easier to think of his making the innovation of extending the scope of a genre he inherited than of inventing a whole new one and then subsequently welding the new work on to another work in the older form. Moreover, Acts several times harks back to the gospel-story, and sometimes specifically to its Lucan formulation, e.g. Acts 1:2–5, 12–14; 10:37–43; 13:26–31; and this is again more naturally explained on the assumption that Acts was, as 1:1 says, written as a continuation of the Gospel.

If this is so, we may proceed the more safely to identify at many points a continuity of themes binding the two volumes together. The Apostles are a bridge linking the mission of Jesus with that of the church; the Gentiles have no direct access to Jesus during his earthly life, because that theme will be expounded in the second volume; and so on. These and other such topics will be explored in detail in the following chapters. But at the outset we can accept it as a reasonable starting-point that what we are looking for is 'the purpose of Luke–Acts' rather than separate purposes for two separate books. This is not to deny that Luke may have had more than a single purpose, or, to put it another way, that his overall purpose may have a variety of aspects. Especially if we can confirm the point after consideration of the date or dates of composition, we may affirm that it is a single work with which we are dealing.

3 The Author and the Date of Composition

(a) We do not know who 'Luke' is. There is a Luke mentioned as a companion of Paul's in the Pauline and deutero-Pauline epistles (Phlm. 24; Col. 4:14; 2 Tim. 4:11). These references are probably all to the same person, though even that is not certain, as the name is not uncommon,[28] and nowhere is he mentioned prominently enough for us to be sure that there was one person self-evidently meant by this name in the early church (as may be the case with the even commoner name Titus). In Col. 4:14 Luke is called 'the beloved physician', and ancient church-tradition, represented for us from the late second century onwards (the Muratorian Canon, Irenaeus, Clement of Alexandria, etc.),[29] identified this Luke with the author of our Luke–Acts. It is possible that this is a reliable tradition, but it is equally possible that ancient scholars did what modern ones have done, that is, to work from the 'we'-sections of Acts and the colleagues mentioned in Paul's epistles and settle on Luke by eliminating all other contenders. That can only be conclusive on the assumption that the preserved epistles give us a complete account of Paul's career and of his fellow-workers, which is most unlikely. A third possibility is that there was indeed a sound tradition which named the author as 'Luke', but that it was only later supposition which identified him with 'the beloved physician'. There may have been just as many Lukes as Johns in the early church! Some parts of early church-tradition (e.g. the Muratorian Canon) had no difficulty about identifying John the Apostle with the authorship of both the Fourth Gospel and the Revelation. In any case, the argument that the language of Luke–Acts has a medical colouring has never recovered from its demolition in H. J. Cadbury's doctoral thesis of 1913.[30]

The only fairly tangible point about the author's identity is the famous 'we'-sections. Some scholars in recent times have asserted that the 'we' must be fictitious, on the ground that the author's view of Paul's biography fits awkwardly beside the information given by Paul's own letters, and his view of Paul's theology perhaps even worse.[31] Against this, I find much more persuasive the judgement of A. D. Nock, who, out of a probably unsurpassed knowledge of Hellenistic and Roman literature, declared a fictitious 'we' of such a kind to be virtually unparalleled and most improbable for a writer who makes as much claim as Luke does to historiography. 'It may well be that the contacts of Luke and Paul were not long intimate; 'beloved' is a word which Paul used freely. If Luke failed to understand Paul's theology, he was not alone in that. Further, when with Paul, he had no literary plans . . . ; he was no Boswell. Nor was he a Thucydides, seeing promptly the significance of the Peloponnesian War and setting himself from its beginning to chronicle it. . . . It was some thirty years after the point where 'we' starts and it was when others had chronicled the things to do with Jesus, that Luke embarked on his two volume work'.[32] Some passages in Paul's letters (e.g. Phlm. 1, 23f.; Gal. 1:2) and in Acts (20:4f.) suggest that even on his travels Paul was sometimes attended by a sizable group, and it seems best to conclude that Luke had been from time to time in his youth a relatively junior member of this circle.

(b) The theoretically possible limits of the date of composition of Luke's work are quite wide, from two years after Paul's arrival in Rome, around 60 AD, to the first signs of literary dependence on Luke–Acts, probably in Ignatius and the Pastorals, around 110 AD.[33] Most scholars put the date around the 80's or 90's. The chief reasons for this are: (1) Mark is a major source of the Gospel of Luke, and Mark is definitely a second-generation Christian work: many scholars regard it as necessary to date Mark after the destruction of Jerusalem in 70 AD[34], but in any case we have to allow time for the evident development of oral tradition which underlies Mark, and we have such signs as that Simon of Cyrene, who was young enough to be able to carry Jesus' cross, is now better known through his children (Mark 15:21). Then we have to allow time for the circulation of Mark and for Luke to develop his plan of using it as the basis of a larger work. (2) As we have seen above, Luke may well have been a minor member of Paul's entourage, but that was clearly long before he wrote or even planned Acts. Luke's portrait of Paul is that of a heroic figure from a past time. (On this, see below, Chapter Three.) (3) Ephesus and its church play a fairly important part in Acts (though perhaps not as great as we might have expected from Paul's letters), yet the atmosphere is quite different from that portrayed in Revelation: it is therefore almost certain that Acts must be dated before the outbreak of Domitian's persecution. *A fortiori*, Acts does not belong in the reign of Trajan, when, as Pliny's correspondence with the Emperor shows, simply confessing to be a Christian was regarded as a crime.[35]

(c) These factors all make a date between the late 70's and the early 90's suitable, with some preference for the later end of the period.[36] We must however acknowledge some difficulties, which lead some scholars to assign either Acts alone or both volumes to the early 60's: (1) Acts neither narrates Paul's death nor (more seriously) hints at the Neronian persecution or sees any difficulty in Paul's appealing for justice to Nero (though the Emperor is not named). Good dramatic reasons can be suggested for Luke's omitting to describe Paul's death: that Paul did die in Rome is strongly enough foreshadowed earlier (Acts 20:22–25, 37f.; 21:10–14). But it is remarkable, especially if the author actually accompanied Paul to Rome ('we' in Acts 27:1–28:16), that no trace is found of the deep impression made in other early Christian traditions by Nero's persecution of the Roman church.[37] (2) Perhaps even more remarkably, Acts never mentions the destruction of Jerusalem, for which there would have been ample opportunity, especially in Acts 6–7 or 21–23. (3) Many who hold the unity of Luke–Acts, and believe the whole work was written before 70 AD, appeal to C. H. Dodd's view that Luke 21:20–24 as a variant of Mark 13:14–20 can be explained by Luke's use of various LXX passages, and therefore does not have to be understood as a prophecy phrased in the light of its fulfilment.[38] Of these arguments, (1) and (2) remain real puzzles for a dating of Acts after the events of 64 and 70 AD, but (3) seems to me to be a weak argument for a pre-70 date for Luke. Even if it be granted that Luke 21: 20–24 is explainable by the use of LXX without knowledge of the fulfilment of the prophecy, it would have to be asked why Luke broke off from following Mark at this point, in order to substitute alternative material. Moreover, this Lucan passage does not stand alone: just as important is 19:41–44, and the fall of Jerusalem is also almost certainly presupposed by 23:27–31 and 13:1–5 (,6–9).[39] Taken together, all these strongly suggest that Luke was written in the light of the events of 70 AD.

(d) But was Acts written earlier? Arguments (1) and (2) in the previous paragraph have to be weighed against the considerations mentioned in the quotation from A. D. Nock in paragraph (a) above as well as by those who feel that the character of Acts makes it impossible that Luke and Paul were ever personally associated. We can in fact admit any sort of association between Luke and Paul only at the cost of acknowledging a long gap of time between that association and the writing of the work in which it is mentioned.[40] Moreover, some scholars, far from putting the date of Acts before that of Luke, have argued on quite other grounds that it must be considerably later: e.g. J. C. Hawkins on grounds of language,[41] and S. G. Wilson on the ground that the theology (most particularly the eschatology) expressed in the two volumes is not as similar as has often been assumed, with Acts representing a later stage of development.[42] In my view, such phenomena can reasonably be explained, partly by the shift of subject-matter from volume one to volume two,[43] partly by the fact that, as far as we can tell, Luke was less directly controlled by the use of written sources in Acts than in the Gospel. In fact, much of our discussion in the following chapters will be concerned with showing the high degree to which Luke's ideas and convictions flow through consistently in the entire work. We do not need to enter into unprovable hypotheses about the length of time it may have taken him to write from start to finish. More important is our contention that, on the one hand, the arguments for a date in the 80's or early 90's for both volumes far outweigh arguments that would put either volume before 70 or even 64; and that, on the other hand, the elements of structural unity provide a strong indication that the two volumes were planned and executed as a single work. Further confirmation of this will have to come from the detailed consideration of Luke's doctrines and ideas in our subsequent chapters.

4 The Shape of Luke–Acts

Since Luke opens his work with a preface which refers to his predecessors and to his own decision to write his story, it might seem reasonable to start our inquiry into Luke's purpose there. In fact, the preface gives little direct help for our question, although, as we shall see in the next section, it can provide indirect hints of some value. So, as an alternative, we can make some observations about the total shape of Luke's work, to see what indications it may provide of the author's main concerns and of the main questions to which he was addressing himself.

(a) Luke is the only writer in the New Testament to discuss, in similar form and at similar length, both the story of the earthly Jesus and the activity of the risen Lord Jesus in his disciples. Luke may or may not have been aware of the existence of writings which discuss theologically the nature of the church (e.g. the Epistles to the Romans and to the Ephesians); certainly he does not seem to use them. He clearly does know of existing 'gospels', and uses at least one of them as a source. His innovation is to show that the gospel-story is incomplete without the church-story.[44] Luke thus emphasizes, on the one hand, that the character of Christian life in the church cannot be understood apart from its foundation in the incarnation, mission, death, resurrection and ascension of Jesus. Conversely, the story of Jesus cannot properly be appreciated without following it through to its outcome in the church. Hence, the basic scope and shape of the work show a major concern to explore and explain the nature of the church.

(b) The ascension of Jesus is narrated at the close of the Gospel of Luke and again at the opening of Acts. In the past this fact has sometimes been explained as being the result of the division of an originally single volume, the editor having put the ascension in both of the new volumes because he was uncertain to which it belonged.[45] Indirectly, this now discarded theory points to Luke's meaning. The ascension is the major bridge from volume one to volume two: it is the necessary climax of the one and starting-point of the other. That Luke narrates the same event twice, and with some inconsistency (especially the fact that the ascension seems to take place on Easter day in Luke 24:50–53 but forty days later in Acts 1:3–14) is indeed unique in Luke–Acts, but there are other cases sufficiently similar for us to regard this as part of Luke's narrative technique: thus Paul twice repeats in speeches the story of his experience on the Damascus road (Acts 9; 22; 26), and Peter immediately relates to the church in Jerusalem the story of the conversion and baptism of Cornelius and his friends (Acts 10–11); and in both these examples there are inconsistencies of detail in the retelling. Luke seems to use this method as a way of underlining the significance of the story concerned. In the case of the ascension, this underlining is the more emphatic by reason of the prominent location of the two accounts. The ascension as a distinct event in the story of Jesus is far more important to Luke than to any other New Testament writer.[46] To put the matter in terms of theological doctrines, the ascension is for Luke the point of intersection of Christology, eschatology and ecclesiology. The chief destiny of the earthly Jesus is to ascend to the right hand of the Father (Luke 9:51; 22:69; cf. Mark 10:1, 32ff.; 14:62); the ascension is a preparation for the fulfilment of the promise of the Son of Man's heavenly coming (Luke 21:27 adapts the 'clouds' of Dan. 7:13 and Mark 13:26 to point forward to Acts 1:9); the ascended Jesus gives the Holy Spirit to his disciples (Acts 2:33) and through the Spirit encourages and guides the church (e.g. Acts 4:29–31; 7:55f.; 13:2f; 16:6f.). Thus these themes are marked out by the location and prominence of the ascension-story as deserving special attention as we look through the whole work for indications of Luke's purpose.

(c) Another significant bridge between the two volumes is the function of Jerusalem as a sort of geographical sign-post. For Luke geography has a quasi-theological significance. (This idea is more convincing in the dynamic sense suggested by W. C. Robinson[47] than in the static sense argued by H. Conzelmann.[48]) In this respect Luke makes two important innovations by comparison with Mark (and Matthew). The first is the artificial extension of Jesus' journey from Galilee to Jerusalem (Luke 9:51–19:40), which emphasizes Jerusalem as the goal of his mission, which is dramatically set forth as his 'visitation' of the city (19:44). The second is Luke's direct contradiction of Mark (and Matthew) in having Jesus command the disciples not to leave Jerusalem after his resurrection: it is there, and not in Galilee, that they will meet him and receive the gift of the Spirit and the charge of world-mission (Luke 24:49, cf. Mark 16:6f./Luke 24:6; Luke omits Mark 14:28). So Jerusalem becomes the dramatic goal of volume one and the starting-point of volume two (Acts 1:8). Rome has a similar, but less important function. Only from Acts 19:21 onwards does it become explicitly the goal of Paul and implicitly a kind of symbol of the mission 'to the end of the earth' in Acts 1:8; Rome is mentioned much less often as the ultimate goal of Paul than Jerusalem is as that of Jesus. But these two cities help to emphasize what is in any case otherwise strongly represented in Luke–Acts: that the story of Jesus and of the church is a story full of purposeful movement. This sense of movement suggests that the story is one in which change and development have a proper place. We shall therefore need to be alert for the kinds of changes and developments which Luke is describing, and perhaps advocating or defending.

(d) It is reasonable to expect that Luke's purpose may also be partly indicated by the major opening and closing sections of his work. Another major innovation of Luke over against Mark (but this time one shared, in a slightly different form, by Matthew) is the addition of the infancy and childhood-stories in Luke 1:5–2:52. The atmosphere conjured up by Luke in the depiction of these first few scenes is one of simple and humble, but devoted Jewish piety. The impact which this makes is all the more striking because of the sharp contrast of mood and literary style from the very Greek-sounding preface. Luke thus seems to be emphasizing to a Hellenistic audience the fact that the chief character of his story was born and brought up in the heart of Israel. All the same, there are a few hints, such as the dating of Jesus' birth by an edict of the Roman emperor (Luke 2:1–3) and Symeon's quotation with respect to Jesus of the Servant's vocation to be 'a light for revelation of the Gentiles' (Luke 2:32), that the implications of the story will be universal in scope. So right from the outset a hint is given of the theme later to be represented by 'Jerusalem' and 'Rome', that the relationship of 'Israel' and 'the Gentiles' may be a major concern of Luke's book.

G. Lohfink has tackled the question just mentioned, and traces how in Luke–Acts the concept 'Israel' shifts in its connotations from the nation-church of Judaism to a new people of God embracing Gentiles.[49] But when he concludes that this process is complete by the time we reach Acts 21,[50] and says nothing about the remaining chapters of Acts, it is clear that his solution is methodologically incomplete. Lohfink and others have rightly seen that the major opening section of Luke–Acts must not be ignored as was done, with serious consequences, in H. Conzelmann's pioneering work on Lucan theology, *Die Mitte der Zeit*.[51] But neither must the major concluding section, Acts 21–28. This section contributes nothing to the description of the geographical and cultural spread of Christianity, which has often been taken to the essential theme of Acts, but concentrates on Paul's imprisonment and trial. So, to judge from the structure of Luke's work, it seems that the climax towards which he is bringing his story is 'Paul under prosecution'. What does this mean for the interpretation of the whole? Who are Paul's accusers, what are their accusations, and how does he respond? Why should *this* be the concluding section of a work whose first half is in the form of a gospel? Considerations of dating (section 3 above) have already ruled out the old idea that this section was aimed at the defence of Paul at his final trial: but clearly, not only because of its position in the book but also because of its relatively great length, this section must be important to Luke's overall purpose. To this question we shall need to return in Chapters Two, Three and Four.

5 The Audience Addressed by Luke

Obviously we shall be greatly helped towards defining Luke's purpose if we can determine the audience to which he primarily aimed his work.

(a) The natural place to begin is the preface, Luke 1:1–4, with its dedicatory address to 'your excellency Theophilus'.[52] In accordance with contemporary custom, the address is much more than personal to Theophilus, who may be presumed to be a leading figure in whichever group Luke had in mind as his first readers. Theophilus' identity is unfortunately even less clear than that of the author. That he is addressed as *κράτιστος* suggests that he was a person of social prominence. In the first century the title was used of high government officials (so of the Roman governor of Judaea, Acts 23:26; 24:3; 26:25), but not necessarily restricted to such: so we can make no assumption such as that Luke was addressing government-circles through Theophilus. It would be most useful to know whether Theophilus was a Christian, or what kind of relationship he had with Christians, such as would have caused Luke to dedicate his work to him. The preface itself gives us no certain answer to that. A difficult point here is the meaning of *κατηχεῖσθαι*. Had Theophilus received 'instruction' in the Christian faith, as a new or prospective member of the church? The use of this verb in a technical sense of formal, catechetical instruction in the church does not occur before the second century (2 Clem. 17:1), but it is at least foreshadowed in Paul's usage (Gal. 6:6, 1 Cor. 14:19; Rom. 2:18) and in one of the four examples in Luke–Acts (Acts 18:25). But Luke also has it twice in the sense of 'to receive an unfavourable report' (Acts 21:21,24). The verb may indeed be used in a quite neutral sense, 'to be informed': but its use in Luke 1:4 presupposes an active interest of some kind by Theophilus, and so a nuance, either positive or negative, may be presumed. Two more words in v.4 have a bearing on our understanding of Luke's meaning. *'Επιγινώσκειν* means 'to recognize' or 'perceive' – 'not so much fuller or more perfect knowing, as knowing arrived at by the attention being directed to a particular person or object'.[53] What Theophilus is meant to recognize or perceive is the *ἀσφάλεια* of the instruction or information he has received. This noun means 'security', 'safety', 'assurance', 'certainty'.[54] It has often been remarked that in v. 1–3 Luke differs from the procedure of other ancient preface-writers in aligning himself with his predecessors rather than criticizing their inadequacies. Yet some hint of criticism does shine through in v.4, and its nature is interesting. When we compare Luke's work with that of Mark, his only predecessor whom we can identify for certain, we might expect Luke to justify his book by the claim to add further information to what the reader already has. But this is what he does not do. Rather, there is a dimension of 'security' or 'assurance' that is so far lacking, which Luke feels the need to supply.[54a]

From these details we may derive the following possible interpretations of the address to Theophilus: (1) Theophilus is a magistrate of some kind, and he and his colleagues have received unfavourable reports about Christianity, such as later was to lead to official persecution. Luke writes to correct the misinformation, i.e. his work is an apology for Christianity. In this case *ἀσφάλεια* means 'correct facts'.[55] The reference in v.1f. to Luke's predecessors is hardly relevant, except perhaps to suggest to the officials that they were guilty of overlooking reliable information about Christianity which was already accessible to them: but then it is strange that Luke proceeds to write such a long work, rather than a short letter drawing attention to the available literature. (2) The readers had received instruction as Christian believers or inquirers, but it was of an inadequate or defective kind. In that case the 'many' predecessors may have included some whose works Luke regarded as heretical or otherwise misleading, though one wonders about Luke's including Mark without distinction among those implicitly criticized. In this case *ἀσφάλεια* means 'correct doctrine'. (3) The readers were instructed Christians, but they were inclined to waver in their faith. Luke writes so that they may perceive the 'reliability' or 'convincing nature' of the doctrines they have received. This interpretation implies much less criticism of Luke's predecessors, but it means that Luke seeks to add some new dimension or perspective to what they have taught, which will help to reassure his readers of the significance of what they have believed.

These possibilities will need to be reconsidered in the light of other factors which will emerge in the process of our study. But we must at this stage note an objection which has been raised to regarding Theophilus as a Christian, at least in the full sense of a baptized member of the church. T. Zahn noted that we have no clear examples until the early third century of one Christian's addressing another by an honorific title.[56] In view of the pervasive use of the language of 'fraternity' among Christians, throughout the New Testament, this is an argument well worth pondering. But it may not be conclusive. For Luke may have been an innovator here, just as he was an innovator in using a literary preface at all in a Christian book. That such an address to a fellow-Christian does not recur for more than a century may be due simply to the fact that no Christian work from the second century has survived, which is strictly comparable with Luke–Acts in subject-matter and intention.

(b) Apart from the details of the preface, and the intention stated in it, the very fact of its existence may give us some hint towards Luke's purpose. It has often been assumed that Luke's adoption of a literary convention whose milieu is the wide world of Graeco-Roman culture, rather than the more private fellowship of Christians, shows that it is this wider public which he addresses.[57] It is suggested that Luke wanted either to introduce the Christian message to educated pagans, so as to win their interest in it and their conversion, or (alternatively or in addition) to disabuse them of false information which might lead them to despise or even try to suppress the Christian movement.

There are, however, good reasons for doubting that Luke was writing for an audience outside the Christian fellowship. It is interesting that the ancient, so-called 'anti-Marcionite' and 'Monarchian' prologues do not think of Luke as addressing outsiders: it was his aim, they say, to set forth for Gentile believers the details of the divine economy, so that they might not fall prey to Jewish mythologies and legalism or heretical and empty fantasies; and they give this interpretation with explicit reference to Luke's preface.[58] For the intention of the preface has to be checked against what is actually said in the body of the work, and it may turn out that these ancient prologues are rather nearer the mark than has been supposed by many modern scholars.

The case of the apologies of the second century is quite distinct from Luke–Acts. There we have not only an address to leading figures of the Roman world but also a discussion thoroughly couched in terms at home in the context of classical literature and philosophy. But Luke plunges his reader immediately into the atmosphere of Judaism and the Old Testament. Frequently the Old Testament is quoted, and that is regarded as self-evident proof of an argument or assertion. Sometimes Old Testament themes are alluded to without explanation, in a way which is highly significant to a reader versed in the Old Testament, but opaque to one without that background: to take just two examples out of scores, the reason for Jesus' teaching in parables (Luke 8:9f.) and the significance of Moses and Elijah at the transfiguration of Jesus (Luke 9:28–36). It is true that Luke has Paul say, in Acts 26:26, that the events concerning Jesus and his disciples have 'not taken place in a corner': but that very passage makes it plain that it is Agrippa, an expert on Jewish religious lore, rather than the uninstructed Festus, whom Paul expects to understand what he is driving at. With respect to Acts, A. D. Nock raised the question, 'If it had come into the hands of a pagan, would he have understood it, unless he was already half-converted?'[59] The same applies even more strongly to the Gospel. For example, it is never explained what Jesus means by the self-designation 'the Son of Man', or by 'the Kingdom of God'. If the work were addressed to pagans, one would expect to find much more in the way of explanatory comment by the evangelist, as he presents teachings of Jesus and incidents concerning him.

The considerations so far mentioned indicate that Luke presupposes in his readers at least a solid grounding in the Old Testament. But he also presupposes a specifically Christian background. Such parts of Jesus' teaching as the Beatitudes and the eschatological discourses have an esoteric sound. Many of Jesus' parables are specifically addressed to disciples, e.g. Luke 11:5–8; 12:35–48; 16:1–9; 17:7–10; cf. 8:9–15; 12:1–12; and others make considerably more sense on the assumption that the book is primarily addressed to Christians, e.g. 16:19–31 (NB v.31!); 18:1–8. And the question has been well asked, whether Luke would have written the Lord's Prayer and the words of institution of the Lord's Supper into a work meant for readers who were not already Christian.[60]

If, then, Luke's address is after all internal to the church, what is the point of the Hellenistic-style preface? It may perhaps be taken as indicating a shift in the church's self-consciousness: either one which has taken place, or one which Luke wishes to suggest. By the time Luke writes, the Christian churches are a far-flung network across the Greek-speaking world. Acts does not tell all there is to be told about the establishment and growth of congregations, even in the 30's, 40's and 50's, but it gives a vigorous enough picture of expansion, which certainly did not abate in the next three decades. Luke may well be understood as encouraging the Christians to take themselves seriously as in themselves a large and important 'public', whom an author should approach with all the dignity and care usual in serious literature among educated people.

6 The 'Genre' of Luke–Acts

By determining the 'genre' in which Luke wrote, we may see some indication of his purpose by analogy with the purpose of his models or compeers. We must however be careful of expecting too much from this part of our inquiry. Luke no doubt had literary models in mind, as all authors do, but he may have adapted whatever genre he was following, to suit a new purpose.

(a) How far afield should we look? It has recently been argued that a useful analogy is provided by the *Lives of Eminent Philosophers* by Diogenes Laertius; or rather, since his work is more than a century later than Luke's by the now lost, earlier representatives of a strong literary tradition, on which Laertius drew. It is suggested that Jesus is portrayed as the founder of a school, with the apostles and others forming the tradition stemming from him.[61] But this analogy is at best a very remote one. Luke never uses of Jesus language suggesting that he is a philosopher: Luke is no Philo. Nor can we see distinctly from the work of Laertius the motives which prompted his predecessors. Laertius himself has been described by his translator and editor R. D. Hicks as 'a Dryasdust, vain and credulous, of multifarious reading, amazing industry, and insatiable curiosity' – but not himself a philosopher: his work is 'a contribution to the biography of men of letters who happened to be philosophers'.[62]

It has been argued persuasively by W. C. van Unnik that Luke fits better than has often been supposed into the category of Graeco-Roman 'history'.[63] In particular, van Unnik pointed to interesting examples of Luke's vocabulary and procedure, to show that he was familiar with the habits and methods of Greek historical writers. Luke's alleged deficiencies as a historian are often shared by the greatest Roman historians: Sallust is confused and careless on chronology and topography, even though he was in a good position to check his facts; Tacitus is inadequate on topography and conceived of character as a wholly static and immutable thing; and the same is true of Plutarch. Still, though this strengthened demonstration of Luke's links with the Graeco-Roman historiographic tradition is illuminating for our appreciation of Luke's background, it does not take us too far with regard to Luke's purpose, for ancient historians were not agreed about the purpose which history should fulfil.

(b) The most obvious model for Luke to have followed is the Gospel of Mark: but, as we have seen, Luke substantially modifies the genre 'gospel' as he received it from Mark, especially by more than doubling its length and greatly increasing the time-span of his story. Beyond Mark (and any other gospels he may have known), the best analogies for Luke's work are the historical works of the Old Testament, and perhaps post-Old Testament Jewish histories such as 1 Maccabees. In this tradition, the aim of historiography is more unified than in the Greek world: it is a form of confessional proclamation. History is meant to instruct in the character of God, to appeal for allegiance to him, and to inspire in his service. If Luke is to some extent shaped by the style and technique of Greek historiography, he is steeped in the motivation of biblical historiography. This analogy prepares us to appreciate what has been richly demonstrated by the 'redaction-critical' studies of the gospels over the last quarter-century: Luke is an historian, but he is at the same time a theologian: he uses history to express his theology. Perhaps we might designate the genre of Luke–Acts as 'theological history'.

(c) So far, what has been said in this section is quite well known, and perhaps rather obvious. But here we come to a point of great importance, which has not always been properly observed. If Luke is a theological historian, this may well mean that not everything in his book is *directly* addressed to his readers. He may be describing past situations which only indirectly, by imaginative reapplication, have relevance for the new situation of his readers; or, to take the matter further, he may be describing past situations whose only relevance is to reveal to the readers the nature of the situation in which they now live.

A couple of examples will explain what is involved here. In Luke 21:12–19 are words of Jesus warning his disciples of persecution that will come upon them. From this it is assumed by many interpreters that the church for which Luke is writing is under persecution, and that these sayings are meant to guide and encourage them through that experience. If, however, Luke is a theologically oriented *historian*, it may be that the time of persecution referred to is actually over by the time Luke writes: it will indeed be argued below that this is the case (Chapter Five, section 4). Luke may not be saying to his contemporaries, 'You are undergoing persecution, but the Holy Spirit will help you through it', but rather 'Our fathers in the faith went through a bad time of persecution, but the Holy Spirit helped them through it'. This may have for their own time a relevance of a quite different kind, i.e. to reassure them of the reality of the divine blessing on the tradition of faith they have entered into.

Again, it is assumed by H. Flender that Luke, as a Gentile Christian, was not himself deeply involved in the meaning of the traditions he received about God's judgement on the Jews, and so he took them over and reapplied them for Christians of his own day as warnings against complacency. Flender speaks of 'Judaism as a type of God's ways with the world'.[64] But in fact this interpretation has to be read into the text: it is based on the gratuitous assumption that everything in the text must have a direct spiritual appeal to the readers. Luke may well have a keen interest in the fate of Judaism, in the light of the events of 66–70 AD, precisely because these past events, taken together with the response of the Jews of Palestine to the mission of Jesus, help to reveal the nature of the situation in which Christians live in the time after 70 AD.

Another example may be taken from the complex sayings in Luke 12:49–13:9, where Jesus speaks of his coming to bring fire to the earth and to cause divisions; about judging the signs of the times; about the Galilaeans slaughtered in the Temple and the eighteen killed by the tower at Siloam; and about the unfruitful figtree. It seems to me that in the second half of this cluster of sayings, 13:1–9, there is an unmistakable reference to the coming destruction of Jerusalem: unless you repent, you will be butchered by the Romans even within the Temple-court; unless you repent, the towers of Jerusalem will fall on you; unless Judaism becomes a fruitful tree, she is to be chopped down. But in his very detailed study, 'Die Prüfung der Zeit (Lukas 12:54–56)'[65], G. Klein rejects this reference to the destruction of Jerusalem in Luke 13:1–9, at least in Luke's redactional intention (though the tradition may have included some such reference): he thinks the reference in Luke as we now have it is to the need for each individual to repent before his death. Klein is concerned that the more obvious historical reference would rob the passage of its force as a call to repentance, since the threatened punishment is past from Luke's standpoint, and his readers are not the Jews addressed by the original sayings. So he has to seek a far less obvious interpretation, whereby the call to repentance is maintained for those who live after the destruction of Jerusalem.

Klein's procedure, like Flender's is based on the tacit assumption that every pericope in a gospel must have direct kerygmatic or paraenetic relevance to its readers: but this assumption may be wrong, and we do better to take the text of Luke as it stands. Klein rightly sees in 12:49–53 a reference to the divisions among people to be caused by the preaching of the gospel after the death of Jesus ('from now on', 12:52, cf. 22:69). But he presses the unity of 12:49–59 too hard when he says that 'this time' which must be 'tested' (12:56) must also be the time after Jesus' death, and that the 'testing' consists of rightly understanding the divisions among people as signifying the distinction between those destined for salvation and for destruction. Again, Klein has unnecessarily avoided the more obvious meaning of the text in its Lucan dramatic setting. Rather, 'this time' is primarily intended as the time of Jesus' mission: failure to 'test' it rightly, i.e. to see it as God's 'visitation' (cf. 1:78, 19:44), will let loose the judgement referred to in both 12:49ff. and in 57ff. To point out in opposition to this that Jesus 'desired' the judgement (12:49), i.e. that judgement was inevitable, whatever the response of the Jews to Jesus' mission, is to mistake the irony of Jesus' 'intention' (cf. God's 'intention' to harden the hearts of Israel in Isaiah 6:9ff., and the application of this passage to Jesus' 'intention' to conceal his teaching by means of parables, Luke 8:9f.). That is, God's 'visitation' in the mission of Jesus brings the possibility of grace or judgement: it depends on the response of the hearers. Therefore Klein is also wrong in trying to argue away the forensic implications of 12:57ff. His interpretation, that the Christian (individual) must escape from the company of unbelievers, lest by association with them he be caught up in judgement (at his death), has the further disadvantage that such an attitude of Christians to unbelievers does not seem to be advocated elsewhere in Luke–Acts (and only seldom in the rest of the New Testament), but is contradicted by the call for faithful and courageous witnessing, e.g. Luke 12:2–12. In the pre-Lucan tradition, the material in 12:57ff. presumably had an eschatological reference: what Luke has done (and the setting between 12:54–56 and 13:1–9 makes this clear) is to add to the eschatological an historical reference.

From our point of view many centuries later, it may seem that Luke is running the risk of opening the way to complacency in his readers.[66] But we have to allow him to speak in his own terms to his own time. In many cases, it is clear that Luke is talking about a past situation, which may be considerably different from that in which his readers stand. It is up to us to do justice to his genre of 'theological history', and inquire what relevance this procedure may have for his readers: i.e., in what way this procedure serves the purpose of his writing.

7 Theories about Luke's Purpose

In the recent literature, we are reasonably well off for surveys of research on the question of Luke's purpose. On the one hand, in the detailed reviews by W. Gasque (1975)[67] and E. Gräßer (1976–77)[68] of studies on Acts, some attention is given to Luke's purpose; on the other hand, an essay by G. Schneider (1977) on the methodology of the question includes a good bibliography of special studies on Luke's purpose down to 1975, and some discussion of recent work.[69]

One problem is that the Gospel of Luke is so often treated along with Mark and Matthew from the perspective of 'the synoptic gospels' that Acts tends to be treated separately. Yet both Gasque and Gräßer, for example, acknowledge the unity of Luke–Acts (Gasque, as we have mentioned, even declares it to be the most important outcome of the history of research on Acts).[70] This leads to a certain imbalance in their studies: they acknowledge that the work they are discussing is properly speaking 'Luke–Acts', yet most of the detailed discussion is devoted to Luke's second volume. Schneider's bibliography lists twenty-one works dealing specifically with Luke's purpose: of these, only seven titles speak of 'the purpose of Luke–Acts', but fourteen of 'the purpose of Acts' – none inquires into the purpose of Luke's Gospel as a separate volume. This fact seems to suggest that scholars assume the purpose of a gospel to be self-evident, whereas it is Acts whose purpose needs to be explained.

But the works listed in this bibliography also reflect some uncertainty about the goal: for example, P. S. Minear's article of 1973 refers in its title only to Acts but actually discusses Luke–Acts as a whole,[71] whereas A. J. Mattill's essay of 1972 has a title referring to the purpose of Luke–Acts but really deals only with Acts.[72] We shall only make proper progress here if we make it quite clear (as Schneider does) that the object of our inquiry must be the purpose of Luke–Acts as a whole.

A second problem is that the question of Luke's purpose has many facets, whose importance is quite diversely estimated by scholars. Much of value for our theme is discussed in works dealing for example with Luke's theology, or with one aspect of it, such as his understanding of eschatology; or with such a problem as the relationship of Luke's church with Judaism. It will therefore be convenient to postpone much of our discussion of the literature of research until we come to the relevant chapters. For the time being, however, it will be helpful to list the chief suggestions that have been made about Luke's purpose, with some brief comments.

It has been remarked by W. Gasque that the suggestions made are so numerous and diverse that one is readily tempted to scepticism about the possibility of a convincing solution, or even about the reality of the question.[73] However, G. Schneider, who also notes the lack of agreement among those who have studied the question, has pointed to the correct first step, which has been too seldom taken: we must reflect on the method appropriate for a solution.[74] Schneider suggests proceeding by the following four questions: 1. What aim is stated in the preface(s)? 2. What details in the work may help to clarify the author's aim? 3. What main themes are discussed in the work? 4. Can the author's purpose be illuminated by the literary genre of his work? This seems to me to be a good beginning towards the needed method. Schneider's four steps are not necessarily of equal importance: his question no.3 turns out to be by far the most fruitful.[75] As has been argued in the earlier part of this chapter, it is also important to give more specific attention, which Schneider has not done, to the unity and literary shape or construction of Luke–Acts, and to the date of composition and the audience addressed.

For a variety of reasons, the theories of Luke's purpose which have been suggested hitherto cannot be accepted as they stand. But many of them are based on valid if partial insights, and part of our effort must be to see whether a new perspective can do justice to those insights without incurring the difficulties to which the respective theories are otherwise subject.

The current theories may be broadly classified according to whether they presume that Luke's address is to people outside the church or within it. As we have argued in section 5 of this chapter, the former are made very difficult by the nature of the work's contents, which at many points assume the reader's familiarity with the main outlines and especially the presuppositions of Christian teaching.

If this is correct, the following three theories are already excluded:

(a) That the chief purpose of Luke–Acts is *evangelism:* so especially F. F. Bruce and J. C. O'Neill.[76] This theory suffers further because of our observations about the shape of Luke's work, for the concluding section, Acts 21–28, is hard to reconcile with this idea. There may however be an element of truth in this suggestion, for, if Theophilus and his friends are Christians instructed in the gospel (see above, section 5 (a) (3)), Luke may perhaps be understood as seeking to undergird their faith.

(b) That Luke wrote *to defend Paul at his trial*, i.e. during Paul's lifetime: so, among recent contributions, especially A. J. Mattill.[77] This theory is made impossible because of the date of Luke's composition; moreover, Luke's volume one is, despite Mattill's efforts, at best only very vaguely relevant to that aim. But his view will not let us forget that Acts 21–28 is indeed the climax towards which Luke builds up his work. One way or another, 'Paul the prisoner' is an important element in Luke's purpose.

(c) That Luke wrote *to defend the Christians in the eyes of the Roman government*. This theory occurs in two forms: i. that Luke wanted to establish Christianity as a *religio licita*, to share the protection extended by Rome to Judaism; ii. without recourse to the 'religio licita'-idea, to show Rome that Christians were not politically subversive. The former, argued most forcefully by B. S. Easton in 1936,[78] has continued to be espoused by E. Haenchen,[79] the latter by many others. In either form, it was dealt a heavy blow by a single, much-quoted sentence of C. K. Barrett: 'No Roman official would ever have filtered out so much of what to him would be theological and ecclesiastical rubbish in order to reach so tiny a grain of relevant apology'.[80] But we shall devote a short chapter to it (Chapter Four), partly because it has continued to command such impressive support, and partly because there is indeed an unmistakably and surprisingly irenic attitude towards Rome in Luke–Acts, which deserves to be explored and taken into account.

The remaining four theories to be listed have the advantage (according to our earlier discussion) of presuming an address internal to the church:

(d) That Luke wrote *to defend Paul's memory* against attacks upon it by Jewish Christians. This theory occurs in a variety of forms, going back to M. Schneckenburger and F. C. Baur in the 1840's.[81] A view rather like Schneckenburger's has been impressively stated recently by J. Jervell.[82] In the older form of Baur and Schneckenberger, this theory suffers from the separation made between Luke and Acts: the purpose here discussed is attributed to Acts alone. Jervell acknowledges the unity of Luke–Acts, but in practice devotes most of his attention to volume two. For him, the all-important problem is the relationship of Christians to the Jewish Law. He holds that Luke presents Paul as a Law-keeping Jew, because the church cannot be the new Israel if it goes back to a Jewish apostate. The criticism immediately arises once more, that Paul is indeed important in Luke–Acts, but a purpose focussed on him does not do justice to the full scope and plan of the work. However, the question of the relationship of Christians to Judaism is indeed a pressing one throughout the book, and in this wider sense will occupy our attention in Chapter Two; the more particular question about Paul's place in Luke's purpose will be discussed in Chapter Three.

(e) A theory of a quite different kind has been prominent in recent years, since the 'redaction-critical' method of interpretation brought *theology* into prominence as a consideration with respect to Luke's purpose. In particular, H. Conzelmann and others have identified Luke's purpose as that of seeking to solve an alleged crisis of faith in the church, due to the *delay of the parousia*.[83] This theory has received very wide assent, and therefore we must take into account the question of *Luke's understanding of eschatology* as a possible aspect of his purpose. This is the subject of our Chapter Five.

(f) Another purpose of a doctrinal kind is suggested by C. H. Talbert.[84] It has often been suggested that this or that aspect of Luke–Acts is formulated with a view to combatting Gnosticism,[85] but Talbert aims to show 'that Luke–Acts was written *for the express purpose of serving as a defense against Gnosticism*'.[86] As this theory will not be discussed further in the following chapters, a few remarks may be made here. Luke's strong emphasis on the physicality of Jesus' resurrection-body may well be a tilt against Docetism. That the instruction of the apostles by Jesus was limited to forty days after the resurrection may be a way of fore-stalling Gnostic claims, such as are represented by the Gospel of Thomas and other Gnostic writings, of secret revelation going beyond the tradition embodied in the canonical gospels.

But other elements alleged to be directed against Gnosticism have other, probably better explanations. The virgin-birth of Jesus has more to do with the fulfilment of God's promises to Israel (Isa. 7:14 LXX, cf. the miraculous births of Isaac, Samuel, etc.). Elements of 'early Catholicism' are much slighter in Luke–Acts than alleged by E. Käsemann,[87] but are in any case better to be explained in a wider way: a far flung, rapidly-growing movement needs institutional forms so as to maintain cohesion, and threats to this may come from other sources. (We shall return to 'early Catholicism' in Chapter Seven.) It is quite likely that anti-Gnosticism is a minor aspect of Luke's purpose, but it is no more than that. How slight a basis Talbert's theory has in Luke's text is illustrated by the heavy recourse to a single passage, Acts 20:17–35, needed to prove the point that 'there is a remarkable similarity between the picture of Paul we find in Acts and that of the Pastorals', where the heresy combatted is Gnosticism.[88]

(g) Finally, Luke's work has been described as '*the confirmation of the gospel*'. W. C. van Unnik took a clue from Hebr. 2:2–4, where the writer, seeking to encourage the wavering faith of his readers, says that the 'salvation' which was first proclaimed by the Lord has been 'confirmed to us' by the Lord's hearers, supported by the testimony of God himself with signs, wonders, miracles and the bestowing of the Holy Spirit.[89] Many of these themes recur in Acts, which may therefore have the purpose of reassuring the faith of Luke's readers. In the form presented by van Unnik, this hypothesis is not very clear. Van Unnik confined the suggested purpose to Acts, and he did not explain what relationship he saw between Luke's two volumes, though he did note that the testimony of Acts as thus understood may be somehow related to the term ἀσφάλεια in Luke 1:4.[90] Nor did he inquire closely into the audience Luke was addressing, or into Luke's literary plan. A rather similar interpretation was presented, apparently independently, in an imaginative article by P. S. Minear.[91] This article has the defect of being rather too lively, for it jumps so energetically from point to point that it seldom has time to penetrate below the surface. But it has the one important merit, which I have not found elsewhere (except gropingly hinted at in van Unnik's article, as just noted) of recognizing the likelihood that the last word of Luke's preface, ἀσφάλεια, is deliberately put in an emphatic position, and that it may mean not merely 'correct factual information' but 'certainty' or 'dependability', in the sense of 'having important significance'.[92] This is a promising insight, to which we shall return in Chapter Seven.

In the preceding paragraphs I have noted in broad terms the chapters of this book in which the various theories of previous researchers will be taken up. There has been no occasion so far to glance forward to Chapter Six. In so far as the special affinities of Luke and John have been studied, this has usually been done from the perspective of a principal interest in John, and mainly with regard to the question of a direct or indirect source-relationship, i.e. whether Luke was used as a source by John (or vice versa!), or whether these two evangelists may have had special sources in common. It has however been noted from time to time by students of Luke that it would be worth while to examine also the possibility that Luke and John share to some extent a common point of view in interpreting their material.[93] So a theological and redactional comparison between Luke–Acts and John will be undertaken, to see whether this, too, may bring forth some illumination of Luke's purpose.

Notes to Chapter One

1. H. J. Cadbury, *Making*, 301–303; cf. 315: 'It is quite possible to overemphasize this factor (purpose) in composition, to assign to it the most fanciful and exaggerated role'.
2. Op. cit., 303–316.
3. See the bibliography in G. Schneider, 'Zweck', 45, n. 1, with works ranging in date from 1841 (M. Schneckenburger) to 1975. In 1960 W. C. van Unnik remarked that the question of Luke's purpose was not prominent between 1897 (J. Weiß) and his own tackling of it in 1955: 'The "Book of Acts" the Confirmation of the Gospel', 342f.
4. C. K. Barrett, *Luke the Historian*, 53.
5. See J. Rohde, *Die redaktionsgeschichtliche Methode* (ET, with additions, *Rediscovering the Teaching of the Evangelists); N. Perrin, What is Redaction Criticism*?
6. H. J. Cadbury, op. cit., 303. An opinion quite like Cadbury's on this point has however been put forward by I. H. Marshall, *Luke: Historian*, 64–66.
7. See H. J. Cadbury, 'The Tradition', 259f.
8. The most important pioneering work was H. Conzelmann, *Die Mitte der Zeit* (ET). For a critical review of the movement mostly stemming from Conzelmann's initiative, see W. C. van Unnik, 'Luke–Acts'; U. Wilckens, 'Interpreting Luke–Acts'; W. G. Kümmel, 'Anklage'. A review more sympathetic to Conzelmann's interpretation, and also covering the range of recent studies more widely, is given by E. Gräßer, 'Zur Theologie des Lukas in der Apg', *ThR* 42/1977, 51–66.
9. E.g., S. G. Wilson, *Gentiles*, 85f.; P. S. Minear, 'Dear Theo', 148f.
10. Luke's purpose and his theology are related but not identical questions, though the distinction between them is often not clearly made: e.g. in the recent work of E. Franklin, *Christ the Lord*, which in reality has much more to do with 'theology' than with 'purpose'. To the literature on Lucan theology there is now added M. Dömer, *Das Heil Gottes*. The author's starting points are on the one hand the great influence of H. Conzelmann's *Die Mitte der Zeit* on modern Lucan studies, on the other hand the increasingly widespread criticisms of Conzelmann's conclusions, and in particular the assertion of H. Schürmann (*Das Lukasevangelium* and other writings) that the idea of Luke as a 'theologian' is unjustified. According to Dömer, the high points of Luke's theology are summarized in Luke 24:44–47 and Acts 26:22f. They are 1. Jesus' death, 2. his resurrection, 3. the Gentile mission. Luke wants to show the

church of his day that its situation and mission are continuous with God's act in Jesus. Dömer makes no observation about the total structure of Luke–Acts and does not offer a justification of his concentrating his study on a few selected passages (Luke 1–2; 3:21f.; 4:16–30; Luke 24–Acts 1; Acts 2; 15; 20:17–38). He essentially picks up and elaborates the theme of J. Dupont's important essay 'Le salut des gentils' (see below, Chapter Two, n. 88). Despite some useful observations on Luke's theology, this work is of no great relevance to the search for Luke's purpose.

11. E.g., G. Schneider, 'Zweck', 55; E. Franklin, *Christ the Lord*, 6.
12. H. J. Cadbury, 'The Knowledge Claimed in Luke's Preface', 401–420; 'Commentary on the Preface of Luke', 489–510; *Making, ch. 1.*
13. W. Gasque, *Criticism*, 309.
14. E. Haenchen, *Die Apostelgeschichte*, 143, n. 3 (ET), also 'Das "Wir" in der Apostelgeschichte und das Itinerar', 260–263, rejects Cadbury's view that Luke 1:1–4 is the preface to the whole work, but still treats Luke and Acts as a closely-paired set. H. Conzelmann, *MdZ*, 7, n. 1 (ET, 15, n. 1), seems to go further and regard Luke and Acts as two separate monographs, though he too finds a common theology and point of view in the two volumes. A clearer motive for wishing to see Luke and Acts as two separate works comes in the attempt of H. W. Bartsch, *Wachet aber zu jeder Zeit!* 11–14, to argue that Luke 1:1–4 is the preface only of the Gospel and not also of Acts: for the author wants to reject the contention, accepted by Conzelmann and others from P. Vielhauer, 'Zum "Paulinismus" der Apostelgeschichte', 1–15 (ET, 33–50), that 'Luke thinks uneschatologically', but finds this easier to reject for the Gospel than for Acts. Bartsch borrows from Haenchen the argument 'daß Lukas das Evangelium als feste Gattung vorfand' and from Conzelmann the idea 'daß der Stil des Prologs zur Monographie gehörte und nicht ursprünglich zur Historiographie. Erst später ist der Brauch derartiger Prologe auch in die Geschichtsschreibung eingedrungen': op. cit., 14. The force of the distinction between 'monography' and 'historiography' is not clear to me. We shall discuss below the possibility that Luke wrote the preface for the Gospel alone and subsequently wrote a match for it in Acts 1:1. But the argument that sequential prefaces for multi-volume historical works were not used before Luke's time is disproved by the case of Diodorus Siculus, though there the prefaces are not so closely similar to Luke's as in the case of Josephus' *Against Apion*. See J. M. Creed, *The Gospel According to St. Luke*, 1. The fact that 'gospel' was an established *genre* before Luke cannot be taken as proof that Acts was not part of Luke's original plan, for that would be to beg the question whether Luke was making a creative innovation by extending the scope of the genre.

    A more radical separation between Luke and Acts is proposed by G. Bouwman, *Das dritte Evangelium*, 62–67. Following the suggestion of H. G. Russell, 'Which Was Written First, Luke Or Acts?', 167–174, that Acts may have been written before the Gospel, Bouwman dates Acts 61–63 AD and the Gospel after 70. This suggestion has won no support: for criticism, see I. H. Marshall, *Luke: Historian*, 157, n. 1. Bouwman rightly rejects the earlier, complicated theory of C. S. C. Williams, 'The Date of Luke–Acts', 283ff., that Luke first wrote a now lost form of his Gospel, then, after reading Mark, wrote Acts, and finally published a revised Gospel in the form now extant.
15. By A. C. Clark, *The Acts of the Apostles*, 393–408. The argument is based on

linguistic differences between Luke and Acts; but the overwhelming consensus of scholars is that the linguistic connexions far outweigh the differences.

16. For literatur, review and criticisms, see W. G. Kümmel, *Einleitung*, 125f. (ET, 157f.).
17. E. Haenchen, *Apg*, 109, n. 2 (ET, 99, n. 1).
18. See below, page 26, on H. G. Russell.
19. See above, n. 12.
20. See J. M. Creed, *St. Luke*, 1; I. H. Marshall, *The Gospel of Luke*, 39.
21. See above, n. 14.
22. H. J. Cadbury, 'Knowledge Claimed', 401ff.; 'Commentary on the Preface', 501f.
23. W. G. Kümmel, *Einleitung*, 146 (ET, 179), claims that it was refuted by E. Haenchen, 'Das "Wir" in der Apostelgeschichte' 260ff. Kümmel and Haenchen appeal to the Demosthenes-passages cited in Bauer's lexicon under *παρακολουθέω*, 3. 'einer Sache nachgehen'. These are (a) 18 (*De Corona*): 172 and (b) 19 (*De Falsa Legatione*): 257. But both these passages are in a much longer list cited by Cadbury, 'Knowledge Claimed', and clearly support his case. (a)*ἐκεῖνος ὁ καιρὸς. . . : οὐ μόνον εὔνουν και πλούσιον ἄνδρα ἐκάλει, ἀλλὰ καὶ παρηκολουθηκότα τοῖς πράγμασιν ἐξ ἀρχης..* C. A. Vince and J. H. Vince, in the Loeb edition (*Demosthenes*) translate: 'The call of the crisis was not only for the wealthy patriot but for the man who from first to last had closely watched the sequence of events . . .' (b) *ὁ τὰ τούτου πονηρεύματ ἀκριβέστατ εἰδὼς ἐγὼ καὶ παρηκολουθηκὼς ἅπασι. . .*: 'I, who have the most accurate knowledge of his villainies, and have watched him closely throughout . . .' Haenchen, 'Wir', 262, n. 3, claims in the first case that *ἐξετάζειν* in the following sentence means that 'Demosthenes hat sich informiert', and seems to assume that this implies historical research! The Loeb translators here take *ἐξετάζειν* to mean 'study' in the sense of pondering or mentally scrutinizing information known from personal experience: and as far as I can see the text bears out that rendering. The whole context emphasizes Demosthenes' *current* involvement in the whole affair. I cannot understand what Haenchen means by his objection to the second example as favouring Cadbury's interpretation. Bauer also cites, under the meaning 'einer Sache nachgehen', Josephus, *Against Apion*, 1:53, 218. But the first of these has the same meaning as in Demosthenes: Josephus speaks of his having 'been in close touch' with events in his description of the Jewish War, and actually contrasts *παρηκολουθηκότα* with *παρὰ τῶν εἰδότων πυνθανόμενον*. The second, *οὐ γὰρ ἐνῆν αὐτοῖς μετὰ πάσης ἀκριβείας τοῖς ἡμετέροις γράμμασι παρακολουθεῖν*, '. . . their inability to follow quite accurately the meaning of our records', gives a meaning allowed for by Cadbury and quite different from 'research'. See also *M-M*, 485f.

Haenchen and Kümmel really seem to base their objection to Cadbury not so much on a thorough lexicographical study of *παρακολουθεῖν* as on what they feel to be the awkwardness of its use with *ἀκριβως*, if the verb means 'to keep in touch with'. So Haenchen, 262f.: 'Ich kann mich genau informieren, aber ich kann nicht genau am Kriege teilnehmen'. But this misunderstands both Cadbury's view of *παρακολουθεῖν* and the range of meanings of *ἀκριβῶς*. Cadbury does not mean that Luke had necessarily 'participated' in all the events referred to, but he had 'kept in touch' with them, as they were happening. *LSJ*, 55, list the following verbs commonly found with *ἀκριβῶς*: '*εἰδέναι ἐπίστασθαι, καθορᾶν, μαθεῖν*, etc.': and these are not far from

Cadbury's sense of παρακολουθεῖν. It is interesting to note that in three of the four examples from Demosthenes and Josephus examined above παρακολουθεῖν is used in close proximity to ἀκριβῶς or ἀκρίβεια, though only in *Against Apion* 1:218 are they directly connected. In Justin, *Apology* I, 16:4, παρακολουθήσαντες is used in much the same sense as κατανοήσαντες.

24. So 'Knowledge Claimed', part I, in contrast with 'Commentary on the Preface', 502f., where the two expressions are said to be 'practically synonymous'.
25. J. H. Ropes, 'St. Luke's Preface; ἀσφάλεια and παρακολουθεῖν', 70f.
26. However, the proximity of Luke 24:48 to Acts 1:8, 22; 2:32; etc. makes it likely that this theme is meant as a bridge from the first volume to the second.
27. H. G. Russell, op. cit. (n. 14, above), 173.
28. See H. J. Cadbury, 'Lucius of Cyrene', 489–495; J. B. Lightfoot, *Commentary on the Epistles to the Colossians and to Philemon*, 307.
29. See H. J. Cadbury, 'The Tradition'.
30. H. J. Cadbury, *The Style and Literary Method of Luke*.
31. See the review in J. Dupont, *The Sources of Acts*, ch. 5.
32. A. D. Nock, 'The Book of Acts', 827f.
33. For this definition of the lower limit, see W. L. Knox, *The Acts of the Apostles*, 2. A more concrete limit is set by Marcion's use of Luke around 150 AD. But very few scholars these days wish to date Luke's work later than the time of Ignatius, partly because of the difficulty posed by Luke's apparent ignorance of Paul's letters, and partly because the alleged 'early Catholic' mood in Luke–Acts is not so advanced as in Clement of Rome, not to mention Ignatius himself.
34. See F. Hahn, 'Die Rede von der Parusie des Menschensohnes', 254f.
35. Pliny, *Letters*, X:96, 97.
36. See below, n. 40.
37. See Eusebius, *Hist. Eccl.* II:22:2–8; 25:1–5; III:17; 20:7; IV:26:9; Augustine, *Civ. Dei*, XX:19.
38. W. Gasque, *Criticism*, 265, with n. 31, with reference to C. H. Dodd, 'The Fall of Jerusalem', 69–83.
39. E. E. Ellis, *Luke*, 170–172, also suggests that Luke 11:49–51 refers to an incident that took place in 68 AD.
40. The problem of dating Acts after the Neronian persecution and the fall of Jerusalem is somewhat alleviated by putting the date as *far* after these events as possible, i.e. shortly before the outbreak of Domitian's persecution in Asia. These events are no longer so acutely painful memories, and Luke preferred to reflect the happier relations with the state which developed in the 70's and 80's.
41. J. C. Hawkins, *Horae Synopticae*, 177–182. H. J. Cadbury's much more detailed studies of Luke's language, especially in *Style*, Part II, did not lead him to the same conclusion.
42. S. G. Wilson, *Gentiles*, 80, 86.
43. H. J. Cadbury, *Making*, 218f., observes that Luke tends (a) to adapt his style and vocabulary to suit the atmosphere of the story being narrated, and (b) to re-use words or phrases he has recently used.
44. Cf. C. K. Barrett, *Luke*, 54ff.
45. See above, n. 16.
46. See G. Lohfink, and the detailed review by F. Hahn, 'Die Himmelfahrt Jesu'.

47. W. C. Robinson, *Der Weg des Herrn*, 30–43.
48. H. Conzelmann, *MdZ*, Part I.
49. G. Lohfink, *Die Sammlung Israels*.
50. Op. cit., 89–92, 95: Acts 20:28 marks the end of the process.
51. See H. H. Oliver, 'The Lucan Birth Stories', 215ff., and P. S. Minear, 'Luke's Use of the Birth Stories', 120–125.
52. The most thorough studies of Luke's preface are still those of H. J. Cadbury; see, in addition to the works mentioned in n. 12 above, 'The Purpose Expressed in Luke's Preface'. See also G. Klein, 'Lukas 1:1–4 als theologisches Programm', 193–216; but this article is problematic in much of its detailed argument as well as in its conclusion, that Luke wanted to make knowledge of salvation dependent on knowledge of historical facts, and thus set Christian faith off in a false direction. An elaborate refutation of Klein's view is undertaken by R. Glöckner, *Die Verkündigung des Heils*, 3–41. Glöckner argues that Luke cannot be seen as eliminating the need for a response of faith on the part of his readers, but that he rightly lays emphasis on the reality of the historical facts established by the church's tradition.
53. *M-M*, 236.
54. See *LSJ*, 266; *M-M*, 88. The range of meanings of *ἀσφάλεια* is important, and has too often been neglected by commentators on the preface, who mostly assume that it means simply 'correct facts'. It is frequently used in commercial and legal contexts, meaning 'bond', 'pledge', 'title-deeds'. Xenophon, *Memorabilia,* IV:6:15, says that Socrates carried his reasoning forward by steps that met with the agreement of his hearers, *νομίζων ταύτην ἀσφάλειαν εἶναι λόγου,* 'regarding this (sc. *τὴν ὁδόν*?) as the sure basis of argument'. *'Ασφάλεια* is 'the condition of being secure', but it can also mean 'confidence' or 'that which gives confidence'.

    One of the few writers to note the significance of the prominent position of *ἀσφάλεια* in Luke's preface is R. Glöckner, loc. cit. (n. 52). However, Glöckner fails to examine this word lexicographically outside Luke's own work; nor does he inquire into its significance as indicating what Luke aims to add to the work of his predecessors. Consequently, the very long discussion sheds little light on the question of Luke's purpose.
54a. J. Ernst, *Das Evangelium nach Lukas*, remarks in his introduction (9) that Luke has the aim of writing 'eine "bessere", d.h. für die veränderte Situation geeignetere Darstellung der Heilsereignisse'; but in his commentary ad. loc. (53f.) he confines his attention to drawing out Luke's concern to mark the need for interaction between critical, historical research and faithful acceptance of the church's tradition. The 'changed situation', according to this interpretation, is simply one in which the church and her theologians are more aware, because of the passage of time, that the church must clarify her understanding of the historical dimension of her own existence.
55. Cf. *γνῶναι τὸ ἀσφαλές,* Acts 21:34; 22:30.
56. T. Zahn, *Das Evangelium des Lucas*, 56–58.
57. E. Plümacher, *Lukas als hellenistischer Schriftsteller* gathers an impressive amount of material from the Graeco-Roman world to show, by comparison with various aspects of Acts, that Luke knew and deliberately strove to forge links with the broad literary traditions of the educated world of his time. His aim was to prove 'daß das Christentum durchaus den Anspruch erheben könne, in der hellenistischen Welt als Faktor von Rang und Bedeutung zu

gelten' (22). From this, Plümacher assumes in general terms that Luke was addressing 'Hellenistic readers' (14, 97) to prove to them 'that these things were not done in a corner', Acts 26:26 (14, 97). Plümacher's case rests almost entirely on Acts: the Gospel of Luke is rarely mentioned, and Luke 1:1–4 not at all! Despite the intrinsic interest and value of Plümacher's work, its relevance for our present discussion is limited: for the author does not examine the relationship of Luke's two volumes, or even the structure of Acts; nor does he inquire critically into the identity of Luke's 'Hellenistic readers', or ask why Luke was seeking to impress them with the success and respectability of the Christian movement.

58. The texts of these prologues are conveniently available in K. Aland (ed.), *Synopsis Quattuor Evangeliorum*, 533, 539. On their origins and significance, see R. G. Heard, 'The Old Gospel Prologues', 1–16; E. Haenchen, *Apg*, 24–26 (ET, 10–12).
59. A.D. Nock, 'Acts', 825.
60. J. Jeremias, as reported by C. Burchard, *Der dreizehnte Zeuge*, 184, n. 4.
61. C. H. Talbert, *Literary Patterns*, G. Schneider, 'Zweck', 61–66, finds this a promising approach.
62. R. D. Hicks, *Diogenes Laertius*, I, xiv, xvii.
63. W. C. van Unnik, 'Éléments artistiques dans l'évangile de Luc', 129–140.
64. H. Flender, *Heil*, 100–102 (ET, *Luke*, 109–111).
65. *ZThK* 61/1964, 373–390.
66. H. Flender, Heil, 100 (ET, 109).
67. See above, n. 13.
68. See above, n. 8.
69. See above, n. 3. A useful, though not comprehensive, review of opinions about Luke's purpose is given by C. H. Talbert, *Luke and the Gnostics*, ch. 7.
70. W. Gasque, *Criticism*, 309.
71. See above, n. 9.
72. A. J. Mattill, 'Naherwartung, Fernerwartung', 276–293.
73. W. Gasque, *Criticism*, 308: 'If anything has been learned from our study, it is that it is impossible to isolate one exclusive purpose or theological idea which is the key to the interpretation of the Third Gospel and Acts'. Cf. 302f.
74. G. Schneider, 'Zweck', 47.
75. According to Schneider, the most important themes running through Luke–Acts are eschatology and the future of Israel. Luke holds firm to the promise of the End, though rejecting the question 'when?'. Luke shows the fulfilment of the OT prophecies concerning Israel: of these the most important is Isa. 6:9f.: Jesus is not only light for the Gentiles but (going beyond Isa. 42) set for the fall as well as the rising of many in Israel. The Paul-part of Acts must be important to Luke's purpose. Acts 21–28 has two aspects: (a) the defence of Paul against Jewish accusations, (b) an irenic attitude towards Rome. Both these themes have significance within the church: (b) does not indicate an apology directed towards Rome. Schneider thinks that (a) has been correctly explained by J. Jervell as Luke's attempt to defend the church, through Paul as one of its leading founders, against Jewish charges of illegitimacy; and (b) by E. Plümacher as Luke's attempt to discourage among Christians an attitude of uncompromising hostility against the state, but also an attitude of resignation which could lead to a too ready compliance with the wishes of the state and to the laming of the Christian mission. (These theories

will be taken up in detail in Chapters Two and Four respectively.) Schneider however thinks that Luke–Acts 'ist allenfalls auch für Nichtchristen bestimmt' (61), though no attempt is made to demonstrate this.

76. F. F. Bruce, *The Book of Acts*, 17–24, begins with noting what have often been regarded as the apologetic elements of Acts, but observes that the combination of Acts with the Gospel of Luke makes apology as such an inadequate description of Luke's purpose: through the demonstration of the political innocence of Paul, and of Christianity generally, Luke seeks to lead sympathetic Romans on to an interest in Jesus. J. C. O'Neill, *The Theology of Acts*, 172–185, makes a more forthright assertion that Luke's purpose is to win educated pagans for faith in Jesus. See also C. H. Talbert, *Gnostics*, 101f.
77. In a series of articles since 1970: see Schneider's bibliography, 'Zweck', 45, n. 1.
78. B. S. Easton, *The Purpose of Acts*.
79. Especially in 'Judentum und Christentum'; also *Apg*, 111–113 (ET, 100–102).
80. C. K. Barrett, *Luke*, 63.
81. See W. Gasque, *Criticism*, 26–40; C. H. Talbert, *Gnostics*, 98–101.
82. J. Jervell, *Luke and the People of God*. The resemblance to Schneckenburger is noted by G. Schneider, 'Zweck', 60, n. 78. Also in the Schneckenburger-tradition is E. Trocmé, *Le 'Livre des Actes'* see W. Gasque, *Criticism*, 268-270.
83. Especially H. Conzelmann, *MdZ*, Parts II-V.
84. C. H. Talbert, *Gnostics*.
85. See especially C. K. Barrett, *Luke*, 62f.
86. *Gnostics*, 15, cf. 13f.
87. See C. H. Talbert, *Gnostics*, with references to Käsemann's well-known view. See also C. K. Barrett, *Luke*, 24–26.
88. *Gnostics*, 114. Talbert has continued to advocate this view of Luke's purpose in the articles 'An anti-Gnostic Tendency in Lucan Christology', NTS 14/1967–8, 259–271, and 'The Redaction Critical Quest for Luke the Theologian' in D. G. Buttrick (ed.), *Jesus and Man's Hope*, Pittsburgh 1970, 171–222. The latter article argues that Luke's editorial handling of eschatology is designed to rebut the view, to which members of his church were inclined, that the parousia had already occurred, being identical with the gift of the Spirit at Pentecost. Here Talbert collects much evidence for the existence of such a view of eschatology in Christian circles in the second and even the first century, but the exegetical demonstration of the thesis from Luke's own text is not persuasive. The passages seen as providing the most direct evidence of such a concern on Luke's part are Luke 19:11–27; Acts 1:6ff.; and Luke 17:20–37; but even here Talbert has to argue very subtly to expose his theme. Below I offer quite different explanations of these passages (Chapter Two, section 5; Chapter Five, sections 3(a) and 6).
89. W.C. van Unnik, 'Confirmation', especially 360–363. It is curious that this essay has not received more notice in recent studies on Luke's purpose. It is briefly summarized by W. Gasque, *Criticism*, 298f., but there its thrust with respect to Luke's purpose is not explained. G. Schneider does not discuss it, though it is in his bibliography. It is not mentioned at all by C. H. Talbert, or by P. S. Minear (see below).
90. 'Confirmation', 370.
91. P. S. Minear, 'Dear Theo'.
92. Op. cit., 133f.

93. E.g., C. Burchard, *Der dreizehnte Zeuge*, 21, n. 31: In the search for Luke's place in the development of early Christianity 'müßte Lukas auch Johannes gegenübergestellt werden, was m.W. bisher abgesehen vom Problem der parallelen Überlierferung besonders in der Passions- und Ostergeschichte kaum geschehen ist . . .; auch ein theologischer Vergleich würde nicht nur Gegensätze erbringen'.

2. Jews, Gentiles and Christians

1 Who Are the Christians?

'It was at Antioch that the disciples were first called "Christians"' (Acts 11:26b). Luke mentions this just after reporting that Saul, on the invitation of Barnabas, had come from Tarsus and spent a whole year instructing the new believers, mainly Greeks, who were streaming into the Antiochene congregation. Significantly, the new name, indicating a new sense of identity, is linked not only with the first large accession of non-Jews to the church but also with the activity of Saul.[1]

In Luke the concept has not yet been reached of the Christians as a 'third race', distinct from Jews and Gentiles.[2] But Luke is caught up, as Paul and Stephen were before him, in fast-moving historical developments whereby the original inherence of Jesus' followers within the community of Israel was becoming increasingly problematic. The question, where do the Christians stand with respect to the age-old distinction between Jews and Gentiles, is an acute one for Luke, as it was for Paul. Both Paul and Luke give confident answers to it, but along substantially different lines. That Luke is aware how important Paul was in the history of this problem is shown by his focusing much of his answer in the narration of Paul's career.

K. Stendahl has recently emphasized that Paul was, in his own understanding, and always remained, a Jew: he did not see his experience on the Damascus road as a 'conversion' from one 'religion' called Judaism to another called Christianity, but rather as a call to a son of Abraham from the God of Abraham to become his apostle to the nations, because of the new situation caused by the coming of the Messiah.[3]

That perspective is vital, as Stendahl explains, if we are to read Paul's letters intelligently and interpret his theology correctly: for example, it makes a great difference whom Paul means, and what he means, by the pronouns 'we' and 'you'.[4] But it was not necessarily the perspective of Paul's Jewish contemporaries. He did not see himself as converted from Judaism to something else, but he certainly was redirected in his theological perception of what it means to be a Jew, now that (as he believed) the Messiah had come. If for him personally, from the inside, his new experience intensified rather than dissolved his sense of belonging to the covenant of God with the patriarchs, from the outside, to those Jews who did not share his call and rejected the theological convictions that went with it, there was a serious question whether Paul was any longer a true Jew. Such opponents may not have seen his change of convictions as 'conversion to' some new entity, but they saw it as 'conversion from' the faith of Israel, that is as apostasy. This raised a severe practical problem for Paul and all who shared his views, a problem which also soon raised acute theoretical issues. As Luke lets us see, this problem had existed at least since the time of Stephen, and is really the same problem as that of the crucifixion of Jesus. These disciples of Jesus may not see themselves, and may not wish to be seen, as anything other than Jews: but if the established leaders of Judaism, and large parts of the Jewish community in general, refuse to accept them any longer as such, who are they? And as to those Gentiles, welcomed by Paul and others into community with themselves in the name of Jesus as the Messiah, what relationship can they have with Israel, unless they accept the Law and become proselytes in the regular way?

It has not always been appreciated that Luke is among those early Christian writers who are concerned with this group of problems. Traditionally Luke has been viewed as a Gentile Christian, with little knowledge of or interest in Judaism and Jewish Christians.[5] He indeed accepts, as anyone must, that Jesus was a Jew and that the understanding of his function as saviour is based on the messianic promises of the Old Testament. But in his own day, we have mostly assumed, Luke lived in a church now predominantly of Gentile origin and engaged in a mission almost solely directed towards Gentiles: the audience for which he writes is a Gentile one, and the only point usually debated is whether these Gentile readers are already Christian or are pagan.[6] According to this view of Luke, the church has now cheerfully and confidently accepted its inevitable break from Judaism as an accomplished fact, and regards itself as 'the new Israel' to which the fulfilment of the old messianic promises to Israel has been bequeathed.

2 Luke's 'Orientation Towards Judaism'

In recent years, this assumption of Luke's thoroughly Gentile orientation has been challenged with some vigour, and notably by J. Jervell[7] and G. D. Kilpatrick.[8] They argue that Luke belongs to a predominantly Jewish church, where Jewish theology is still influential. The church, especially as represented by Paul, is being charged by non-Christian Jews with disloyalty to the Law. Luke's aim is to rebut this charge and show that the church remains within the Law: in the renewed Israel the Law must be fulfilled. This new perspective deserves careful consideration, for it has drawn attention to aspects of Luke's work which have not been sufficiently regarded.

It is a pity that, like many other Lucan scholars, Jervell has directed his studies disproportionately towards Acts. He does however make some remarks about the Gospel of Luke. In Luke 1–2 he notes the emphasis on the Jewishness of Jesus, and especially on his circumcision, which marks him as Messiah for the people of Israel.[9] He regards some of Luke's omissions from Mark as evidence of a pro-Jewish point of view: e.g. Luke omits Mark 12:28–34/Matt. 22:34–40, where Jesus summarized the Law in two commandments, which a Rabbi would hardly do.[10] He has a novel interpretation of Luke's omission of Mark 7:1–23 (the question about cleanliness and defilement): whereas most interpreters have seen this as a sign of Luke's Gentile orientation, in that the matters discussed have to do with Jewish ritual and would be irrelevant to Luke's Gentile audience, Jervell contends, on the contrary, that Luke omits this section because he does not want to show Jesus as critical of Rabbinic halakah: Jesus is too loyal a Jew![11] Luke gives us three times (against once each in Mark and Matthew, and twice in John) a story of Jesus' healing on the Sabbath and being criticized for it by Jewish authorities. Luke's purpose, according to Jervell, is 'to show that Jesus acted in complete accordance with the Law . . . His principle may be found in Luke 13:10–17: It is no transgression to free a daughter of Abraham, an Israelite, on the Sabbath. On the contrary, this is what the Law demands.'[12]

On these examples the following comments can be made. The Jewishness of Jesus in Luke 1–2 is a clear phenomenon, which must be taken into account in any explanation of Luke's theology and purpose.[13] Jervell's reason for the omission of Mark 7:1–23 needs to be checked against other passages bearing on the question whether Jesus is a 'loyal Jew' with respect to the Law.[14] As for the healings on the Sabbath, Jervell can support his explanation only by citing John 7:22f., where Jesus defends his acting in this way by a sort of inverse analogy with the permission of circumcision on the Sabbath. As commentary on John 7:23, Billerbeck adduces a number of Rabbinic passages which teach that on the Sabbath it is permitted to rescue a person who is in danger of his life: but this has nothing to say as to whether Jesus was within the Jewish Law as commonly understood and practised when on the Sabbath he healed people of chronic, non-fatal disabilities.[15] In order to set these matters in correct perspective we need to consider also, for example, the pericope where Jesus defends his disciples when they pluck ears of wheat on the Sabbath (Luke 6:1–6/Mark 2:23–28). Luke apparently has no qualms about showing Jesus here in conflict with the Law. Rather than showing Jesus to have consistent respect for the Law, Luke is content to follow Mark in reporting that Jesus on occasions deliberately set the Law aside, without needing to include every such Marcan passage.[16]

The observations of Kilpatrick about the Gospel of Luke tend in a similar direction to those of Jervell, though for him the point of departure is not the Law but the alleged 'universalism' of Luke. In a number of short papers spread over some twenty years Kilpatrick[17] has been pursuing the program of showing that Jesus did not command a mission to the Gentiles, that the gospel-writers were at any rate very reserved in representing Jesus as commanding a world-mission, and that in general the church of the first century was not greatly interested in mission to the Gentiles as a matter of policy: the Gentiles only gradually forced themselves on the attention of the

Jewish leaders of the church, as they began to be converted in considerable numbers, but only incidentally, in the course of the mission of Paul and others to the Diaspora. Luke, too, according to Kilpatrick, fits into this general pattern. The first clue comes from Luke's use of certain significant words: κύριος and its vocative κύριε, γραμματεύς and νομικός, λαός and ἔθνος: and especially the distribution of these words in various parts or 'strata' of Luke's two books.[18] Kilpatrick finds that Luke's vocabulary has a more Jewish cast in the Marcan parts of his material than in the non-Marcan, and yet that some of these words of Jewish flavour recur in Acts. It was Luke's use of λαός, and especially its frequency, which first made him 'doubt the customary description of Luke as the Gospel of the Gentiles'.[19] This prepares the way for a more definite statement in a lecture entitled 'Luke – Not a Gentile Gospel'.[20] Here Kilpatrick briefly reviews a number of passages in Luke–Acts which have usually been taken as signs of a universalist attitude on the part of Luke, and warns us that this may be merely a convention of interpretation, rather than something inherent in the text. The nearest we come to universalism in Luke's Gospel is 24:47, 'that repentance for the forgiveness of sins should be proclaimed in his name to all the nations': but even here universalism is less marked than in Matt. 28:16–20. From these various observations Kilpatrick draws some debatable conclusions.[21] But, unlike Jervell, he has drawn attention to details of Luke's Gospel which have too often been overlooked. There is indeed some kind of 'Jewish orientation' in Luke's work. Whether the significance of this 'orientation' is correctly interpreted is another question.

Jervell is much more impressive when he turns to deal with the book of Acts. He reminds us that most studies of the 'speeches' in Acts (and there have been many) have dealt only with the mission-speeches, or sermons, in ch. 2–17. But Paul's defence-speeches in the later chapters (22:1–21; 24:10–21; 26:1–23; plus his briefer statements under interrogation before the Sanhedrin, 23:1–7) also deserve attention.[22] It is remarkable that the last eight chapters of Acts are dominated by Paul's defence against Jewish accusations: this theme in fact receives more space than Paul's mission, and so it may be suspected that in describing Paul's mission in ch. (9–)13–20 Luke is really aiming to defend it.[23] But it is important, says Jervell, that what is being defended is not the Christian mission in general, or the policy of a mission to Gentiles, but specifically and personally *Paul's* mission, as is made plain by the repeated and detailed biographical element in these speeches.[24]

Jervell sees the broad sequence of ideas in Acts like this: in ch. 1–8 a renewed Israel is established, on the basis of repentance, piety according to the Law, and faith in Jesus.[25] Luke repeatedly mentions the enormous numerical success of the mission among the Jews, a success which is to be understood as continuing while the diaspora-mission is going on, for by the time we come to 21:20 a high proportion of the population of Judaea must be Christian, if we are to take the figures seriously.[26] Ch. 9–15 deal with the question of Gentiles, and show how they are allowed, both in principle and in practice, to be 'associated' with Israel.[27] (This concept of 'association' is used also by Kilpatrick:[28] it is at the heart of the problem with which this chapter is concerned, and to it we shall return.[29]) In ch. 16–21 Paul carries out a mission to the Jewish dispersion, geographically complete except for Rome; and on his return to Jerusalem he proves that he has been throughout, and still remains, a loyal, Law-keeping Jew. Now this point dominates the last eight chapters, a section which might be entitled, 'Paul and the Jews'.[30] Paul's arrest and trial lead not, as we at first expect, to the Emperor, but to the Jews in Rome. The Roman state is almost completely ignored.[31] And when, on arrival in Rome, Paul summons the leading Jews to visit him, it is not primarily so that he may preach the gospel to them, but that he may assert his loyalty to Judaism.[32] The charge against Paul is stated at the beginning and end of this section (21:21, 28; 28:17) as well as several times within it, and what it amounts to is that Paul has spoken against the λαός and the νόμος, i.e. he is an apostate Jew: and Luke's whole effort in ch. 21–28 is to clear him of this – and through him the whole church; for Paul is acknowledged as πρωτοστάτης of the sect of the Nazarenes (24:5).[33] Luke emphasizes repeatedly that Paul believes all that Moses and the prophets taught: and paramount in this teaching is the resurrection, which all true Jews believe in. So it is Paul's accusers who are heretics, not he.[34] All this is reinforced by Paul's speeches. In the two biographical speeches, ch. 22 and 26, Luke is not freely composing, but is controlled by a tradition going back to Paul himself[35] (though it is not claimed that Luke had access to any of Paul's letters): from these two speeches one gets the impression that Paul's exemplary Pharisaism belongs to the past, to his pre-Christian period. But in ch. 23 and 24, where Luke is composing freely,[36] this impression is corrected: Paul *is still* a faithful, Pharisaic Jew, both in his practice and in his teaching; indeed, he is more faithful to the Law than the High Priest is (23:1ff.).[37] In all this, 'Luke's concern is the struggle for the right of citizenship in the people of God'.[38] According to Jervell, Luke is writing for Christian readers: and he writes history as a way of dealing with problems that confronted his readers in their own time. The church had to defend itself against Jewish attacks, which were especially directed against Paul and his statements about the Law.[39] This leads Jervell to conclude that in Luke's church Jewish Christians are an influential element, whose opinions must be respected. Their opinions have so far prevailed that in the renewed Israel the Law must be fulfilled and the customs of the fathers upheld.[40]

The value of these studies, and especially those of Jervell, is that they force us to come to terms with those parts of Luke–Acts which speak about Judaism and its interests, which have been too easily and frequently ignored. It is certainly odd to come from, say, Mark or Galatians, and hear Paul say, 'I am a Pharisee'. But have these elements been correctly interpreted?

3 The 'People of God' and the Law

The most fundamental problem lies in the relation of Acts 10–11 to ch. 15 – of the conversion of Cornelius to the apostolic council and its decree. According to Jervell, 'Luke knows of but one Israel, one people of God, one covenant': and this people and this covenant are still based on the Law.[41] The Jewish Christians are the 'restored' Israel, and it is precisely by 'being zealous for the law' that they 'prove their identity as the people of God, entitled to salvation'.[42] With the renewed, Law-keeping Israel, according to Acts 15:14, a 'people of the Gentiles' is 'associated'. 'The idea is that of a people and an associate people . . . Luke labours to prove that the salvation of the gentiles occurs in complete accordance with the law; no transgression has taken place, the law is not invalidated, abridged or outmoded.'[43]

At this point the logic of the argument must be watched carefully. On the one hand, it is quite true that 'Luke knows of but one Israel'. This has been well shown by G. Lohfink, who emphasizes that the mission of Jesus is deeply rooted in Israel and is addressed to Israel:[44] the alternative concept 'church' never occurs in the Gospel of Luke and only gradually and almost imperceptibly replaces 'Israel' during the course of Acts.[45] Lohfink further shows that, right from the opening scenes, Luke 1:5–2:40, Israel is being divided in accordance with its response to God's visitation in Jesus[46] (so far in agreement with Jervell); but also that as from the resurrection of Jesus (Luke 24:47) the concept of 'Israel' is widened to include the Gentiles.[47] If this is true, it means that for Luke Israel is no longer the same: it is no longer simply identical with the community based on the Law. Perhaps Lohfink has read too much into Luke 24:47: the Law is not mentioned there.[48] But these words of Jesus after the resurrection serve to prepare the way for Acts 10, where the problem of the Gentiles and the Law is directly tackled. In 1963, in an article on Judaism and Christianity in Acts, E. Haenchen had already shown that Luke was here saying something very different from what Jervell asserts.[49] In Acts 10 it is stressed that Peter is a legalistic Jew who would never have entertained the idea of a Gentile-mission of his own accord. He is shown, not through theological argument of the Pauline kind, but through a vision and a command given by God, that he must call no person unclean. But this strikes at the basis of the Jewish Law: there is no 'chosen people'![50] In ch. 11 the message of ch. 10 is reinforced when the Jewish Christians in Jerusalem at first bitterly object to Peter's actions (11:3f.), but after hearing him narrate what has happened acknowledge that God has given 'repentance leading to life' to the Gentiles as well. It is a matter of astonishment to them, but they yield to God's *force majeure* (11:17f.).[51] The conclusion is complete and unqualified: God's gift has been given to the Gentiles on equal terms with the Jewish believers, and the qualification for it is belief in the Lord Jesus Christ, without any mention of the Law (v. 17). It is misleading when Jervell says, on the basis of Acts 10:2,

4, 22, 'Significantly, Cornelius himself keeps the law . . . but without the one necessary thing, circumcision.'[52] That pious behaviour, without the 'one necessary thing', is of no significance for the question of Peter's abiding within the Jewish Law. If God has 'cleansed' the Gentiles, it is incorrect to say that therefore 'Peter has not transgressed the Law'.[53] Of course Peter has transgressed the Law (10:28a; 11:2f.), and he has done so because God has done so before him (10:15, 19f., 28b): which is to say, God has abolished the Law.[54] There is no hint in Acts 10–11 that the Gentiles are to be only 'an associate people', a separate group enjoying only limited status in or access to the fellowship of God's people.

How, then, are we to understand Luke's report of the council-meeting and its decision in Acts 15? Jervell rightly emphasizes the surprising prominence of James at the council – surprising, because Luke has barely introduced James before (12:17) and does not explain how he came to have such a dominant position.[55] The decree is described not as a decision by the whole group but as James' personal decision (v. 19) which the others then accept.[56] Jervell then proceeds to argue that Luke has gone to the limits of compositional freedom in portraying, contrary to the facts known by both Luke and his readers, a 'liberal' James who defends a 'conservative' Paul against the criticisms of Jewish Christians.[57] Paul's only negative statement about the Law in Acts is 13:38f. (through Jesus comes freedom from all those things from which there is no release through the Law of Moses), and this, says Jervell, is far less critical than James' remark that the Law is a 'trouble' (15:19).[58] Jervell also regards the decree itself as a 'liberal' measure, since a conservative Jewish-Christian might well have demanded much more: and it is James, not Paul, who takes this 'liberal' step. 'This decree . . . is not to be attributed to Paul. He shares no responsibility for Gentiles' being exempted from details of the Law.'[59]

But does not this stand the question on its head? Luke has narrated in detail how Paul accepted Gentile believers in Antioch-in-Pisidia, Iconium, Derbe and even pagan Lystra, and in no case has he said anything to indicate that these Gentiles are required to keep the Law. Rather, Luke is most hesitant about ascribing to Paul a share of responsibility for *demanding anything* of the Gentiles with respect to the Law. It is not true that when Luke ascribes the decree to James 'the explanation . . . can only be that Luke's readers have little confidence in Paul'.[60] It is arbitrary to assume, as Jervell does here, that Luke is freely composing a story about James and Paul, guided only by his apologetic purpose and without regard for the historical facts. (Here we come across a remarkable feature of Jervell's book. The opening chapter, 'The Problem of Traditions in Acts', argues, especially against E. Haenchen, that in the first century conditions were favourable 'for the formation of a tradition about apostolic times' and that therefore historical traditions lying behind the book of Acts are to be sought with more confidence than Haenchen has allowed; but in the remaining chapters this insight is largely abandoned: to an astonishing degree the contents of Acts are attributed to Luke's redactional purposes.[61]) Admittedly, this is indeed a liberal James by comparison with the James of Gal. 2:12–14 and the later tradition – but not by comparison with Paul, even the Paul of Acts! Luke's reason for giving Paul so small a place at the council is not that he will not let Paul appear so liberal, but that he knows he is on uncertain ground in letting Paul appear so conservative. Historically, the case can with some confidence be reconstructed as follows.[62] The conversion of Cornelius was neither so well-known nor so influential as a test-case and precedent as Luke implies through his narrative in ch. 10–11:[63] otherwise it is hard to see how the 'believers who had come from the party of the Pharisees' would have been able to mount a case to demand the circumcision of Gentile believers; rather, Cornelius' conversion was one case like the many hinted at in Acts 11:20f. It is hard to believe, in the light of Gal. 2 and of Paul's correspondence generally, that Paul was really a consenting party to the decree, as is implied in Acts 15:2, 12, 22, 25. At a conference of leading Christians representing Antioch and Jerusalem, but at which Paul was not present[64] (and therefore not the meeting referred to in Gal. 2:1–10) the continuing problem, how fellowship could be established between Law-keeping Jewish Christians and non-proselyte Gentile Christians, was thrashed out, and a decision reached in the form preserved by Luke in the decree of Acts 15:20, 29.[65] In the essential point, this decision did not seek to contradict the earlier agreement (Gal. 2:1–10) that God did not require accession to Judaism for salvation through Christ; but the pain that this involved to the sensibilities of conservatively-minded Jewish Christians was to be mitigated at two points: Gentile Christians should eat kosher meat, and not marry within the prohibited degrees of relationship.[66] But does this mean that, after all, the Gentiles are being required to keep the Law, or part of it, and could be described as being 'associated' with Law-keeping Israel? No: the requirements of the decree, in the sense of a distinct group of prescriptions intended for Gentiles, form no part of Jewish halakah of the first century; nor, from the perspective of Jewish orthodoxy, do these reduced requirements constitute a basis for fellowship between Jews and Gentiles.[67] Rabbinic theology knows of a list of six 'Adamic' commandments and a set of seven 'Noachic' commandments which were held to be binding on Gentiles, but these were of merely speculative interest – they were regarded as the minimal standard of behaviour required for the continuance of human life, but not as providing for any kind of associate status of Gentiles in the community of Israel.[68] The origin of the list of four requirements in the decree is obscure. It does not seem to occur in any Jewish sources. Whether they were worked out on the analogy of the Noachic commandments, or, as P. Billerbeck suggested, by Christian exegesis of Lev. 17–18,[69] these requirements may be said to come from 'the Law' only in the sense of the Pentateuch as their ultimate source, but not in such a way as to reflect current Jewish halakah.[70] And if Luke thought otherwise, this would only show how far he was from any lively contact with Jewish theology and Jewish interests.

As even Acts 21:25 probably implies, Paul was only much later informed of the decree promulgated by the council. Paul himself explicitly rejected a prohibition of meat sacrificed to idols: his discussion of the matter (1 Cor. 8–10) shows that he certainly appreciated the pastoral problem involved, but was determined to deal with it in a more dynamic way, on the one hand insisting on the freedom of the Christian conscience in welcoming social intercourse without concern about the ritual status of the food offered, on the other hand calling for imaginative compassion to avoid using that liberty when to do so would unnecessarily give offence to a less perceptive fellow-Christian.[71] Now it is abundantly clear that Luke had no access to Paul's letters, and his acquaintance with Paul's theology was at best rather fuzzy around the edges.[72] From his point of view, making the small compromise offered by the decree to the strict Jewish-Christian attitude was only a kind and courteous thing to do; and, lacking any definite information to the contrary, he saw no reason to deny Paul's participation in the conference at which the decree was agreed to: nevertheless, some hints of his hesitation on the point are suggested by the small part played by Paul in his report of the conference and in the remark of James and others, informing Paul of the decree, some years later (Acts 21:25).

We have already seen good reason to doubt J. Jervell's conclusion that, when Luke is writing, 'the Jewish element within the church is still a decisive factor, if not numerically, at least theologically'.[73] It is indeed remarkable, as he says, that Luke is at such pains to have Paul emphasize that he himself has always lived according to the Law, including the oral, Rabbinic halakah. But it is also clear that Luke has no real understanding of what this Law is. A good example of this is Paul's assumption of a Nazirite vow (Acts 18:18; cf. 21:23–27), which Jervell cites as an illustration of the Jewishness of Luke's Paul:[74] what he does not mention is that the way the vow is carried out bears little resemblance to what we know from Jewish sources of the Nazirite procedure – it is a garbled description, such as might come from a Gentile Christian at some remove from the ritual practices of orthodox Judaism.[75] In insisting that Paul is a Law-keeping Jew, Luke is no doubt recalling at any rate one aspect of Paul's actual practice, mentioned in 1 Cor. 9:20;[76] and his reason for so insisting is that he wants to make it clear that the breach between Judaism and Christianity is not due to the Christians – least of all Paul. This is for Luke a large and important consideration. He wants to emphasize that the Christians have done their best to behave courteously and to avoid giving offence; nevertheless, they cannot resist God when he so clearly intervenes to show them that a new era has arrived, in which the Gentiles have full access to his grace.

But still, how can Luke go so far as to say that Paul is (not was, but is) a Pharisee (Acts 23:1–9)?

4 Christians and Pharisees

At this point, an attentive reading of Luke–Acts calls for a distinction which J. Jervell has not observed, and thereby introduces into his interpretation of Paul as a Pharisee a confusion which has serious consequences for his total case about Luke's theology.[77]

There are two distinctive characteristics of the Pharisees: on the one hand is their veneration for and fidelity to the Law as elaborated in the Rabbinic halakah; on the other hand their lively eschatology. Luke is well aware of both these aspects. He is aware that the Pharisees are legalists, as is shown not only by the many passages in his Gospel where they come into conflict with Jesus over the Law,[78] but also for example by Acts 15:5, where it is believers 'from the party of the Pharisees' who want to insist that Gentile believers be required to undergo circumcision and to keep the Law of Moses. But it is their eschatology, and especially their doctrine of resurrection, which Luke finds really interesting. In particular we must observe (against Jervell) that it is *only on the latter ground* that Luke suggests some degree of affinity or sympathy between the Pharisees and Jesus, Paul and the Christians in general.[79]

This is shown, for example, by the way Luke expands the pericope containing Jesus' answer to the Sadducees about marriage in the resurrection (Luke 20:27–40 pars.): not only is Jesus' statement of the difference between life in this age and in the resurrection more emphatic than in Mark and Matthew, but Luke also concludes by having the scribes congratulate Jesus on his remarks.[80] And in Acts 23:1–9 this doctrine is the sole reason given for Paul's aligning himself with the Pharisees over against the Sadducees in the Sanhedrin: not only does Paul say so, 'I am a Pharisee and a son of Pharisees: I am on trial concerning the Hope and the resurrection of the dead' (v. 6), but Luke also adds a note explaining for his readers that the difference between Sadducees and Pharisees lies in their respective denial and affirmation of resurrection, angel and spirit – with not a word about their different attitudes to Torah. (In contrast with this passage stands the only place in Paul's letters where the word 'Pharisee' occurs (Phil. 3:5): Paul repudiates his former life as a Pharisee, blameless in the performance of righteousness in the Law.) Early in Acts, it is explicitly the Sadducees who take offence and initiate action against the apostles for preaching in Jerusalem that Jesus has been raised from the dead (Acts 4:1f., 5f.; 5:17f.), and it is 'a Pharisee called Gamaliel' who tentatively suggests that the truth or falsity of their preaching be left an open question (Acts 5:34–39). Through the various scenes following his arrest, Paul keeps returning to this theme. In the hearing before Felix Paul declares, 'I hold the hope in God, which these people themselves also accept, that there will be a resurrection of just and unjust' (24:15), and he completes this speech by harking back to his statement to the Sanhedrin in 23:6. In the hearing before Festus (25:6–12) attention is fixed on Paul's appeal to Caesar; but when Festus afterwards tells Agrippa about the case he explains that it is concerning questions of Jewish religion and Paul's claim that a certain Jesus who has died is alive (25:19). In his address to Agrippa and a distinguished Caesarean audience (ch. 26) Paul again affirms that it is because of his adherence to Israel's ancient hope of the resurrection of the dead that he is on trial (v. 6–8); and he finishes this speech, too, by claiming that his testimony to the suffering and resurrection of the Messiah is based on what was foretold by the prophets and Moses (v. 22f.). Finally, in his encounter with the Jewish leaders in Rome, Paul repeats, 'It is because of the hope of Israel that I am wearing this chain' (28:20). Thus Paul consistently maintains that his teaching has been based not only on the testimony of the Twelve and the other eye-witnesses of Jesus' ministry about the way God had fulfilled his promise to send the Messiah (13:31); not only on the clear witness of scripture to the meaning of what had happened in Jesus and was happening among his disciples (13:32–39); not only on God's continuing confirmation of his revelation through Jesus by wonders, signs, miracles and visions (15:12; 16:9, 18; 18:9; etc.); but even on the Pharisees' own theology. The Sadducees, perhaps, can't be helped: they never did believe in resurrection anyway. But the Pharisees, at least, *ought* to believe, since what the Christians proclaim is nothing other than the fulfilment of their own hope and expectation – a fulfilment attested not only by impeccable witnesses and abundant proofs of the resurrection of Jesus itself, but also by the continuing evidence of the corollary of the resurrection, namely, the Holy Spirit.

Clearly, then, Luke is appealing to the common ground between Christians and Pharisees *on the doctrine of resurrection*. It is not because of the Law that Luke has a positive attitude to the Pharisees. When Pharisees come forward as champions of the Law, either as opponents of Jesus or as 'believers', they are either decisively repudiated (Acts 15:5, 19f.) or at least do not appear in a very good light: the 'many myriads' of Jewish Christians who are 'zealots for the Law' (Acts 21:20) do nothing to support Paul when he is shamefully treated in the Temple and then kept under arrest.[81]

What then is Luke's line in all this? Jervell rightly rejects E. Haenchen's view that the alliance Luke suggests between Christians and Pharisees can be explained by Tertullian's phrase (too often referred to and too little understood) about bringing Christianity 'under the umbrella of a most distinguished and certainly permitted religion',[82] i.e. to use this alliance as a way of appealing for Roman toleration and protection.[83] (The theory of a 'religio licita' will be examined below, in Chapter Four.) Jervell has rightly seen that the 'bond of sympathy'-theme has to do not with the relations of Christians to the Roman state but with relations between Christians and Jews.[84] It is a doctrinal matter: but the doctrine in question is not the Law, as Jervell supposes, but the resurrection.

From the prominence of this theme in the last few chapters of Acts it is evident that Luke is indeed deeply concerned about the relationships of

Jews and Christians. For Luke 'the Jews' means especially 'the Pharisees'.[85] No doubt this partly reflects the situation after 70 AD, when the Pharisaic group led by Johanan ben Zakkai provided the only effective impetus for the restoration of Jewish life after the war against Rome; but it may also be due to the fact that of all the groups within Judaism it was the Pharisees with whom first Jesus and then Paul shared the most in common, and from whose opposition they suffered their worst disappointments. In Acts 23–28 Luke stresses two things: first, that in principle there exists the possibility of agreement between Pharisaic Judaism and Christianity; but secondly, that on the whole this possibility has not been realized, because the Jews have refused to accept the plain evidence which indicates the fulfilment of their own hopes and expectations.

Thus the strong Jewish orientation of Luke–Acts, which Jervell has rightly detected, especially in the closing chapters of the work, does not mean that the church is still close to Judaism, much less that Luke believes Christians should live within the Law: rather, Luke is sharply aware of the separation that has taken place between the Christians (now largely of Gentile origin) and that part of Law-keeping Judaism which has not accepted Jesus as the Messiah.[86]

5 Luke's Orientation Against Judaism

It may be that the weakness of Jervell's interpretation is due not only to the inadequacy of his exegesis of certain key passages, as I have tried to show, but also to his posing the question of Luke's concerns too narrowly. For there are in Luke–Acts not only an undeniable 'Jewish orientation' but also two other closely related factors, which we might call a 'Gentile orientation' and an 'anti-Jewish orientation',[87] which must be studied if we are to arrive at a proper understanding of Luke's aim. The former is well known,[88] but the latter, though occasionally noticed, does not seem to have been explored systematically.

It is important, in the first place, to take note how Luke has chosen to end his work. As has been well observed, especially by W. C. Robinson, Luke's work is shaped by geographical movement: in the Gospel Jesus moves from Galilee to Jerusalem, in the Acts the message of Jesus is taken from Jerusalem to Rome. Such a theme is undoubtedly meant by Luke to convey an important significance in itself. This movement is 'the way of the Lord', whereby God moves triumphantly through the earth, fulfilling his promise of life, hope and joy as declared by the prophets, especially the second Isaiah.[89] In accord with this theme, the ending of Acts is a joyful one. Though every reader of Acts knows that the actual end of Paul's career was martyrdom (cf. 20:22–25, 28),[90] Luke's last word is that the Christian mission has in spite of all obstacles successfully reached the heart of the Gentile world: the gospel is now in principle open to all people, and Paul is preaching in the imperial capital quite openly and without hindrance.

But to describe the ending of Luke–Acts in this way is to take account of only the last two verses, which stand on their own as a separate, final note.[91] Just as important is the last major unit of Acts. After the long description of Paul's journey to Rome (Acts 21:1–28:15) Luke also gives us a narrative of Paul's activity in Rome in more specific terms (Acts 28:17–25a) followed by comment on the significance of this experience (28:25b–28). The first readers of this passage must have been astonished at its two glaring omissions: first, the complete silence about Paul's trial before Caesar, for which he has been brought to Rome, and second, the slight regard paid to the Roman Christians (v. 14b–15).[92] These omissions bring into sharp focus what Luke has decided to include in this final scene: only Paul's unfruitful preaching to the leading Jews of the city, his solemn pronouncement of God's judgement upon them by the quotation of Isaiah 6:9f., and his final repetition of the 'turning to the Gentiles'. That Acts 28:17–28 is a Lucan composition rather than simply an historical report has often been shown.[93] It is therefore evident that this passage, which Luke has composed to place in so prominent a position in his work, is meant to convey an important part of his message, and deserves more attention than commentators have given it. E. Haenchen and H. Conzelmann[94] are content to observe that Luke wants to emphasize the continuity of Paul's work in Rome with his earlier work (Acts 13:46 and 18:6, where Paul's turning to the Gentiles is provoked by the Jews' rejection of his preaching), and that according to Luke there is no longer hope, as there was for Paul (Romans 11), that the Jews would accept the gospel: in other words, our attention is still drawn to the importance of the Gentile mission. But the negative theme, that the Jews are excluded, is also most important to Luke. It is true that some of the Roman Jews are persuaded by what Paul says (v. 24). But this is by no means where Luke lets the emphasis fall. As the meeting broke up in disagreement Paul 'said one thing' (v. 25), addressed to the Jews as a whole, and its burden is entirely negative.[95]

This remarkable conclusion of Acts does not stand alone, but brings to a climax a theme that has been present throughout the work. In the first place, we must notice the great importance in the structure of Acts of the three passages about Paul's 'turning to the Gentiles': Acts 13:46; 18:6; and 28:28. At a first reading, it seems from Acts 13:46ff. that Paul has made a decision of policy: his preaching to Jews has come to an end. But at the next station on his journey, he immediately sets out to preach in the synagogue as before (14:1). Nor is the 'turning to the Gentiles' in 18:6 a final one: we reach finality on this question only at the end of the book. The almost stereotyped, threefold repetition is clearly meant to mark an important part of Luke's message. Only one other theme is put forward three times in Acts: the narrative of Paul's conversion. In both cases, Luke is especially drawing his readers' attention to the significance of the respective matters in hand. And in the case of the 'turning to the Gentiles', the significance is that, if the Christian message is being heard and accepted more by Gentiles than by

Jews, *that is not Paul's fault*. Though Paul habitually begins his preaching by addressing the Jews, it repeatedly turns out that it is the Gentiles who are responsive to it, and the Jews who are not.[96]

Secondly, we must note that the three passages about Paul's 'turning to the Gentiles' are not merely parallel: there is a progressive intensification of the theme. In 13:46, after Paul's preaching at Antioch-in-Pisidia has stirred up opposition among the Jews, the attitude portrayed is one of reluctance: 'It was necessary that the word of God be spoken to you first; since you repudiate it and judge yourselves unworthy of eternal life, behold, we are turning to the Gentiles.' In 18:6, at Corinth, the mood is of frustration and impatience: 'Your blood is on your heads: I shall from now on go with clean hands to the Gentiles.' In 28:25b–28 Paul's pronouncement, quoting Isaiah 6:9f., has the solemn air of finality. Formal, extended quotations of the Old Testament are rather rare in Luke–Acts, and where they occur they usually underline some important principle or new stage in the advance of the gospel: e.g. Luke 3:4ff. (John the Baptist); 4:18f. (Jesus' sermon at Nazareth); Acts 2:17–21 (the gift of the Holy Spirit); Acts 15:16ff. (the Jerusalem council). Of all the Old Testament quotations in Luke–Acts, only Acts 2:17–21 is longer than 28:26ff. The content of this last quotation deals not with the opening of the gospel to the Gentiles but with the self-exclusion of the Jews: and Luke emphasizes this with the introduction to it in 28:25b, 'Rightly did the Holy Spirit speak through Isaiah the prophet to your fathers . . .'. It is worth recalling here the observation of G. Stählin, that Paul's final words in 28:28, 'to the Gentiles has this salvation of God been sent', have become almost the exact opposite of his words in the synagogue at Antioch-in-Pisidia, 'to us (i.e. to us Jews) the message of this salvation has been sent' (13:26).[97] At the end of Paul's mission the opportunity offered at its beginning has been lost.

In a more general way, the theme of Acts 28:17–28 has been present since early in Luke. It is first hinted at in the prophecy of Symeon that Jesus would be 'a sign spoken against' (Luke 2:34). But it is brought to clear expression at the beginning of Jesus' public work, in his sermon at Nazareth (4:16–30). This sermon has the peculiar feature, which has worried many exegetes, that after the hopeful opening, with a positive response from the congregation in v. 20–22, the words of Jesus in v. 23ff. switch without warning, and apparently without provocation, to rebuke of his townsfolk, in the assumption that they have already rejected his mission. This sudden, harsh turn has been explained by some as due to Luke's use of a new source. G. Lohfink, for example, thinks that the many 'expressions hostile to Israel' in Luke are due to early traditions including those contained in 'Q', whereas Luke's own redaction tends to portray a harmonious relationship between Jesus and his people.[98] But against this it must be observed that, whatever sources he may have used, Luke himself is responsible for the final shape of the passage: and what it clearly says is that, right from the outset, Jesus found his mission rejected by his own people. G. Stählin is again right in pointing out the connexion between this passage and the end of Acts.[99] That Jesus here seems to assume that the Jews oppose him, even before they make any explicit response, is not unique to this passage. In much the same way Paul, at the end of his sermon at Antioch-in-Pisidia (Acts 13:40f.), anticipates the subsequent rejection of his message (v. 45f.), though the initial response is actually positive (v. 42f.). In this connexion we must recall that the Gospel of Luke is not intended as first information about Jesus' career (see 1:4): Luke does not necessarily write a complete and self-explanatory account, but is writing for an audience which already knows a good part of the story he has to tell, and can at many points read between the lines. In other words, he assumes from the outset that his readers will understand that he is writing a work concerned, among other things, with the rejection of the gospel by the Jewish people.

At this point we may raise in a preliminary way the question whether, according to Luke, it is indeed 'the Jewish people' who characteristically resist the mission of Jesus and then of his disciples. It is true, as G. Braumann has said, that in Acts opposition and even persecution of the church come from Gentiles as well as Jews: e.g. at Philippi (16:19ff.) and Ephesus; and at Acts 4:25ff. Psalm 2 is seen as the background to a conspiracy between Jewish and Gentile rulers against Jesus.[100] But the main concentration of Acts is nevertheless on Jewish persecution and rejection of the gospel, both in Judaea and abroad, and in a stereotyped way that does not accord with the evidence of Paul's letters. There is also much truth in H. Conzelmann's observation that Luke does not regard all Jews individually as rejecting the gospel, but rather shows that it is the established leaders of Judaism who resist.[101] However, Luke does not maintain a clear distinction on this point. Luke received from the gospel-tradition the basic information that the career of Jesus was marked by constant clashes with the Jewish leaders, which ultimately led to his crucifixion. Many passages in Luke and the early chapters of Acts distinguish between the friendly attitude of 'the people' or 'the crowds' and the hostility of various groups among their leaders. But this is complicated by at least two factors, as G. Lohfink has pointed out.[102] First, the attitude of 'the people' suddenly and briefly changes in Luke 23:1–5, 13–25, when they call for Jesus to be crucified, though at 23:48 they beat their breasts at his death: apparently this is needed to prepare the way for Acts 2:23 and 3:14, where the Jewish community in general is charged with responsibility for Jesus' death. Second, there are some dozen sayings of Jesus, which Luke has taken up from old tradition, in which the Jewish people as a whole are rebuked for their lack of faith. Lohfink argues that in Luke's narrative passages, where his redaction is more strongly at work than in the sayings of Jesus, the crowd is always friendly, with the exception of Luke 23:1–5, 13–25, until we come to the death of Stephen.[103] There are however in the Gospel of Luke a number of passages, not noticed by Lohfink, where even in Luke's redaction it is implied that the Jewish community in general (though indeed not all individual Jews) stands under judgement for its refusal to respond positively to the mission of Jesus. These passages will be examined below.

In summary we may propose the following hypothesis about Luke's meaning. Although Luke knows that many Jews became disciples of Jesus during his lifetime, and many others became believers in him, especially during the early stages of the apostolic mission in Jerusalem, and some also in the diaspora, and although he puts the main responsibility for the rejection of the gospel on to the Jewish leaders, he nevertheless stands over against Judaism as an organized community, which he in general regards as unbelieving. This is well exemplified in the final scene, Acts 28:17–28, where Paul calls 'the leading people among the Jews' to a discussion with him (v. 17), but at the end he quotes Isaiah's words to 'this people' (v. 26), which is contrasted with the Gentiles, who 'will actually listen' (v. 28).

6 The 'Visitation' of Jerusalem

Between the sermon in Nazareth (Luke 4:16–30) and beginning of Jesus' journey to Jerusalem (9:51) there is not a great deal on our theme. It may be significant that in 6:27–29 the call to 'love your enemies' is placed immediately after the beatitudes and woes, which each end with reference to the way 'their fathers' treated the prophets and the false prophets: it is thereby implied that the 'enemies' envisaged are the persecutors of Jesus' disciples. There may be a still subtler nuance in the sequence from 6:49 through 7:9 to 7:23: the sermon on the plain ends with a warning about those who hear Jesus' teaching and do not act accordingly; it is a Gentile centurion rather than Israel who has great faith in Jesus; the Lord ends his answer to the messengers of John the Baptist with the warning, 'blessed is anyone who is not offended by me'. These hints at least prepare the way for the more explicit words in which the unbelieving 'people of this generation' are rebuked in 7:31–35.

But the theme is greatly intensified once the journey begins. Many suggestions have been made about Luke's reason for so artificially protracting the journey (9:51–19:27, or–19:41a).[103a] In fact Luke has stated the purpose of the journey at its opening, 9:51: 'And it happened, when the days of his ascension were being fulfilled, that he set his face to go to Jerusalem'. The two key expressions in this heavily Septuagintal Greek are *αἱ ἡμέραι τῆς ἀναλήμψεως* and *τὸ πρόσωπον ἐστήρισεν*. Luke prefers to say, Jesus is going to Jerusalem for the ascension, rather than for the crucifixion. (9:51 *ἀναλήμψεως*; Acts 1:2 *ἀνελήμφθη*, v. 11 *ἀναλημφθείς*.)[104] Luke's chief view of the destiny of Jesus is that he is to take his place at God's right hand in heaven (22:69; Acts 7:56; 2:30–35; 5:31).[105] But on the way to this destiny he must, as the Son of God, come to Jerusalem, the city of God's people, to claim the fruits of God's covenant with them (Luke 20:13).[106] This is the 'visitation' which Jerusalem did not recognise (19:44), and therefore the 'son' became the 'stone' on which rebellion is crushed (20:18).[107] This program is already announced in the words 'he set his face to go to Jerusalem'. This is a traditional biblical idiom concerned with judgement, and it is so used here, rather than as a reference to Jesus' resolution to go to Jerusalem to be crucified.[108] It is doubtless true that the journey is useful to Luke in a literary way, so that he can gather up in it much non-Marcan material.[109] But he could easily enough have accommodated this material in some other way. He has cast it in the form of an extended journey so as to heighten the tension of Jesus' challenge to the holy city as he approaches it. During these ten chapters we are often enough told explicitly that Jesus is on his way to Jerusalem, so that the same goal is also implied for those additional passages which simply speak of Jesus as being on his way, or travelling.[110]

Sometimes Luke speaks of the judgement as still being an open question, depending on the response to Jesus which is still in the process of being made as he travels towards Jerusalem; sometimes he implies that a negative response has already been given and that the judgement is merely being worked out: an example of the former is the complex of sayings in 12:49–13–9; of the latter, the parable of the great feast, 14:15–24. Again, the judgement is sometimes described as taking place in the destruction of Jerusalem, sometimes by the exclusion of Judaism from the Kingdom of God: examples of the former are 12:49–13:9 again, and the double parable in 19:11–27; of the latter, 14:15–24 again, and the discourse in 13:22–30.

12:49–13–9 is not constructed as a literary unit, but a continuous line of thought is provided by the theme of judgement. In 13:1–9 this theme is unmistakable: unless you (the Jewish people) repent, you will be butchered by the Romans even within the Temple courts; unless you repent, the towers of Jerusalem will fall on you; unless Judaism becomes a fruitful tree, she is to be chopped down. 12:49–53 follows without interruption a passage addressed to disciples, warning them to remain faithful in their obedience to the Lord: but now the perspective widens to take in a more general judgement brought by Jesus. The signs of this judgement are already available (v. 54–56) in 'this time' (v. 56), the time of Jesus' mission. Failure to 'test' this time rightly, that is to see it as God's 'visitation' (cf. 1:78 as well as 19:44), will let loose the judgement referred to both in 12:49ff. and in 57ff. If we were to assume from Jesus' 'desire' for judgement (12:49) that judgement was inevitable, whatever the response of the Jews to Jesus' mission, this would be to mistake the irony of Jesus' 'intention', as 13:34 and 19:42 make plain. God's 'visitation' in the mission of Jesus brings the possibility of grace or judgement: it depends on the response of the hearers. Presumably 12:57–59 originally had an eschatological reference: by placing these verses between 12:54–56 and 13:1–9 Luke has added to the eschatological reference an historical one: the judgement that threatens is the destruction of Jerusalem.[111]

In 13:22–35, as J. M. Creed observed, 'the rejection of the Jews, the admission of the Gentiles and the fate of Jerusalem are again the determining ideas'.[112] E. E. Ellis, stating the theme more broadly as the giving of unexpected answers to the question, 'Who receives the kingdom of God?', also casts the range of the section farther, 13:22–16:13.[113] There are indeed also hints of the same theme in the passages linking 13:22ff. with the section last discussed. It is curious that Luke has put the two short parables of the mustard seed and the leaven here, 13:18–21 (rather than, as in Matt. 13:31–33, where they are also paired, in the general context of teaching parables); curious too that he has linked them by the words 'he said therefore' (v. 18) with the preceding passages, 13:10–17. Here Jesus heals a 'daughter of Abraham', but the emphasis falls also on his condemnation of those who tried to hinder this deed: 'therefore' Jesus tells the parable of the mustard seed, which in its concluding words hints at the opening of the Kingdom of God to the Gentiles. At any rate, the theme becomes quite clear in 13:22–30 and 31–35. Much of the material in 13:22–30 has parallels in scattered parts of Matthew, but there the meaning because of the different contexts, is also different. Two of the three main corresponding pieces in Matthew occur in the sermon on the mount and are addressed to disciples: in Luke the whole section is a reply to an unidentified questioner, but implicitly addressed to the whole Jewish community. The question, whether those to be saved were few, is significantly raised after the note that Jesus was making his way to Jerusalem. The body of the answer consists of two images, occurring in different form in Matt. 7:13f. and 22f., about the gate hard to enter and about those who will be surprised to be excluded and told that they are 'workers of iniquity'. In Matthew the gate is hard to enter because it is hard to find[114] – it is modest and obscure: so the disciples of Jesus are to accept an unpretentious style of life on their way to the Kingdom. In Luke, entering the gate will require a struggle, calling for strength: the image seems to be that of a crowd stampeding in a last-minute rush to get in. In Matthew those surprised to be excluded are false disciples: they have prophesied, cast out demons and performed miracles in the Lord's name, but are still evildoers. In Luke, they are Jesus' audience during his ministry – people with whom he has shared meals and in whose streets he has taught. It is these same people (ὑμᾶς, Luke 13:28) who will be thrown out when others come from north, south, east and west to join the banquet of the Kingdom of God with Abraham, Isaac and Jacob. The time left for repentance is short. What matters is not an abstract, speculative question about the number ultimately to be saved: Jesus challenges the whole Jewish community to make an urgent, practical decision about his mission in God's name. 13:31–33 and 34f. are two distinct pieces, of separate origin,[115] but Luke has bound them closely with the preceding context. Jesus' death will be brought about not by Herod but by his encounter with Jerusalem in fulfilment of the mission God has given him. But what matters even more than the death of Jesus is the decision Jerusalem is making about him, which will determine her fate. It is remarkable that 13:34f., placed still relatively early in Jesus' march from Galilee to the capital, implies that the negative decision has in fact already been reached. By again anticipating the outcome (cf. 4:23ff.), Luke intensifies the sense of doom as Jesus goes on his way.

It is widely recognized that the parable of the great feast (Luke 14:15–24, par. Matt. 22:1–14) deals not only with the opening of the Kingdom of God to the Gentiles but also with the self-exclusion of the Jews, at least that part of the Jews represented by the Pharisees (and as we have seen, this is the Judaism which for Luke really matters).[116] But it is worth looking again at this passage, because the widely influential interpretation of H. Conzelmann has found here a reference not to the judgement of Judaism but to eschatology, to the so-called 'delay of the parousia': 'Die neue, lukanische Pointe wird in v. 23 sichtbar: Nicht die *Nähe* des Gottesreiches ist betont, sondern die Möglichkeit, *heute* den Zugang zum *künftigen* Mahl zu finden'.[117] However, it is clear from Luke's editorial introduction and conclusion to the pericope that the real question is not 'when?' but 'who?'. A fellow-guest at the Pharisee's dinner-party (14:1, 15) says to Jesus, 'Blessed is he who will eat bread in the Kingdom of God' – and the implication is, that it is 'we Pharisees' who will be so blessed. The culmination of Jesus' answer is that 'none of those men who were invited will taste my feast'. The emphasis falls, then, on the reversal of expectations as to who is and who is not accepted by God. The point of v. 22f. is not, as Conzelmann supposes, that it will take a long time to fulfil the church's mission, but that the Kingdom of God is open to the Gentiles as well as the outcasts of Israel (v. 21). The passage says nothing explicitly about the 'time' of the Kingdom: the only thing that could properly be deduced about time is that the parable arises from the experience of Jesus' mission: those who are excluded could be identified with those who rejected the call of God brought by Jesus.

The parable of the rich man and Lazarus (16:19–31) is rather puzzling, because at first sight we expect it to be about rewards and punishments for moral behaviour. But comparison with Egyptian and Jewish stories using a similar motif shows how the ethical aspect surprisingly falls into the background in the Lucan parable.[118] The real point here, too, is in the end of the pericope. Even the miracle of the resurrection of Jesus will not avail to convince people who did not listen to Moses and the prophets.

Perhaps most important of all for our argument is the double parable in Luke 19:11–27, with which Jesus' journey to Jerusalem virtually ends. It is usually understood as an attempt (in its present form) to explain the delay of the parousia: so C. H. Dodd,[119] J. Jeremias[120] and many others.[121] This passage is among a few on which H. Conzelmann depends most heavily in his contention that Luke's main aim in his two-volume work was to solve the dilemma posed by the delay of the parousia. Conzelmann says, 'The disciples interpret the approach to the city as the approach to the Parousia instead of to the Passion. They have a wrong conception of both Christology and eschatology. It is not yet – not for a long time – the "kairos" of the Parousia'.[122] According to Dodd and Jeremias the nobleman in the parable is Jesus, and his departure and return signify Jesus' death, exaltation and second advent. It must however be observed that the subject of the expectation in 19:11 is 'the Kingdom of God', and there is reason to doubt (as we shall see in Chapter Five) that for Luke the coming of the Kingdom is necessarily equivalent to the 'parousia'. Certainly, Jesus is represented as refuting a false expectation. But is his answer equivalent to saying, 'Not now, but much later', as these scholars suggest? The motive of the false expectation is rather to be illustrated by such passages as Mark 10:37, John 6:15, Luke 24:21, Acts 1:6: both the inner circle of disciples and a wider crowd of admirers are looking to Jesus to bring glory to Israel. Jesus' answer is: for the unfaithful nation, not glory but destruction. Even if it is true, as Jeremias holds, that the parable of the rebellious subjects was already interwoven with the parable of the minae before Luke, at least Luke in his final redaction has left the combined parable with the concluding emphasis falling on the destruction of the rebellious subjects rather than merely on the deprivation of the unfaithful servant. In the light of the fact that the violent destruction of Jerusalem plays an important part in Luke's understanding of God's judgement, it may be argued that the interweaving of the two parables is Luke's own work. Their combination is rather awkward and artificial: such a connexion is hardly to be expected in the natural story-telling of oral tradition.[123] If then the combination is Luke's literary work, his motive must be to sharpen the point of the main parable by hinting at the historical events which have in the meantime brought the fulfilment of the judgement pronounced by Jesus. Not only have the fruitless guardians of God's covenant been repudiated by God's Son (20:9–18, cf. 13:6–9), but also the rebellious city that would not receive God's Son as its rightful King has been violently destroyed. Of course, according to Luke Jesus has not yet entered Jerusalem: but neither had he at 13:34f., where the same point is more briefly made. Once more the outcome of Jesus' challenge to the city (representing the nation) is anticipated.[124] At this first mention of his near approach to the city, its attitude to Jesus is vividly described and the consequence proclaimed: they refused to have him be king over them, so they were slaughtered before him.

The theme of the judgement of Judaism for its refusal of Jesus' mission does not end with the journey, but is maintained into the passion-narrative. It receives no more poignant expression than in the lament of Jesus over the city, immediately as it comes within view, Luke 19:41–44 (no pars.). The allusions to the destruction of Jerusalem by Rome in 70 AD are much more explicit than we have seen earlier in the book: thus Luke prepares the way for his adaptation of the apocalyptic discourse of Mark 13 in ch. 21, where he makes it plain that God's final judgement of the world has already reached a very particular expression in the judgement of Jerusalem through the war against Rome. Luke's account of the so-called 'cleansing' of the Temple in 19:45f. is surprisingly brief by comparison with Mark 11:15–18: at first sight one is tempted to call it perfunctory: and it also lacks the indication given by Mark, in framing this incident with the withering of the barren fig-tree, that Jesus' demonstration in the Temple is a prophetic act of judgement.[125] But when it follows hard on the words 'they will not leave stone on stone in you, because you did not recognize the time of your visitation', we may suspect that Luke was after all expecting his readers to understand that the phrase 'a den of robbers' from Jer. 7:11 refers, both in Jeremiah and here, to the ruins of the Temple which has been destroyed in punishment of the unfaithfulness of the people. The parable of the vineyard, which follows soon after (20:9–19, par. Mark 12:1–12; Matt. 21:33–46), clearly states in all three synoptic Gospels that because of her unfaithfulness Israel is to be displaced as the guardian of God's covenant. Perhaps surprisingly, in view of our usual stereotypes, it is Matthew who most clearly points the story towards the opening of the gospel to the Gentiles (v. 43): in Luke the climax speaks in violent terms of the destruction to which those who oppose Jesus are doomed (v. 18f.).

About the apocalyptic discourse in Luke 21:5ff. only a few brief remarks need be made at this stage. (This passage will need to be considered again with regard to eschatology, in Chapter Five.) As in Mark and Matthew (though with a different setting and audience), Jesus begins by speaking of the coming destruction of the Temple. In Mark apparently (13:4) and Matthew certainly (24:3) this event is immediately linked with the apocalyptic consummation, but in Luke (v. 7) Jesus' hearers only ask when the destruction of the Temple will take place. Thus the destruction of the Temple can be seen as an historical event, and indeed one that is past from Luke's point of view, and is not to be mixed in with the mysterious events of the End. v. 12, 'before all these things', has the effect of placing the persecution of Jesus' followers, mentioned in the next few verses, chronologically before the wars, disturbances and other disasters mentioned in v. 9–11, whereas in Mark and Matthew the persecution of Christians is a part of the general woes of the End;[126] thus Luke allows room for the events to be narrated in Acts,[127] which are not apocalyptic, and thereby allows the language of v. 9 to be understood as relating to the Jewish war against Rome in 66–70 AD. This is followed by references to the siege and capture of Jerusalem by the Romans, in the midst of dreadful sufferings for the inhabitants (v. 20–24). For our present theme the important point is that Luke (alone) interprets this time of suffering in Jerusalem as 'days of vengeance' (v. 22) and as 'wrath for this people' (v. 23).

Finally, in a passage included only by Luke, Jesus on his way out to be crucified tells the women of Jerusalem, who weep for him, that terrible suffering is in store for them too (Luke 23:27–31). J. M. Creed understands 'the dry wood' as referring to 'the guilty Jerusalem' in contrast to 'the innocent Jesus' ('the green wood').[128] This interpretation may be too precise, but in any case the passage envisages a worsening political situation in which the element of judgement is implied.

7 Stephen's Attack on the Temple, the Law and the People

The first five chapters of Acts describe a 'Jerusalem springtime' of the church. Great emphasis is laid on the success which attends the preaching of the Apostles. Opposition arises in ch. 4 and 5, but Luke gives us to understand that in this the Sanhedrin is in a weak position, since its attitude of hostility is not shared by the people at large (4:21; 5:13). Even within the Sanhedrin, it is only the Sadducees who initiate action against the Christian preaching (4:1; 5:17), and their attack is further weakened by the reluctance of the Pharisees (represented by Gamaliel, 5:34–40) to support their policy. With the rest of the community in Jerusalem, however, the growing church enjoys excellent relationships.

The story of Stephen in Acts 6–7 marks a great change in this aspect of the church's life, as in others. This is not the place for a discussion of the important literary and historical questions raised by this passage. But we must note briefly its important bearing on the theme of our discussion in this chapter.[129]

It is in accordance with Luke's literary method to let the individual portrait of Stephen stand as representative of the whole group of 'Hellenists' to which he belongs.[130] Presumably they are diaspora-Jews now settled in Jerusalem, but they hold a distinctive theology, which not only stirs up controversy with other diaspora Jews (6:9f.; 8:3) but also seems to set them in sharper opposition to the authorities in Jerusalem than was the case with the Apostles and their followers (8:1b). On the one hand, this theology was marked by special enthusiasm for Jesus' denunciation of the Temple and of the Rabbinic halakah (6:11–14); on the other hand, Stephen's speech shows affinities with Samaritan ideas, not only in theology but also in the interpretation of biblical history.

In the case of Stephen and the Hellenists, how far is Luke simply bringing forward traditions he had received about a distinctive group in the early church, and how far is he using this part of his narrative to express his own concerns? It seems certain that Luke is indeed using old traditions here. The character of Stephen's speech is quite different from that of all the other speeches in Acts, for example, in the way in which quotations from or allusions to the LXX run all the way through it, and in the fact that it contains no positive affirmation of the possibility of salvation through Jesus. It uses a technique familiar in the Old Testament and post-OT Jewish writings, by putting a theological statement in the form of a speech or song recounting the history of Israel from ancient times (Josh. 24:1–18; Psalm 105:12–45; 106:6–46; Neh. 9:6–31; Judith 5:5–21; 1 Enoch 84–90; Acts 13:16–41): but whereas all these other examples finish with a promise or celebration of God's salvation, this speech builds up to a climax of condemnation. The Israelites of the past are condemned for (a) rejecting Moses in Egypt (7:23–29, 35); (b) practising idolatry in the desert (7:39–43); (c) building the Temple (7:44–50); (d) persecuting and murdering the prophets (7:52). Stephen's hearers in Jerusalem share with their ancestors the same attitude of complete rebellion against God (7:51), shown, in their case, by the betrayal and murder of the Righteous One (7:52b). But in his conclusion (7:53) Stephen goes yet a step further: he addresses the entire Hebrew nation, from the generation of the Exodus until the present, with the accusation of having failed to keep the Law which was given at the commands of angels.

No doubt the strangest feature of this speech is the idea that the building of the Temple was an act of rebellion. This idea is all the more prominent, in that it is from that point that Stephen breaks off his historical survey in order to direct his attack on his contemporary audience. It must have come to Luke from tradition, for there is nothing like it in the other passages of Luke–Acts in which the Temple is mentioned. Elsewhere, as we have seen, Luke emphasizes the destruction of the Temple as punishment for the failure of Israel to produce the fruits of God's covenant with his people, but without any hint that the Temple is intrinsically an evil institution. Presumably this tradition had some affinity with the theology of the Samaritans, who rejected Solomon's temple as blasphemous, did not rebuild their own temple at Gerizim after its destruction in 128 BC, and looked forward to the coming of the Ta'eb who would restore not the Temple but the Tabernacle.[131] This seems to be confirmed by the observation of H. J. Cadbury,[132] that in the details of the history narrated by Stephen special prominence is given to Shechem, which runs counter to the tendency of later Jewish historiography. The Chronicler ignores Samaria altogether; Josephus and the *Bibilical Antiquities* of pseudo-Philo tend to locate elsewhere incidents which according to the Old Testament took place at Shechem or in Samaria generally. But Stephen says that Abraham and all the patriarchs were buried at Shechem, the Samaritan holy place (Acts 7:16: not at Mamre/Hebron, Gen. 23:16f.; 50:13).

Our present concern is not to trace the origins of these traditions, behind which we may suspect a very interesting aspect of early Christian history, but to note the use Luke makes of them. Despite the considerable use of traditional material, the speech as it stands must be regarded as a Lucan composition.[133] This means that Luke has not simply taken over a pre-formed story, but has entered actively into this material, to prepare it for a place in his whole composition. What is his purpose in doing so? It was remembered in the church that Stephen and his followers were responsible for the first great outward thrust of Christian evangelization (Acts 8:4ff.; 11:19f.) and that Stephen's martyrdom was in some way a precursor of the conversion of Saul (7:58–8:3; 9:1ff.). Stephen was, therefore, very much a key-figure of the early history of the church. In editing the traditions about him, Luke does not emphasize his quasi-Samaritan associations, which would brand him as heterodox from the point of view of Judaism: those elements were given to him in the traditions themselves, and are only apparent on a closer inspection. Instead he emphasizes the piety and spiritual force of Stephen: Acts 6:5, 8, 10, 15; 7:55f., 59f. The speech gives the impression of a man who knew the Scriptures thoroughly, and could argue with their authority. Yet such a person had felt deeply that the history of Israel, culminating in the rejection and death of Jesus, was one long tale of rebellion against Israel's God. Nowhere else in Luke–Acts is Christian reaction against Judaism as passionate and complete as in this incident. The other great preachers (Jesus himself, and Peter and Paul) on the whole approach their Jewish hearers with sympathy and hope, and Luke frequently reports on the positive response of individual Jews to the Christian message. Yet Luke himself may well have thought that Stephen's summing up of past and present Jewish history, even if unusually sharp and pessimistic, was on the whole a fair statement of the case. As we have already noted, even Jesus' opening sermon at Nazareth (Luke 4:16–27) contains the assumption (v. 23ff.) that his call will be rejected by the Jewish nation, and hints of the same kind of expectation are found again, e.g. at Luke 13:34f. and Acts 13:40f. All this, taken together with Paul's three-fold turning from the Jews to the Gentiles, and especially the last main scene of Luke–Acts in Acts 28:17–28, presumably reflects the experience of Luke himself and of the church within which he lives. The separation between Christians and non-Christian Judaism had its roots deep in the past, as exemplified especially in the careers of Jesus and Stephen, and more recently of Paul. This separation was a most serious matter, which Luke called on his readers to ponder well, so that they might understand the nature of their life and mission as the people of God, now institutionally cut off from their roots in the Hebrew tradition.

8 'To Give Knowledge of Salvation to His People'

The foregoing pages have shown that, in the Gospel as much as in Acts, Luke keeps reminding his readers that the offer of salvation, coming from the God of Israel and promised in the Old Testament Scriptures, was represented to Israel first by Jesus, then by the Apostles and other preachers, especially Paul. In both cases a large number of individual Jews responded positively, as G. Lohfink has well explained.[134] In the case of the Gospel, 'the people', in contrast to the leading groups, generally welcome Jesus' teaching and lament his death: only, when the crucial decision about his execution is being made, even 'the people' share the responsibility. In the case of Acts, an initial 'Jerusalem springtime' ends with the opposition raised against Stephen, and gradually the Christian message becomes more and more a concern of the Gentiles. Luke has taken great care to emphasize that Jesus himself was born into the heart of Israel[135] and was from his childhood onwards concerned with the revelation of his 'Father', which was centred in the Temple (2:49). Likewise, Paul was born into the heart of Pharisaic Judaism (Acts 22:3; 26:4–7); the Apostles, the Seven,[136] and in general all the early Christian preachers were also Jews.[137] None of them was in any way a renegade from the faith of Israel as attested by the Scriptures. On the contrary, God has shown his approval of this whole movement by the miracles performed by Jesus (Luke 7:18–23; Acts 2:22) and by the Apostles and missionaries in his name (Acts 3:12–16; 16:18), by the resurrection of Jesus (Acts 2:24–36; 13:33–37), and by the presence of the Holy Spirit, not only after Pentecost but even in the circumstances surrounding the birth of Jesus (Luke 1:15, 35, 67; 2:25, 27). The whole career of Jesus and its sequel were in every sense the saving action of the God of Israel towards his own people, the consequence of which should have been great joy for them (Luke 2:10). Yet 'Israel', viewed as an institution (and always excepting many individual Jews), rejected what was offered to them.

It was however God's intention that through the descendants of Abraham all the families of the earth should be blessed (Acts 3:25f.). The coming of the Messiah and of the Holy Spirit mark the time when that should happen, and God has explicitly revealed this to Peter (Acts 10). There are hints enough of this theme in the Gospel (Luke 2:30–32; 4:23–27; 13:29; 14:23; 24:47). But it is quite correct, as G. D. Kilpatrick and S. G. Wilson have said, that the contents of Luke taken on their own, are not particularly 'universalistic'.[138] Indeed, Luke seems deliberately to have gone beyond Mark and his other sources in confining the ministry of Jesus to the Jews and to the land of Palestine: the most obvious evidences of this are, first, the way in which the Capernaum centurion of Luke 7:1–10 approaches Jesus only rather elaborately through Jewish intermediaries (contrast Matt. 8:5–13) and, second, Luke's complete omission of the incident concerning the Syro-Phoenician woman.[139]

But it is short-sighted to deduce from this that Luke is 'not universalistic', or opposed to the Gentiles. For one thing, unlike the other evangelists he has no need to fit into the Gospel a theme which he plans to set forth at length in a second volume. Moreover, his traditions, like those of John, seem to have made it clear that it was only some time after the resurrection that the gospel was in fact opened to the Gentiles. In this regard he shares not only with John (12:20–24) but also with Paul (e.g. Gal. 3:23–29), Matthew (10:5f. and 28:18–20), and the early church generally, a time-table of this kind as to God's purposes. In order to make the point clearer he can afford to omit the rare, striking exceptions in Jesus' own practice.

We have therefore three phenomena to set side by side. First, the judgement of Judaism for its rejection of the offered salvation is displayed with remarkable breadth and force. Second, the leaders of the Christian movement are portrayed as consistently loyal and courteous towards the

Hebrew traditions, in so far as to be so is consistent with God's new revelation in Jesus. Third, the Gentiles, when offered their share in 'this salvation', receive it promptly and joyfully (Acts 10:1–7, 24f., 30–33, 44–48; 11:20ff.; 13:48f.; 18:6ff.; 28:28).

The third of these factors is clear and unmistakable. Yet it is not as prominent as the first two. It may be suggested that this is because Luke does not need to emphasize it.[140] If he is writing to a predominantly Gentile audience, as has been traditionally assumed, he needs to give his readers enough assurance that they are indeed welcome within the fellowship of God's grace: but he does not need to labour the point. On the other hand, the rejection of the Christian message by Judaism (in so far as it is an organized community), despite every effort on the part of Jesus and his followers to open for it the way to faith, is clearly for Luke a major concern, and thereby a major hint towards identifying the purpose of his book.

Notes to Chapter Two

1. He is of course not 'Paul' until 13:9, but by then he has been a leading teacher of the gospel for a considerable time. The change from 'Saul' to 'Paul' marks not the beginning of his missionary activity but of his involvement with the Roman world.
2. This concept does not become relevant until the second century. In recent times we have learnt, e.g. through the work of M. Hengel, *Judentum und Hellenismus* (ET, *Judaism and Hellenism*); cf. E. Lohse, *Umwelt des Neuen Testaments* (ET, *The New Testament Environment*), to be less clear-cut about the distinctions between 'Palestinian Judaism', 'Hellenistic Judaism', 'Jewish Christianity', 'Hellenistic Jewish Christianity' and 'Gentile Christianity', as such terms used to be employed, e.g. by R. Bultmann, *Urchristentum* (ET, *Primitive Christianity*). When Luke speaks of Gentiles, he does not necessarily mean that the people concerned are alien to Jewish theology and culture, for many of them come to faith in Jesus through a prior connexion with Judaism (so Cornelius: Acts 10:2, 22; but he is still clearly identified as a Gentile, 10:28, 45; cf. Acts 13:44–48; 14:1f., 27; etc.). The distinction between Jews and Gentiles, which remains a real and indeed burning issue for Luke, depends only on circumcision and the acceptance of the yoke of the Law (cf. Acts 11:1f., 18; 15:1, 5, 19, 23ff.). Luke speaks several times of Gentiles who have associated themselves with Jewish belief and worship, but without technically becoming Jews, as *φοβούμενοι* or *σεβόμενοι τὸν θεόν* (Acts 10:2, 22 (, 35); 13:16, 26, 50; 16:14; 17:4, 17; 18:7). But this usage falls a little short of being technical terminology, for in Acts 13:43 he speaks of *σεβόμενοι προσήλυτοι*. Though Luke distinguishes 'Jews' and 'proselytes' in Acts 2:11, he nevertheless regards proselytes as being Jews rather than Gentiles, for in 6:5 the proselyte Nicolaus is accepted, without comment, into leadership in the church, but Gentiles are not converted until ch. 10.

   Luke's use of the term 'Christians' in Acts 11:26 has recently been studied afresh by P. Zingg, *Das Wachsen der Kirche*, 217–246. Zingg is sceptical about the view that the name arose as a term of contempt, and holds that at least in Luke's mind it is a term of honour, produced in part by the striking success of the mission in Antioch. In a predominantly Gentile environment the use of a name derived from 'Christ' was as natural as the avoidance of it in a Jewish setting, where 'the sect of the Nazarenes' is the equivalent (Acts 24:5).

3. K. Stendahl, *Paul Among Jews and Gentiles*, 7–23.
4. Ibid., esp. 22f.: In several key-passages 'we' means 'we Jews' over against 'you Gentiles'.
5. E.g., W. G. Kümmel, *Einleitung*, 118 (ET, 124).
6. E.g., Kümmel, op. cit., 98f. (ET, 104f.).
7. J. Jervell, *Luke and the People of God.*
8. See below, n. 17.
9. Op. cit., 138.
10. Op. cit., 139. Cf. G. Barth in G. Bornkamm, G. Barth and H. J. Held, *Überlieferung und Auslegung*, 71–73 (ET, *Tradition and Interpretation*, 76–78).
11. J. Jervell, op. cit., 139f., 146.
12. Op. cit., 140.
13. See below, section 8 of this chapter.
14. In any case, in Luke 11:38 the Pharisees express disapproval of Jesus himself (not of his disciples, as in Mark 7:2–5/Matt. 15:2) for not washing before eating, and Jesus' reply implies criticism of the halakah on at least this point; though v. 42c/Matt. 23:23c expresses loyalty to the halakah.
15. P. Billerbeck, *Kommentar*, II, 488.
16. In Luke 5:33 pars. the Pharisees (cf. v. 30) criticize Jesus and his disciples not for a breach of halakah (regular fasting became binding on all Jews only after 70 AD) but for defective piety: see Billerbeck, II, 241–244. But a breach of halakah by Jesus and his disciples evidently exists in Luke 5:29f. pars., Luke 15:1f., see Billerbeck, I, 498; II, 208.
17. G. D. Kilpatrick: (1) On γραμματεύς and νομικός, 56–60. (2) 'The Gentile Mission', 145–158. (3) 'Mark 13:9–10', 81–86. (4) 'Λαοί', 127. (5) '"Kyrios"', 60–70. (6) 'The Gentiles and the Strata of Luke', 83–88.
18. See previous note, essay no. (6). This article makes some controversial assumptions about the literary criticism of Luke–Acts, implying that Luke's composition was spread over a considerable time, and in four rather clearly defined stages, during which the author's ideas were developing steadily. This aspect need not concern us here.
19. Op. cit., 87.
20. Unpublished lecture given at various universities in the late 1960s.
21. In particular, Kilpatrick seems to hold that in order for Luke to be judged 'universalist' in outlook statements of a 'universalist' character must be located throughout the work: he takes no account of the possibility that Luke argues his case through dramatic development with an element of tragic irony, in that Jesus comes as the Messiah into a completely Jewish community (Luke 1–2) but at the end (Acts 28) the gospel is finally rejected by the Jews and directed to the Gentiles. See above, Chapter One, section 6.
22. Op. cit., 153.
23. Op. cit., 154.
24. Ibid.
25. Op. cit., 158.

26. It is not clear whether the 'many tens of thousands among the Jews' refers to the population of Jerusalem, of Judaea (so the Western text) or of a wider area. (Since Paul is invited to 'see' the numbers on his return to Jerusalem after a long absence, the number referred to presumably relates to Jerusalem and its general neighbourhood.) It is notoriously difficult to estimate the population of Palestine in ancient times (see C. C. McCown, 'Palestine, geography of', 638). J. Jeremias in 1962 calculated the population of Jerusalem in the first century at between 25,000 and 30,000 (*Jerusalem zur Zeit Jesu*, 97f., reducing by about half his estimate of 1923, op. cit., 96 (ET, *Jerusalem in the Time of Jesus*, 84).
27. J. Jervell, loc. cit.
28. G. D. Kilpatrick, 'Luke – Not a Gentile Gospel'.
29. Above, p. 55f.
30. Jervell, op. cit., 159. On the significance of Acts 21–28, see below: section 4 of this chapter and sections 1 and 5 of Chapter Three.
31. Op. cit., 159f. What Jervell does not mention is that the Emperor is not the only Roman conspicuous by his absence in Acts 28:16–31! See below, p. 00.
32. Op. cit., 160–163.
33. Op. cit., 173.
34. Op. cit., 170.
35. Op. cit., 162, referring to Phil. 3:3ff.; Gal. 1:13ff.; 1 Cor. 15:8f.; 2 Cor. 11:22. On this judgement, see the following note.
36. Op. cit., 163: 'In chapters 22 and 26 Luke clearly makes use of pre-formed material without making any alteration, while his commentary on the material is found in Chapters 23 and 24.' Support for the first of these assertions is drawn from 'the inconsistencies in Luke's account in Chapter 9, 22 and 26', which are due to the history of transmission which the Pauline tradition has undergone (op. cit., 162). This is a dubious argument. Luke adapts such features as the description and role of Ananias, and the place and form of the divine call giving Paul his mission to the Gentiles, according to the audiences addressed in the narrative of ch. 9 (Luke's Gentile Christian readers) and the speeches in ch. 22 (the Jews in Jerusalem) and 26 (Agrippa and Festus). Cf. the variations in the accounts of the ascension in Luke 24 and Acts 1 and those of the dealings of Peter with Cornelius in Acts 10 and 11. On the question of tradition and composition in Acts 9, 22 and 26, C. Burchard comes to a conclusion almost the exact opposite of Jervell's: see below, Chapter Three, 72f. The arguments appealed to by both these writers on this matter are equally uncompelling.
37. Jervell, op. cit., 146, 162f., 169, 171.
38. Op. cit., 174.
39. Op. cit., 175–177.
40. Op. cit., 176.
41. Op. cit., 141f.
42. Op. cit., 142.
43. Op. cit., 143.
44. G. Lohfink, *Sammlung*, ch. 1–2.
45. Op. cit., 56. His observations indirectly refute Jervell's criticism of J. Gnilka, *Verstockung Israels*, 145, who speaks of an 'imperceptible process' by which a 'new people' is formed alongside the Jewish people – 'This process is imperceptible because it never occurs!' (Jervell, op. cit., 179, n. 26.)

46. Lohfink, op. cit., 22–31.
47. Op. cit., 79, 95.
48. Just before, Luke 24:44, the risen Jesus reminds his disciples of his earlier prophecy that 'all the things had to be fulfilled, which were written about me in the Law of Moses and the Prophets and the Psalms'. This raises the question, what 'the Law' means in Luke–Acts. In Paul, 'the Law' has two meanings: it can refer to the *commandments* of God, by which Israel lived, but also to the Torah, the contents of the Pentateuch, as the *revelation* of God's purposes and promises, which begins long before the commandments were given, and so outweighs them in importance. This distinction is most important, for example, to Paul's argument in Rom. 3:21–31. In John, the aspect of 'revelation' predominates; the element of 'commandment' is still present (7:23; 19:7), though without the negative connotations found in Paul. In Luke–Acts the usage is as follows: (1) 'The Law' as a designation for 'the Scriptures' as revelation. In this sense 'the Law (of Moses)' mostly stands in combination with 'the prophets': so Luke 24:44; Acts 24:14; 28:23. In this category we should probably include Acts 7:53. Acts 13:15 refers quite neutrally to the reading of the Law and the Prophets as normal procedure in the synagogue-service, though Paul's sermon following imparts to it a sense of revelation. On the other hand, in Luke 16:16 the following context gives the phrase 'the Law and the Prophets' more the sense of commandment. (2) 'The Law (of the Jews)' occasionally occurs as a designation for the Jewish 'religion', especially when spoken by outsiders: so Acts 23:29; 25:8; 18:15: but in the last case the ambiguity of 18:13 shows that we are not far from (3) 'The Law' as commandment. This is clearly the meaning in Luke 2:22–39 (5 times); 10:26; Acts 6:13f. (*νόμος*|*ἔθη*); 13:39; 15:5; 23:3. We are left with the 5 examples in Acts 21–22. What do James and the elders mean when they tell Paul that the many myriads of Jewish believers 'are all zealous for the Law'? The following context shows that their 'zeal' is for circumcision (v. 21f.) and, more generally, for the ritual practices of Jewish piety (v. 23–26). If Paul shares in the Nazirite vow, it will tend to nullify the suspicion (v. 24) that he has been teaching apostasy from Moses among diaspora-Jews by discouraging circumcision and the halakah generally (v. 21). These precautions by the legalistic Christians are followed by the denunciation of Paul by some Asian Jews (v. 27) for precisely those alleged acts of apostasy, plus that of bringing Greeks into the Temple (v. 28). In this light, it is clear that when Paul speaks in 22:3 of his meticulous upbringing in the ancestral Law, and in v. 12 of Ananias' piety according to the Law, it is the Law *as commandment* which he means. Since Paul and Ananias were born and brought up as Jews, Luke sees nothing wrong in their adherence to the commandments of the Law. But in ch. 10 and 15 he is concerned to emphasize that the commandments of the Law are no longer valid as a definite marker of the 'people of God'.
49. E. Haenchen, 'Judentum und Christentum', 155–187.
50. Haenchen, op. cit., par. 12.
51. Op. cit., par. 13.
52. Jervell, op. cit., 138.
53. Op. cit., 149, n. 24.
54. Cf. W. Eltester, 'Israel im lukanischen Werk', 98: 'Die Scheidung zwischen Juden und Heiden durch das mosaische Reinheitsgesetz wird nunmehr durch göttlichen Befehl aufgehoben, die alte Offenbarung also widerrufen'.

55. Jervell, op. cit., 185ff.
56. Op. cit., 190f.
57. Op. cit., 196–199.
58. Op. cit., 197f.
59. Op. cit., 191.
60. Op. cit., 192.
61. This is particularly striking in chapter 4, 'The Lost Sheep of the House of Israel: the Understanding of the Samaritans in Luke–Acts', where no account is taken of possible sources or traditions underlying Acts 8:5–22; and in the section of chapter 5, 'The Law in Luke–Acts', dealing with the decree of the Jerusalem council. In chapter 6, 'Paul – the Teacher of Israel', the relation of tradition and composition in Paul's defence-speeches, Acts 22–26, is dealt with too easily: see above, n. 36.
62. See especially S. G. Wilson, *Gentiles*, 178–191.
63. M. Dibelius, *Aufsätze* (ET, *Studies*), ch. 5.
64. Nor James: E. Haenchen, *Apg.*, 455 (ET, 471).
65. R. Bultmann, 'Zur Frage nach den Quellen der Apostelgeschichte', argues for a written source. The historicity of such a decree, influential in some Christian circles, is not to be doubted. C. K. Barrett, 'Things Sacrificed to Idols', 150, suggests on the basis of 1 Cor. 9 (coming between ch. 8 and 10) that Peter tried to promulgate and enforce the decree at Corinth and in other Pauline churches.

    Since our main concern here is with Luke's intention, rather than with the precise reconstruction of the history, it is not necessary to take up in detail the problem of the traditions underlying Acts 15 and Gal. 2. It is likely that Acts 15 represents a conflation and heavy re-working of accounts of two conferences, perhaps separated by a considerable period of time. The first, in which Paul was an active participant, decided against the need for Gentiles to be circumcised and keep the Law (Gal. 2:1–10; Acts 15: 1f., 4a, 5f., 12), but did not fully resolve the problem of fellowship between Jewish and Gentile Christians. Subsequently, Paul sought to draw radical conclusions from the decisions of this conference, in terms of complete freedom of intercourse between the two groups; but Peter, from the side of Jerusalem, and Barnabas from the Antiochene side, looked for a compromise (Gal. 2:11–13). A second conference, in which Peter and Barnabas may have led the respective delegations, established this compromise in the form of the decree of Acts 15:19f., 28f. That Paul was not present is shown not only by the absence of any mention of the decree from his letters, but also by the separate tradition, reported in Acts 21:25, that Paul was informed of the decree by the Jerusalem church on his last visit to the city. Disagreement over this issue between Barnabas and Paul (Gal. 2:13ff.) must have contributed to the break of their missionary partnership (Acts 15:36ff.) and in Paul's close association with the church in Antioch. (So F. Hahn, *Das Verständnis der Mission*, 65–74; ET, *Mission*, 77–86.)
66. So P. Billerbeck, *Kommentar*, II, 729. The exact force of the four points in the decree is not clear beyond any dispute, but it is now generally agreed that the original intent was ritual rather than moral, as in the Western text.
67. S. G. Wilson, *Gentiles*, 188f.
68. The Rabbis also regarded these laws as required of Gentiles living as resident aliens in Israel, so as to provide minimum offence and disturbance to Israel's

keeping of the Law, and were perhaps mainly concerned to devise arrangements for a future time when Israel would again possess and control her own land: P. Billerbeck, *Kommentar*, II, 722, cf. G. F. Moore, *Judaism*, I, 274f.; II, 75.

69. P. Billerbeck, *Kommentar*, II, 716f.: Rabbinic literature has little to say about 'half-proselytes' or 'God-fearers' and how they stood in relation to Israel: cf. K. Lake in *Beginnings*, V, 207f.
70. This point is repeatedly confused by J. Jervell, e.g. *People of God*, 144: 'The four prescriptions are what the law requires of Gentiles'; 176: 'Uncircumcised Gentiles had already been fully recognized with minimum fulfillment of the law'. The concept of 'minimum fulfillment of the law', without circumcision, is meaningless in Jewish theology. E. Haenchen, *Apg.*, 455f. (ET, 471f.), shows that the requirements of the decree were not only observed but also passionately valued throughout the second century by many Christians who had no general connexion with Judaism or the Jewish Law. C. K. Barrett, 'Things Sacrificed', 150–153, shows that the decree was due at least as much to concern about Gnostic libertarianism as to the pressure of Jewish legalism.
71. See C. K. Barrett, op. cit., especially 147.
72. E.g., W. G. Kümmel, *Einleitung*, 118 (ET, 170).
73. J. Jervell, *People of God*, 147.
74. Op. cit., 169.
75. E. Haenchen, *Apg.*, 523f. (ET, 545f.).
76. G. Bornkamm, 'The Missionary Stance', 204.
77. J. Jervell, *People of God*, especially 158–174.
78. Breach of Sabbath: 6:2, 7; 13:14; 14:1–6.
Blasphemy: 5:21; (7:49); (19:39).
Associating with sinners: 5:30; 15:2; (19:7: πάντες).
79. E. Haenchen, 'Judentum', par. 4.
80. Luke 11:45f., cf. 42ff., seems to distinguish the scribes from the Pharisees. Elsewhere, however, Luke has the combination 'scribes (γραμματεῖς, νομικοί, νομοδιδάσκαλοι) and Pharisees' 8 times, and in Acts 5:34 Gamaliel is both a Pharisee and a νομοδιδάσκαλος. (Matthew has 'scribes and Pharisees' 10 times, but 7 of these examples are concentrated in ch. 23.) Luke 20:39 clearly implies that the scribes are of the Pharisees, cf. 5:30 'the Pharisees and their scribes'.
81. E. Haenchen, 'Judentum', par. 21. On the 'zealots for the Law' in Acts 21:20, see above, n. 48.
82. Tertullian, *Apology*, 21:1.
83. J. Jervell, *People of God*, 155–158; E. Haenchen, 'Judentum', par. 24.
84. J. Jervell, op. cit., 174–177.
85. So too J. Jervell, op. cit., 170.
86. E. Haenchen, 'Judentum', par. 22, mentions how odd it is that Acts contains nothing corresponding to Luke 21:20–24; 19:41–44; etc.: although Luke clearly knows of the destruction of Jerusalem and sees it as the punishment of Judaism for rejecting its Messiah (see below, p. 29–39), he takes no interest in it from the point of view of the Jewish Christians in Acts. See below, Chapter Five, section 3(a).
87. J. Jervell, *People of God*, 203, n. 25: 'Epp [E. J. Epp, *The Theological Tendency*] has convincingly shown that there is a marked anti-Jewish bias in D's textual revision. For D, Acts is obviously too Jewish, and D attempts to modify this feature'. This last sentence is wide of the mark. On the contrary, D tends to

exaggerate tendencies that are already there: it is not that Acts is 'too Jewish' but that Acts is already somewhat anti-Jewish in the 'neutral' text: see C. K. Barrett, *New Testament Essays*, 102–104.

88. Among recent studies, see especially J. Dupont, 'Le salut des gentils'; S. G. Wilson, *Gentiles*.
89. W. C. Robinson, *Der Weg des Herrn*.
90. See especially H.-J. Michel, *Abschiedsrede*, 77: Paul's speech at Miletus makes it clear that Luke ends his story deliberately with the end of the career of Paul, who represents a generation that had worked closely with the Twelve and with eye-witnesses of Jesus' activity.
91. They are not unimportant, as will be explained below: see Chapter Three, section 5.
92. On these two omissions, see below: Chapter Three, section 5, with notes 48–50.
93. This was recognized with respect to this passage long before Haenchen's commentary, which first attributed the matter of Acts very generally to Luke's own composition: e.g. by H. J. Holtzmann, *Apostelgeschichte*, 14f., 155.
94. E. Haenchen, 'Judentum', par. 24; H. Conzelmann, *Apostelgeschichte*, 149.
95. J. Jervell, *People of God*, 63: 'Acts closes with a description of a people divided over the Christian message.' This interpretation gives too much weight to v. 24. Luke here as elsewhere in Paul's mission says that some Jews believed: but these are always exceptions. The official view of 'Judaism' is expressed in v. 22: 'what we know of this sect is that it is denounced everywhere'. And Paul's address in v. 25 is not partitive: 'your fathers'! Nowhere does Jervell examine the dramatic function served by this closing scene in the structure of Luke's whole work. The outcome of Paul's sermon at Antioch-in-Pisidia is similarly misunderstood by Jervell, when he says that the usual interpretation of 13:46 (that Paul turned to the Gentiles because the Jews rejected the gospel) is contradicted by the quotation from Isaiah 49:6 in v. 47: 'Even before the speech in the synagogue, the missionaries were under command to turn to Gentiles. The partial rejection on the part of the Jews does not provide the basis for preaching to Gentiles because the Gentile mission is already contained in the missionary command of God. Sent to Gentiles, the missionaries turn, because of the commandment of God (v. 46), to Jews! The meaning is clear, provided that the object of the quotation of Scripture is Israel, which is to be set as a light to Gentiles, and provided the missionaries represent Israel' (61). But the 'usual interpretation' here criticized is only the plain, literal statement of the text: '*since* you reject (the word of God) and judge yourselves unworthy of eternal life, look, we are turning to the Gentiles'. And the 'you' is 'the Jews' (v. 45): the expression is not partitive. It is indeed remarkable, not only here but throughout Paul's mission, that he who was called to preach to the Gentiles (9:15; 22:21; 26:17f., 23) always preaches first to Jews (even in Athens, 17:17). But this is not because Luke understands 13:47 as applying to Israel as a whole: this text only supplies a justification of what Paul and Barnabas now proceed to do. Paul always begins with the Jews because it must be made plain that the failure of the Jews (on the whole) to believe in Jesus is not because they have been by-passed by the missionaries but because they have deliberately rejected their message.
96. This theme in Acts recalls Paul's 'to the Jew first, and also to the Greek' (Rom. 1:16; cf. 3.1f.; 9:3–5; etc.). It is Paul's Epistles, more than Acts, where we find

insistence on Paul's vocation as (apostle) 'to the Gentiles' (Gal. 1:15; 2:9; Rom. 1:5; 11:13; 15:16; etc.). It is not clear how the demarcation of mission-fields in Gal. 2:9 was intended to be carried out in practice. But it no doubt represented a general line of strategy. When Paul says 'to the Jew first', he does not mean, as in Acts, that in each new city he seeks out the Jews first, but rather that the Jews have as it were a theological priority, as bearers of the tradition through which God has chosen to act for the salvation of the world. Rom. 9–11 shows that he has experienced just such a response as Acts describes, but still expects the Jews ultimately to take their rightful place as senior members of the new fellowship of the gospel of Christ. Luke no longer holds out such a hope.

97. G. Stählin, *Apostelgeschichte*, 328.
98. G. Lohfink, *Sammlung*, 41–46. J. Ernst likewise believes that Luke is not seriously concerned about the rejection of the gospel by Israel: it is only a negative foil, against which he can set his chief theme, the growth of the church. He notes that the saying about blindness in Mark 4:12 is milder in Luke 8:10b, and regards this editorial modification as 'für die Gesamttendenz des 3. Ev. kennzeichnend' (*Lukas*, 15). This generalization fails to take account of the dramatic development unfolding through Luke–Acts, and especially of the emphatic place and manner in which Luke again quotes Isa. 6:9f. at the end of his work.
99. G. Stählin, loc. cit.: 'Von Lk 4:25ff. zu Apg. 28:28 spannt sich ein großer Bogen: gewiß gilt das "den Juden zuerst"; aber gleichfalls von Anfang an richtet sich der Heilsplan Gottes auf die Heiden.'
100. G. Braumann, 'Das Mittel der Zeit', 135ff.
101. H. Conzelmann, *MdZ*, 136 (ET, 146).
102. G. Lohfink, *Sammlung*, 42, 43f.
103. This generalization is contradicted by Luke 11:15f., where it is people from the crowds who associate Jesus with Beelzebul, against Mark 3:22 (the scribes who came down from Jerusalem) and Matt. 12:24 (the Pharisees), and 'test' him by seeking a sign from heaven.

103a. After the manuscript was completed, my attention was drawn to H. L. Egelkraut, *Jesus' Mission to Jerusalem: A redaction critical study of the Travel Narrative in the Gospel of Luke, Lk 9:51–19:48*, Bern/Frankfurt a.M. 1978 (Europ. Hochshulschr. 23/80). This work anticipates, and works out in great detail, the interpretation of the travel-narrative adopted here. It provides a clear, thorough and convincing interpretation of the travel-narrative, set over against a review of previous interpretations, with fresh and illuminating exegesis of many passages. It should now be regarded as the definitive study of this part of Luke. The author makes only a brief attempt to place the travel-narrative within the total theological scheme of Luke–Acts (223–234). Here he only notes (224f.) that the theme, so strongly expounded in the travel-narrative, of Israel's rejection of the mission of Jesus and consequent exclusion from the Kingdom of God, is announced in Luke 4:16–30 and brought to a conclusion in Acts 28:17–28 (see above, 63f.). The author's concentration on the travel-narrative at the expense of the rest of Luke's work leads him (231f.) to exaggerate somewhat the significance of the former as the decisive point at which Israel's doom was sealed. With respect to Luke's purpose, he is content to note (235–237) that a number of writers, notably Schütz, Flender and Conzelmann, have too hastily made assumptions about

Luke's historical situation and aims, assumptions which his analysis of the travel-narrative has falsified. Rather than venture into this field himself, he simply observes that he has achieved a necessary preliminary task, that of clarifying Luke's historical perspective.

104. G. Lohfink, *Himmelfahrt*, 212–214, regards ἀνάλημψις here as primarily a reference in solemn language to Jesus' death, but with allusion to the ascension as well.
105. See also E. Franklin, *Christ the Lord*, 29–47.
106. Cf. F. Schütz, *Der leidende Christus*, 62–79.
107. On the Semitic word-play underlying 'son' and 'stone' see M. Black, 'The Christological Use', 11–14.
108. So too G. Lohfink, *Himmelfahrt*, 215f., who explains Luke's wording as a conscious combination of 4 Kgdm 12:18 with Ezek. 21:7. Cf. K. W. Carley, *Ezekiel*, 40–42, esp. 41: 'The instructions to Ezekiel to set his face towards the subjects of his prophecies . . . were as much a part of Yahwe's message as the words Ezekiel had to speak. Moreover, they are all found in prophecies of doom.' See now also H. L. Egelkraut, op. cit., 79–81.
109. So e.g. A. Wikenhauser/J. Schmid, *Einleitung*, 262. But W. G. Kümmel, *Einleitung*, 110f. (ET, 141f.), shows that in recent studies of Luke some sort of theological or dramatic motive for the journey-section is almost universally assumed, though there are very diverse suggestions about what Luke's motive is.
110. Going to Jerusalem: Luke 9:53; 13:22, 33; 17:11; 18:31, (35; 19:1); 19:11, 28. Travelling: Luke 9:57; 10:1, 38; 14:25.
111. See above, Chapter One, p. 12f., for criticism of G. Klein's detailed study of this passage in 'Die Prüfung der Zeit'.
112. J. M. Creed, *St Luke*, 184.
113. E. E. Ellis, *Luke*, 187.
114. K. Stendahl, 'Matthew', 681n (p. 780).
115. For a thorough literary and form-critical analysis see A. Denaux, 'L'Hypocrisie'.
116. For a detailed study of Matt. 22:1–10/Luke 14:16–24 see F. Hahn, 'Einladung zum Festmahl'.
117. H. Conzelmann, *MdZ*, 102: this passage was added in the 4th edn., 1962, and therefore does not occur in the English translation of 1960; see above, Chapter One, n. 8.
118. See J. M. Creed, *St Luke*, 208–210.
119. C. H. Dodd, *Parables of the Kingdom*, 114–121.
120. J. Jeremias, *Gleichnisse*, 58–63 (ET, *Parables*, 58–63).
121. E.g. H. J. Cadbury, *Making*, 293; S. G. Wilson, 'Lukan Eschatology', 337; G. Bouwman, *Das dritte Evangelium*, 60. Contra G. H. P. Thompson, *Luke*, 231: 'The parable is intended as a sobering influence: will the Jews be ready for the kingdom of God . . . ? "Into a far country" (v. 12), best taken as merely a feature of the story, should not be pressed to mean that Luke is suggesting that the final advent of Jesus will be interminably delayed.'
122. H. Conzelmann, *MdZ*, 67 (ET, 74).
123. However, G. H. P. Thompson, *Luke*, points out that in the main body of the parable of the minae the master has authority to appoint his servants to have charge of many cities. This feature does not exist in the other version of this parable, Matt. 25:14–30, and can be explained as a modification introduced

when the parable of the minae was combined with that of the rebellious subjects.

124. See above, p. 36, 46.
125. See E. Schweizer, *Markus*, 130 (ET, *Mark*, 229) where Mark 11:12–26 has the heading 'The End of Israel's Temple and God's Turning to the Gentiles'.
126. In Mark 13, the events belonging to the End strictly speaking begin to be described in v. 14ff.: but there is no great gap between those still future events and the events already being experienced by the church in v. 7ff. On this see F. Hahn, 'Markus 13', esp. 247 and n. 33. The same view is taken by R. Pesch, *Naherwartungen*, 237ff.: Mark saw the church of his own day as 'bereits in den Wehen der Endzeit . . . Das Vorspiel des Endes hat schon begonnen' (238). Cf. R. Pesch, *Das Markusevangelium*, 2. Teil, 277–282. (In this later work, Pesch accepts Hahn's article as substantially superseding *Naherwartungen*, especially with regard to the nature of Mark's source for ch. 13 and Mark's redaction of it: see *Mk–Ev.*, 2. Teil, 266. Against *Naherwartungen*, 203f., 207ff., Pesch now agrees with Hahn that Mark's source for Jesus' apocalyptic speech arose in Judaea in the early stages of the War of 66–70; and that Mark himself followed this source, though with some caution, in seeing a close connexion between the 'wars and rumours of wars' and the imminent End.)
127. In Mark 13, v. 10 is a subsequent modification of the apocalyptic discourse in a similar direction: on this see F. Hahn, *Mission*, 29f., 57ff., 99ff. (ET, 37f., 68ff., 116ff.).
128. Creed, *St. Luke*, 286.
129. See M. Simon, *St. Stephen;* J. Bihler, *Stephanusgeschichte*; M. H. Scharlemann, *Stephen*; cf. E. Graßer, 'Acta-Forschung', *TR* 42, 17–25.
130. On this literary device in Luke–Acts, see below, Chapter Three, p. 76f.
131. M. Simon, *St Stephen*, 35–38.
132. H. J. Cadbury, *Book of Acts*, 102–106.
133. See J. Bihler, *Stephanusgeschichte*, 81–86.
134. G. Lohfink, *Sammlung*, ch. 2 and 3.
135. See esp. W. Eltester, 'Israel', 79f., also G. Lohfink, *Sammlung*, ch. 1. The continuity between Israel and the church is also rightly stressed by H. Flender, *Heil*, 107–122 (ET, 117–135), though not all the passages he adduces are convincing for this argument.
136. H. J. Cadbury, 'Note VII. The Hellenists', in *Beginnings* V, 59–74, argued on linguistic grounds that 'Hellenists' means 'Greeks', i.e. pagans. This has rightly been rejected by most subsequent commentators on exegetical grounds: for Luke Gentiles have no part in the church until Acts 10.
137. J. Jervell, *People of God*, 50.
138. G. D. Kilpatrick, 'Gentiles', 88; 'Luke – Not a Gentile Gospel'; S. G. Wilson, *Gentiles*, 51f.
139. S. G. Wilson, *Gentiles*, 49, believes that 'all of Mark 7 is the sort of material which Luke could well have used', and revives the old idea that the 'great omission' of Mark 6:45–8:26 by Luke is due to Luke's not having this section in his copy of Mark. But it was shown by H. J. Cadbury, *Style*, 96–103, that Luke betrays knowledge of the matter omitted.
140. E. Gräßer, 'Acta-Forschung', *TR* 42, 54f., criticizes Jervell for failing to recognize that, when Luke was writing, the Gentile character of the church was self-evident.

3. The Picture of Paul in Acts

In the previous chapter we noted the importance of Acts 21–28 as the last major section of Luke–Acts and of 27:17–28 as the last major scene, and examined them from the perspective of understanding the identity of Christians in relation to Jews and Gentiles. We must now go further and ask why Luke has so planned his work that the latter part of Acts, more than half the volume, and therefore more than a quarter of the whole book Luke–Acts, is dominated by the figure of Paul. Why is Paul so important to Luke? And what are the chief things Luke wants to say about him?

1 Analysis of What Luke Says about Paul

Luke reports the following information about Paul:

(a) Paul persecutes Christians: 7:58; 8:1, 3; 9:1f.
(b) Paul is converted: 9:3–19.
(c) For the first time, in Damascus and Jerusalem, Paul preaches in the name of Jesus and is persecuted: 9:20–29.
(d) Paul retires to Tarsus: 9:30, and then is active as a leader and teacher in the church at Antioch: 11:25–30; 12:24–13:3, 15:1–35.
(e) Paul travels as a missionary
  i. (with Barnabas) on behalf of the church at Antioch: 13:4–14:28;
  ii. independently: 15:36–20:1.
(f) Paul returns to Jerusalem under the shadow of predictions that he will soon die: 20:2–21:26.
(g) Paul is arrested and held as a prisoner: 21:27–28:31.

This tabulation underlines again the fact, remarkable in view of the way in which we usually read Acts, that the section on Paul's arrest and imprisonment (g) is slightly longer than that describing his mission (e) – 239 verses against 226: similarly, sections (c), (d) and (e) together are a little shorter than the total of sections (f) and (g) – 283 verses against 302. Moreover, section (g) alone comprises some 23.5% of the text of Acts and 12% of the whole of Luke–Acts. Since we have on other grounds every reason to judge that Luke composes with a careful eye to the dramatic movement and balance of his work, we may regard this long, final section as intended by the author to carry an emphasis and to form at least in some degree the goal and climax of his composition. It may indeed be asked whether Luke has described at greater length Paul's career as a prisoner simply because he knew more about it – because he had more extensive sources, either from other informants or, if the 'we'-sections be taken at their face-value, from his own recollections. We cannot here enter into the most perplexing question of the sources of Acts,[1] but the following observations will quickly show how unlikely it is that Luke had more extensive sources for Paul's imprisonment than for the period of his real work, namely his mission. First, it is generally acknowledged that Luke's hand is more strongly at work in the speeches than in the narrative.[2] If we count as 'speeches' all consecutive words of a single speaker amounting to more than two verses, our section (e), the mission, contains 47 verses of speeches, 21% of the whole section, including the long synagogue-sermon at Antioch-in-Pisidia (13:16–41) and the Areopagus-speech (17:22–31): section (g), the imprisonment, contains 94 verses of speeches, 39% of the whole section, despite the great space taken up by the shipwreck-narrative in ch. 27. Second, the speeches in section (g) do not all represent new matter, for the two longest of them (22:1–21 and 26:2–23) largely recapitulate the narrative of 9:1–19a. There are excellent *dramatic* reasons for these speeches, but they do not represent greater information. We may conclude that Luke made section (g) slightly longer than section (e) despite having less information for it, not because he had more.

When we read Acts as a whole, rather than selectively, it is Paul the prisoner even more than Paul the missionary whom we are meant to remember.

2 Paul's Theology according to Acts

Luke's representation of Paul's theology has been studied so throroughly in recent years[3] that we need refer to it only briefly here. It is not, in any case, the most important aspect of Luke's picture of Paul. The theology which Paul preaches and teaches in Acts is Lucan rather than Pauline: or, better, it is not distinctively Pauline but shares the general character of early Christian theology as Luke understands it. There are indeed a couple of passages where the Lucan Paul speaks with slight undertones of the old Pauline language, e.g. 13:38f. (justification is possible by faith in Jesus but not through the Law of Moses, cf. Rom. 3:21–26; 5:1) and 20:28 (the church has been bought by God through the blood of his own Son, cf. 1 Cor. 6:20; 7:23). But Luke either knows nothing or wants to know nothing of the vigorous controversies within the church, through which Paul had to hew out the shape of his theology. He only describes how some Christians in Jerusalem, who came from the sect of the Pharisees (15:5), wanted to have the newly-converted Gentile believers submitted to the Law: but according to Luke this controversy was settled quickly and easily; Paul does not even have to come forward as advocate for the Gentiles, for the supposedly 'Pauline' attitude is represented by Peter and James, and Paul only has to support their argument with reports of the tangible signs of God's favour evident in the experience of his mission. But the solution of this controversy within the church, the only one affecting Paul, was not really Pauline, for it involved a compromise with legalism nevertheless, Paul without hesitation conveys the decree in which it is expressed to his own churches (Acts 16:4, cf. 15:36–16:1).

It is today generally recognized that Luke did not know the Pauline letters, and that if he had any personal contact with Paul at all, it was not in such a way that he could get to know his theology in any more than a superficial way. The difference between the theology of Paul's letters and that of the Lucan Paul have been described sharply and extensively by P. Vielhauer, more concisely by E. Haenchen.[4] These treatments have been criticized, notably by U. Wilckens, P. Borgen and C. K. Barrett, for exaggeration of the differences and for failure to pay due regard to the respective historical circumstances in which Paul and Luke had to do their work.[5] Whatever may be the case with Luke's knowledge of Paul's theology, and it was in any case slight, it probably seems to us still slighter: for Luke's intention, corresponding to his new historical situation, was a different one from Paul's. For example, Paul in his time had to struggle for the truth of the Christian faith through the theology of the cross. It is a question how far Luke understood or sympathized with a theology of the cross:[6] but he did have before him the Gospel of Mark (which Paul did not have); and what Mark had already done Luke did not need to repeat, especially since there were new challenges confronting the church, which had to be met. It has been extensively debated, whether behind Paul's speech on the Areopagus in Acts 17:22–31 there lie recollections of the ideas found in Rom. 1:18ff. Certainly Paul and Luke use natural theology in quite different ways: Paul to rebuke the Gentile world for its idolatory, since it could have known the true God through creation and reason, Luke to suggest a praeparatio evangelica.[7] But it must be recalled that Acts 17: 22–31 represents a missionary speech addressed to Gentiles, and Rom. 1:18ff. an argument addressed to a controversy within the church: we do not know how Paul would have composed a mission-speech for Gentiles. Further discussion of the differences between Paul's own theology and Luke's representation of it is not necessary here. Used with caution, Acts can enlarge our knowledge of Paul's biography, but hardly of his theology. That does not mean that Luke's portrait of Paul is theologically unimportant or uninteresting: but the theology it can open up for us is Luke's not Paul's.

3 Why Paul is Important to Luke

It is obvious from the structure of Acts and the disposition of material within it that Paul is immensely important to Luke. And since his importance does not consist in a distinctive theology, it must consist in his historical function – either his actual function within the early history of Christianity as Luke understood it, or the dramatic function which Luke assigned to him. This pair of alternative interpretations is worth considering carefully. J. Jervell has argued that Luke was forced to grapple with the problem of Paul's actual historical function as a missionary and theologian, to whom 'the greatest segment of the Christian church' owes its origin.[8] In the previous chapter we discussed, with respect to Luke's attitude to the Jews, Jervell's argument that Luke was forced to defend Paul *personally* against charges of apostasy from the Law of Moses, because if the charges stuck they would invalidate the greatest part of Christendom. We must now consider this argument with respect to Luke's attitude to Paul.

It runs into two serious historical difficulties. First, it requires the general belief, among Jews and Christians in Luke's day, that Paul *had* founded most of the Christian congregations. But this is most unlikely, despite the evidence of the deutero-Pauline literature.[9] For instance, the complete silence of Revelation, especially in ch. 2 and 3, about Paul, is remarkable in view of the fact that Ephesus and its hinterland were one of the most intensive areas of the Pauline mission. Clement of Rome mentions Paul to the Corinthians, but as a figure of the past whose memory is not too lively among them (1 Clem. 5:5–7, cf. 6:1). If even in the areas of his most intensive missionary effort the memory of Paul has become rather dim in the 90's AD (Revelation and 1 Clement), it is unlikely that in Luke's time, however precisely we date that, Paul was held to have been so comprehensively responsible for the planting of Christianity in the 40's and 50's – not to mention the many churches that presumably were founded between Paul's death and the writing of Luke–Acts. Second, Jervell's argument requires the belief by Luke himself that Paul had founded most of the churches. At first sight Acts gives just this impression. But in fact Luke acknowledges quite clearly that Paul did not found the church in Caesarea (Acts 8:40; 10:1–48), Antioch (11:19), Rome (28:15) or Alexandria (not mentioned in Acts, unless 18:24f.), or a large number of less prominent congregations ranging from Damascus (9:10), Lydda and Joppa (9:32, 36), Samaria and Galilee (8:5–25; 9:31 – surprisingly the *only* mention in Acts of churches in Galilee!), Tyre (21:3f.) and Sidon (27:3), Phoenicia generally, Cyprus and Cyrene (11:19f.), across to Puteoli (28:13f., presumably an offshoot of the church in Rome). Paul was indeed a great missionary, but Luke and his contemporaries knew quite well that there was a vigorous and successful expansion of Christianity quite independent of Paul.

Nor can Luke's remarkable concentration on Paul in Acts 13–28 be explained by supposing that Luke was specially concerned about the Pauline churches, as distinct from the rest. In their dealings with Paul, or in their behaviour generally, the churches founded by him do not seem to differ from other churches.[10] Nor is Luke interested in their subsequent history. In Paul's address to the Ephesian elders at Miletus, Acts 20:18–35, Luke seems at first sight to be reflecting on the later development of this congregation: but this speech is expressed in very general terms and is really concerned not specifically with Ephesus but with all the churches of the post-Pauline generation. (With respect to Ephesus in this period we actually receive more precise information from Rev. 2:1–7, the first of the letters to the seven churches.)

There remains the possibility that Paul is important to Luke as a representative or symbol of the whole of Christianity in the generation before Luke's own. Clearly Luke admired Paul greatly and revered his memory: for him Paul is the hero of the earlier period of Christianity. In Acts we glimpse almost nothing of the picture drawn large in the epistles, of Paul as the centre of controversy in the church: his image here is always splendid and inspiring. On the other hand, Paul in Acts has no very distinctive character: in his style of thinking and acting he is not noticeably different from Peter or Barnabas, Stephen or Philip, and he can even agree with James. His distinction lies simply in the fact that he is the greatest of the early Christian leaders and missionaries.

Luke's concentration on Paul is only partly due to his personal interest in him. It also owes much to Luke's narrative method. Luke is much more inclined to paint an individual portrait or an individual scene than to describe a general development. We can take as a good example of this Acts 8, where Luke tells in detail two stories about Philip's mission, his encounter with Simon Magus in Samaria and the conversion of the Ethiopian eunuch, and then at the end there comes this quite short note: 'Philip turned up at Azotus: and passing on he evangelized all the cities until he came to Caesarea'. Behind this laconic statement lies hidden an extensive history, which is actually presupposed as the basis for the events to be narrated in the next two chapters (apart from the conversion of Paul): for according to 9:31 the church existed 'in all Judaea and Galilee and Samaria' – Luke has not explained this, nor has he explained how it was that Peter found Christian congregations already exisiting in Lydda and Joppa (9:32, 36). For him it was more important to illustrate the general development with a few vivid examples. This should warn us against taking Luke's concentration on Paul as necessarily implying a strictly personal interest in him: and all the more so, because he avoids reporting Paul's death, which he could hardly have done if his interest was really in the person of Paul as such. In Acts 24:5 Tertullus calls Paul a *πρωτοστάτης*, champion or ring-leader, of the sect of the Nazarenes, and (apart from the hostile overtones) it is precisely as such that Luke himself wants to portray him. He is more important for what he represents than for his own sake.

4 For Luke Paul is Not an Apostle

This brings us up against the well-known problem, that in Acts Paul does not receive the title of apostle, a fact which stands in sharp contradiction to the evidence of Paul's letters. Why is Paul not an apostle? In early Christianity we can distinguish three chief ways in which the term 'apostle' was used. First there is the meaning which was so important to Paul: an apostle is a missionary in the service of the exalted Lord Jesus, who has appeared to him after his resurrection in order to call him personally (1 Cor. 9:1f.; 15:7f.; cf. Gal. 1:1, 15f.). Secondly we find this same concept in a debased form, according to which an apostle is simply a wandering preacher (Didache 11:3–6; perhaps Rev. 2:2). Thirdly the term is confined to the closed group of the Twelve Apostles.[11] Luke uses the term only in this last sense (apart from Acts 14:4, 14, which will be discussed below). In our surviving literature it first occurs towards the end of the first century, probably first of all in Luke, but soon afterwards also in Rev. 21:14 and in the title of the Didache. It has not yet been satisfactorily explained how the two titles 'the Twelve' and 'the Apostles', clearly distinguished in Paul's terminology (1 Cor. 15:5–9), came to be fused in the next generation.[12] The most serious attempt so far made to answer this question is that of G. Klein, who concludes that it was Luke himself who first made the identification, as a deliberate literary device.[13] Klein argues that Luke restricted the title 'apostle' to the Twelve simply so as to deprive Paul of it. In Luke's time, says Klein, Paul's heritage was being claimed vigorously by Gnostic heretics, who set Paul over against the conservative orthodoxy represented by the church in Jerusalem: Luke's tactic, then, was to deprive Paul of this theological and ecclesiastical independence by subordinating him to the Twelve, who, as the only 'apostles', possess the only authentic revelation of the earthly and the risen Jesus. This theory cannot be sustained,[14] for it runs up against a serious historical difficulty through the existence of Rev. 21:14: 'The wall of the city had twelve foundations, and on them were written twelve names, the names of the twelve apostles of the Lamb', Klein tries to argue this evidence away by refusing to acknowledge that 'the Twelve Apostles' is a title here: he contends that there simply had to be twelve apostles (out of an indefinite number) because there were twelve foundation stones.[15] However, the conscious co-ordination of the twelve foundations represented by the twelve apostles with the twelve gates represented by the twelve tribes of Israel (v. 12) brings the number twelve into sharp prominence: here John is presumably recalling the tradition of the saying of Jesus about the eschatological function of the Twelve in Matt. 19:28/Luke 22:29f.; the only new element is that John adds to the Twelve the title 'Apostles', and in such a way as to suggest that this identification will not be unfamiliar to his readers. The difficulty which this creates for Klein's interpretation is all the greater since he dates Luke–Acts early in the second century,[16] i.e. later than Revelation. There is also the problem, how convincing Luke would have been to his readers if, as suggested, he was artificially giving a new meaning to a term well established in a quite different sense. We must in fact assume that the identification of 'the Twelve' with 'the Apostles' had been attained through a broad consensus in the church, by some process which we can no longer discern, between the time of Paul's letters and the writing of Luke–Acts and Revelation.[17] All the same, it seems clear that Luke cannot have been ignorant of Paul's claim to be an apostle, or at least that Paul had once been known by this title, because in the exceptional case of Acts 14 he twice incidentally refers to Barnabas and Paul as 'the apostles': here presumably the old tradition is shining through,[18] and Luke has for once neglected to amend the language to conform it to his own conception. His otherwise consistently maintained view that only the Twelve are apostles can only be explained on the assumption that by the late first century this restriction of the term had come widely to be taken for granted: either Luke regarded it as an error when the traditions he received spoke of Paul as an apostle, or else he himself had reasons to emphasize the newer terminology and suppress the older.

Klein's theory suffers further from the fact that in Acts Paul is not in reality subordinated either to the Twelve in particular or to the church of Jerusalem in general. The aid given Paul by Ananias in Acts 9:10–17 and 22:12–16 seems at first sight to contradict the immediacy of his call by Jesus, on which Paul insists in Gal. 1:11–17. But it is not at all certain that Paul would have denied the truth of Luke's story about Ananias, or that he would have regarded it as invalidating his claim to have been given his commission directly by the Lord himself.[19] In any case, Ananias does not represent the Twelve or Jerusalem. Luke does indeed hasten to mention that Paul was accepted by the Twelve and that he worked in harmony with them, and even in partnership with them so long as circumstances permitted (Acts: 9:26f., 28–30): but that is a different matter. The nearest we come to a hint of subordination is the minor rôle played by Paul in the council-meeting in Acts 15, but even here Luke's meaning is different: the problem that made the council necessary arose from an error originating within the Jerusalem congregation (Acts 15:1, 5), and since Luke regards the leaders of the church as all acting in harmony it was fitting that the rejection of this error should be proposed by Peter and James, who represented Jerusalem, rather than by Paul and Barnabas as the representatives of Antioch.

There is indeed no question in Acts of Paul's being subordinated to others. Out of the recognition of this fact has arisen a theory almost the direct opposite of Klein's: C. Burchard has asserted that in his portrait of Paul Luke's purpose is to *equate* him with the Twelve Apostles through the terminology of 'witness', while acknowledging that he is not an apostle.[20] Burchard unfortunately does not inquire about the origin of the concept 'the twelve apostles': he simply assumes without argument the conclusion suggested above, that the restriction of 'apostles' to the Twelve was already firmly fixed in the church's language before Luke; and then goes further to suggest that Luke's effort was directed towards redressing the balance, so to speak, by trying to find a way to overcome the separation thus set up between the Twelve and Paul.[21] Burchard does not consider why Luke should not simply have reasserted the earlier terminology, of which he was aware, as we can see through Acts 14:4, 14, and which could not have lain so far buried in the past that its resuscitation was impossible. Instead he seeks to clarify Luke's meaning by seeking to distinguish in the three accounts of Paul's Damascus-experience (Acts 9:3–19a; 22:5–16; 26:12–18) between tradition and redaction.[22] He concludes that the narrative in ch. 9 substantially represents tradition received by Luke (though not originating from Paul), with only slight touches of Lucan redaction, and setting the experience forth as one of conversion.[23] In ch. 22 and 26, on the other hand, Lucan redaction has played a much more active part, and the event is now interpreted rather as a call.[24] Of great significance in the latter two passages is the application to Paul of terminology otherwise used only of the Apostles: Jesus has *appeared* to Paul (26:16: cf. 22:14–18 and 9:17 – the latter is one of the few traces of Lucan redaction in 9:3–19a) because he has *chosen* him (22:14; 26:16) to be a *servant* (26:16) and *witness* (22:15; 26:16) of what he has seen and heard: cf. Luke 1:2; 24:48; Acts 1:2–8, 22; 2:32; 3:15; 4:33; 5:32; 10:39, 41; 13:31.[25] In this way, according to Burchard, Luke uses the concept 'witness' to remove the basic difference between Paul and the Apostles caused by his not belonging to the circle of the Twelve.[26] But why should Luke have been concerned to do this? Burchard rejects (without argument) an interpretation frequently given of Acts 28:30f., that Luke–Acts breaks off as it were with an open end, implying the continuation of Paul's mission after the death of Paul himself and down into Luke's own times:[27] he holds instead that the importance of Paul lies in the historical fact that it was he and not the Twelve who literally fulfilled the commission of Acts 1:8;[28] with Paul's death (implied by the end of Acts) a 'caesura' is marked:[29] the 'thirteen witnesses' established in the early days the truth of the gospel, which is to give Luke's readers confidence to hold fast to their faith through the time in which they must simply wait for the parousia.[30]

Burchard has rightly emphasized the methodological importance of distinguishing as clearly as possible between the traditions Luke received and the use made of them by the author, if we are truly to understand Luke's theology and purpose.[31] With respect to the picture of Paul, Burchard believes that tradition gave Luke a Paul separate from the Twelve Apostles and that Luke's aim was to bring him as close to them as possible.

But may not the case be just the reverse? It is doubtless true, as many have said, that Haenchen was too sceptical about recovering written and oral sources behind Acts: but the difficulty of achieving convincing results should not be underestimated.[32] Burchard's case rests heavily on the argument that Acts 9:1–19a is essentially a pre-formed narrative, not Luke's composition and not in all points representing Luke's own view.[33] The crucial point is that Luke's own view, to be seen in his adaptation of the original story in ch. 22 and 26, sees Paul's experience as a *call* to be a witness, in which Jesus *appears* to him, as he did to the Apostles between the resurrection and ascension; whereas in 9:1–19a the incident is told as a *conversion*, without any call, and there is no appearance of Jesus to Paul except in Ananias' words 'Jesus who appeared to you on the road', 9:17, which according to Burchard is one of the few traces of Lucan redaction in the passage.[34]

A serious weakness in this line of argument is that Burchard takes too little account of dramatic development in Luke's composition. The distinction between 'conversion' in ch. 9 and 'call' in ch. 22 and 26 is perfectly well explained by the respective contexts in Luke's whole story. In ch. 9 Luke is not yet ready to get Paul fully launched on his great mission, so the 'call'-aspect can for the present be played down in favour of emphasizing the overwhelming power of the Risen Lord in swinging the arch-persecutor over to his side. Conversely, by the time the reader reaches ch. 22 and 26 he is very familiar with Paul as a devout Christian: it is the legitimacy of his mission, and therefore the authenticity of his call, which now claims the centre of attention. The matter of Jesus' 'appearing' to Paul is even more interesting. In none of the three accounts is there any detailed description of Paul's seeing Jesus. (22:17–21 is a special case: it is a vision Paul sees ἐν ἐκστάσει in Jerusalem and is not directly part of the experience near Damascus.) The central narrative of what Paul experienced is told in remarkably similar language in all three chapters: Paul sees a bright light and hears a voice, to which he responds and is answered again: but it is not said that he saw Jesus (9:3–5; 22:6–8; 26:13–15). In the sequel, however, in different words in each case, it is hinted that Paul did after all see Jesus (9:17, 'Jesus who appeared to you on the road'; 22:14, 'to see the Righteous One'; 26:16, 'I appeared to you'). Which side of this picture represents the tradition Luke received, and which is due to his own interpretation? We have no concrete evidence of any tradition external to Luke which denied that Jesus had appeared to Paul, but in Paul's letters we have emphatic proof that Paul himself claimed to have seen the risen Jesus in the same way as those who had been apostles before him (1 Cor. 9:1; 15:5–8; Gal. 1:15–17).

On the other hand, it is Luke himself whose general theory will not allow Paul to have seen Jesus in the same way as the Twelve, for it is he who in Acts 1:1–11 first sets the Ascension as a very early time-barrier, long before the conversion of Paul, after which there are no more resurrection-appearances. The old, Pauline tradition that Paul had 'seen the Lord' (1 Cor. 9:1), that the Lord had 'appeared to' Paul (1 Cor. 15:8), or that God had 'revealed his Son to' him (Gal. 1:16) was too powerful to be ignored altogether, and Luke lets it shine through, not only in the three verses mentioned but also in 9:27. But the fundamental description of Paul's experience in 9:3–5 pars. is fully in accord with the Ascension-schema of Acts 1:1–11. Just as the Ascension-narrative itself is Luke's own construction[35] (at least in its form in Luke–Acts),[36] so is the narrative of the Damascus-experience. And its function is not to assimilate Paul to the Twelve Apostles but to distinguish him from them.

It is indeed remarkable that the two themes we have just been discussing, the title 'apostle' and the seeing of the risen Lord Jesus, are closely linked by both Paul (1 Cor. 9:1) and Luke (Acts 1:21f.). The traditions available to Luke would have made it quite possible for him to include Paul at both points, and thus assimilate him to the Twelve. In fact he has gone the other way. This is not to say that Luke *invented* the restriction of the title 'apostle' to the Twelve: he most likely had a tradition to that effect, side by side with the tradition that Paul too had been called an apostle. What is significant is that he chose to accept and develop the tradition that set Paul apart from the Twelve: and his interpretation of the Ascension and the Resurrection-appearances serves the same purpose.

What then of the concept 'witness', which according to Burchard Luke uses in order to point in the opposite direction? It is true that μάρτυς, occurring twice in Luke and thirteen times in Acts, is most often (nine times) used of the Apostles, and that the two passages in which it is used of Paul (Acts 22:15; 26:16) are specially significant in that they have to do with Paul's vocation. But this is not enough to show that μάρτυς is a technical term specially connecting Paul with the Twelve as the 'thirteen witnesses'.[37] In Acts 22:20 Paul speaks to Stephen as the μάρτυς of Jesus – so there are not only thirteen. And in 13:31 it is Paul who says of the Twelve that the Lord had appeared to them 'for many days' and that they were now his witnesses to the nation – so the concept is used here to distinguish Paul from the Apostles rather than to link him with them.

We can thus see, over against the arguments of Klein on the one hand and of Burchard on the other, that Luke's purpose with respect to Paul and the Twelve Apostles is neither to subordinate him to them nor to minimize the distinction between him and them. Rather, there is an important distinction, but it has to do not with rank but with differentiation of time and function. Paul's ministry largely overlaps in time with that of the Apostles, but by setting Paul's conversion as late as ch. 9, and mentioning the Apostles no more after 16:4, Luke heightens the impression that Paul came on the scene long after them and continued to be active long after them. Within the basic continuity and harmony of the life of the church there is also a necessary distinction of functions in different periods.[38] The Twelve Apostles had the special, unrepeatable function of bearing witness to their own experience of the transition from the Lord's earthly life through his cross, resurrection and ascension to his heavenly enthronement. After them the whole church, represented by the great preachers and missionaries, like Stephen and especially Paul, had to carry the same testimony on throughout the world. The Apostles had to lay the true, historical foundation of faith in Jesus, but Paul and his contemporaries had the honour of carrying out a geographically far greater part of the Lord's commission in Acts 1:8: 'you shall be my witnesses in Jerusalem . . . and to the end of the earth'. The chronological differentiation between the Apostles and Paul is very important.[39] From the perspective of Luke and his contemporaries the origins of the church now lay a long time back in the past. But with Paul it was a different matter. Whatever may be the historical and literary origin of the 'we'-style, which Luke uses at the beginning of the European mission, on Paul's return-journey to Jerusalem and in the voyage to Rome,[40] its dramatic function is clear. The author wants to hint that he himself had had a share, even if only a rather marginal one, in the career of Paul: thus he indicates that Paul was the bridge leading from the original, apostolic age down into his own day.[41] But we should add (bearing in mind the conclusion of section 3 of this chapter): it is not specifically and exclusively Paul himself that Luke means, but Paul as chief representative and symbol of that great second generation of Christians, to whom Luke and his friends are indebted for their faith.

5 The Function of Luke's Picture of Paul

Paul, then, is a bridge: but of what kind? What significance has this bridge in Luke's scheme? This may be clarified by noting the outlines of Luke's sketch of Paul's career after his conversion. It falls into three periods. The first period is an extended one of missionary work and pastoral leadership in Cilicia and Syria, i.e. in Tarsus and Antioch and their surroundings. Luke gives no dates, but he hints that this period lasted a number of years:[42] however, he seems to have little information about it. The second period is that of the great missionary journeys, lasting from the late 40's and through the 50's.[43] The third period is that of Paul's imprisonment, which lasted at least four and a half years. Now it is most interesting that Luke describes this period of imprisonment at greater length than that of the mission, even though he knows less about it. As we noted in section 1 of this chapter, Paul's imprisonment serves as the climax not only of Acts but of Luke's whole work. If in Luke's eyes the main thing about Paul was his mission, then the final section of Acts is disappointing, for in the last nine chapters no one is converted![45] The narrative momentum of Acts 21:27 – 28:31 is provided by Paul's trial. The whole section begins and is carried along by the fact that Paul has been falsely accused by the Jewish authorities and that he is one day to be juridically acquitted of those charges. No fewer than four times in this section we read rather detailed accounts of trials or legal inquiries in the case of the Jews versus Paul (22:30–23:10; 24:1–23; 25:6–12; and 25:23–26:32), and in the meantime the case is also privately discussed at some length by Festus and Agrippa (25:13–22). There is a great heightening of tension when at the end of the third hearing Paul appeals to Caesar (25:11f.). All the same, there is reason to doubt whether it was the juridical aspect of Paul's situation in which Luke was really interested. The trial-theme serves to emphasize the unjust suffering to which Paul was subjected in his last few years. It is most significant that after Paul had lodged his appeal to the Emperor the latter is virtually not heard of again. It has sometimes been argued that Luke's silence on the further progress of Paul's trial in Rome is for historical reasons. For example, Burchard has suggested that Luke says nothing about the outcome of the imperial trial because he knew nothing about it: it could be that in the Neronian persecution all the witnesses of Paul's trial in Rome, and presumably of his death there, had been killed or scattered.[46] But that seems to me to be based on too unimaginative and too unsympathetic a view of Luke's method of composition. Luke is no mere pedantic chronographer. The Christian church in Rome was certainly not completely wiped out by the Neronian persecution: and even if only a few small, general pieces of information about Paul's end had been handed on, Luke was quite capable of shaping some sort of historical picture out of them, as Burchard himself has convincingly shown with respect to Luke's treatment of the period between Paul's experience on the Damascus-road and his settling in Tarsus (Acts 9:20–30).[47] No, Luke says no more about the imperial trial because for him that is not the point. The trial as such is important only because it is the means whereby Paul, despite his imprisonment, eventually succeeds in getting to Rome. Even the angel's words of encouragement before the shipwreck, 27:24, 'Do not be afraid, Paul! You must stand before Caesar', do not signify anything else: Paul must fulfil the purpose of the journey, i.e. he must come to Rome.

What Luke really intends to convey to his readers through the last great section of his work, Acts 21:27–28:31, seems to me to be threefold:

1. Before Paul reached Rome, there were already Christians there, as Luke clearly knows (28:15). But these were ordinary, anonymous Christians. From the perspective of Luke's dramatic concept of historiography, it is with the arrival in Rome of Paul, a great *πρωτοστάτης*, that Christianity has really reached the imperial capital. Luke certainly has in mind the programme announced in Acts 1:8 'witnesses . . . to the end of the earth'. He does not mean that that program has now been fulfilled: its fulfilment still lies in the future in Luke's own day, not to mention Paul's.[48] But the arrival of Paul in Rome at least marks a most important step forward along the way. Luke wants to show the commission as being *in process* of fulfilment. This is the meaning of that most carefully constructed sentence with which he ends his work, Acts 28:30f. The ending is certainly intended as 'open': but it points forward not to a third volume[49] but to Luke himself and his contemporary fellow-Christians. To them Luke is saying: 'This is the same mission which is committed to us, too'.

2. By contrast with Gal. 2:1–9, Paul in Acts is not the head of the Gentile Department, so to speak, of the Christian world-mission. Paul's old title of 'missionary to the Gentiles' does indeed shine through in Acts: but his commission now is to bear his witness to Jesus not only before Gentiles but also before Jews. We have already noted (in Chapter Two) the importance of the last half-chapter, Acts 28:17–28, where Paul on arrival in Rome concerns himself neither with the Gentile pagans nor with the Christians[50] but only seeks out the leading Jews. During his career as a Christian preacher, from its very beginnings in 9:20 on, Paul has striven to convince the Jews about the Lord Jesus Christ. The fact that twice during his

missionary journeys, disappointed by the rejection of his message by Jews of the diaspora, he solemnly turns to the Gentiles (13:46; 18:6), does nothing to change his plan. Right at the end of the book, 28:25–28, the same turning to the Gentiles has to take place. It is the merit of J. Jervell's essay, 'Paul – the Teacher of Israel', to have shown that a major function of Acts 21:27–28:31 is to prove that the Jewish accusations against Paul have no basis. But if, as we have argued, Paul for Luke stands essentially as a symbol of the whole Christian movement, or at least of its great leaders in the second generation, then what Luke is saying to his contemporary fellow-Christians is: 'The separation between Jews and Christians, which is going on before our eyes, is not the fault of us Christians'.

3. Within the last section Paul as a prisoner twice repeats in detail the narrative of his conversion from 9:1–19a in 22:3–22 and 26:4–24. The differences in content and emphasis between these three passages have often been studied,[51] and are not of major importance for our present purpose. Nor do we need to emphasize again the familiar observation that Luke must have regarded this story as of extraordinary importance, to have told it at length three times over. What has not received so much notice is the significant context in which Luke has set the two repetitions of the original narration. If Luke's only intention with this literary procedure was to underline the importance of the Damascus-experience (whether for Paul personally or for the Christian movement as a whole), why did he in this case wait until so late a stage in the book before bringing the repetitions forward? In the case of the almost equally important story of the conversion of Cornelius, which Luke also underlines by a detailed repetition, the second narration follows the first *at once*, 11:1–18 after ch. 10. It would for example have made good sense to let the suspicious Apostles be persuaded of the genuineness of Paul's conversion by letting him relate his experience of 9:1–19a in detail as soon as he meets them in Jerusalem, 9:26: instead we simply read, 9:27: 'But Barnabas took him in hand and brought him to the Apostles, and reported to them how he had seen the Lord on the road, and that he had spoken to him, and how he had at Damascus spoken publicly in the name of Jesus'. One could also think of a number of good opportunities during the missionary journeys for the desired repetitions.[52] But it is Paul *under arrest* who twice recalls his conversion, though the emphasis has been shifted, for it is now interpreted as a call. But that means that his imprisonment is closely linked with his vocation: in fact it is to imprisonment that Paul is called, i.e. to rejection and suffering.[53] If we turn back to the first Damascus-narrative in ch. 9, we find no direct call addressed to Paul; however the Lord explains to Ananias, 'This man is my chosen instrument, to carry my name before the Gentiles and kings and the sons of Israel, for I myself will show him all that he must suffer for my name'. The conjunction 'for', *γάρ*, which connects v. 16 to v. 15, has given many commentators and translators[54] difficulty: the reader is expecting a 'but', for 'carrying the name' is mostly understood as

missionary activity, and it is not clear why suffering should be a precondition for that. But C. Burchard has convincingly shown that 'carrying the name' of Christ is the terminology not of mission but of martyrdom.[55] This means that God has declared from the very beginning that Paul is to bear his witness for Jesus even more through persecution and suffering than through his famous mission.[56] This, then, is the nature of the 'bridge' of Christendom that leads from the Apostles to Luke and his contemporaries.

Note: Paul and Jesus: The view has often been held that Luke's picture of Paul, and therewith his purpose in drawing that picture, can be significantly illuminated by a comparison with the picture of Jesus in the Gospel of Luke. The latest full study on this theme, by W. Radl,[57] traces the discussion back to tentative beginnings in the eighteenth century but sees its first full expression in R. B. Rackham's Acts-commentary of 1901. Advocates of this line of research regard Luke as setting up a parallel structure in his two volumes, usually with the person and career of Paul, as the chief figure of volume 2, corresponding in many features to those of Jesus in volume 1. Thus Radl himself draws up a list of several elements in which he believes Luke is deliberately emphasizing the parallelism: in particular he believes that Paul's trial and 'passion' in Acts 21:27–26:32 are an echo of Luke 22:47–23:25, and further that Paul's journey to Rome is an elaborate parallel to Jesus' death and resurrection. Luke's purpose in doing this, according to Radl, is to demonstrate that there is a continuity between Jesus and the church – that the life of the church is a genuine extension of the activity of Jesus. A variation of this is the view of V. Stolle,[58] that the Paul-story in Acts *is* the Jesus-story again: when Paul is arraigned and justified, this is Jesus being tried again and being acquitted by the truth to which Paul witnesses. Jesus is present in his faithful disciples.

In very general terms this line of approach is true enough. The Christian life is an imitation, or better a following, of Christ: the Christian is one who takes up his cross 'daily' and follows Jesus (Luke 9:23); the disciple is one who is shaped into the pattern of his teacher (Luke 6:40). But one may be sceptical as to how far this is worked out by Luke in the form of typological narrative. Certainly Paul suffers, and his suffering is prophesied, as is the case with Jesus. But it is not too persuasive when Luke 2:32, 34b is compared with Acts 9:15f. as 'prophecy of suffering in preparatory scenes', or when Acts 13:14–52 is called a 'programmatic sermon' parallel to that of Luke 4:16–30. Still more remote, of course, is the alleged parallelism of Paul's journey to Rome with the death and resurrection of Jesus.

What seems to be overlooked here is that for the rest of the NT writers the figure of Jesus is unique and unrepeatable. Luke is indeed not averse to seeing a certain poignancy when some aspects of the career of Jesus are repeated in the lives of his disciples: but at this point one thinks not of Paul so much as of Stephen,[59] who is nevertheless for Luke a relatively minor figure, at least by comparison with Paul. That Luke is concerned about continuity between Jesus and the church is not to be denied – quite the reverse. But the means by which he sees this continuity being expressed are neither the repetition of a pattern of events (Radl) nor a sort of reincarnation of Jesus in his disciples (Stolle) but the Scriptures, the Apostles and the Holy Spirit. Luke takes great care to prove that the mission of the church, like the death and resurrection of Jesus, has been predicted by or is in accordance with the commands of Scripture.[60] The Apostles provide the historical continuity from the life and work of Jesus to the life of the church. The Holy Spirit, prophesied in Scripture and now an actual reality, expresses the will and gives the power of Jesus, who is neither simply a figure of the past, nor immanent within the lives of his disciples, but is enthroned at the right hand of God and from there maintains a lively intercourse with his church on earth.[60a]

6 The Persecution of Christians according to Luke

The Lucan Paul, we have argued stands as a representative and symbol of Christianity, and precisely as one who is persecuted and suffers. Therefore Luke is saying through his picture of Paul something about the persecution and suffering to be expected by all Christians.

How serious a matter was persecution for the church in Luke's day? We have of course virtually no external evidence for the history of the church in the period between the persecutions of Nero and Domitian, during the latter part of which period we presume Luke to have written his book, so we must rely on internal evidence. Some interpreters, notably G. Braumann[61] and F. Schütz,[62] believe that the church for which Luke is writing was severely persecuted, and that this persecution was indeed the chief problem which provoked Luke's writing.[63] The evidence adduced to support this view comes from the Gospel of Luke more than from Acts, and consists either of passages where sayings of Jesus referring to future persecution for his disciples are felt to be more sharply worded in Luke than in the synoptic parallels (Schütz)[64], or of themes such as the rôle of John the Baptist as forerunner of Jesus' suffering rather than of his messiahship, and the baptism and genealogy of Jesus as contrasting his divine Sonship with his rejection at Nazareth as Joseph's son (Braumann).[65] In my judgement the texts are in each case capable of a different interpretation, and there is indeed good evidence to the contrary. It is striking for example that the phrase in Mark 4:17, 'when affliction or persecution arises because of the Word', retained without change in Matt. 13:21, is weakened in Luke 8:13 to read 'in time of testing'. One of the more important passages in Luke where Jesus warns his disciples of coming persecution is 12:2–12. In the context provided by Luke in setting these words after 12:1 the passage calls for disciples not to dissemble their faith when Jewish opposition becomes threatening. By a different arrangement of the material, also found in Matt. 10:26–33, 19–20, Luke brings the passage to an optimistic conclusion with the promise that the Holy Spirit will come to their aid. In the still stronger prophecy of persecution, in 21:12–19, the promise of divine aid which makes anxiety superfluous is repeated in a variant form, not mentioning the Holy Spirit but declaring that all the disciples' opponents will not be able to withstand or contradict the eloquence and wisdom which will be given them (21:14f.): the saying in this second form does not occur in the equivalent passage Mark 13:9–13/Matt. 24:9–14, and in general the discourses in Matt. 10 and 24 give a more alarming picture of coming persecution than is found in Luke 12 and 21. As is well known, Luke has a tendency to abbreviate and weaken passages in Mark about the suffering and death of Jesus, which also have implications for the suffering to be expected by his disciples: e.g. Mark 10:33–45/Luke 18:31–33; 12:50; 22:24–27; Mark 8:27–33/Luke 9:18–22; Luke omits Mark 9:9–13. This means that while Luke acknowledges, along with the whole gospel-tradition, that the Christian life is one in which persecution is part of the cost of discipleship, he does not emphasize this more than the other evangelists, and may even be seen to hold out a stronger hope that persecution can be withstood successfully. In Acts this note of confidence in the face of opposition is still stronger.

One sign of this is the way in which Luke handles the theme of Paul's death. In Acts 20–21 Luke quite clearly presupposes that Paul's imprisonment will end with his execution, but at the end of the book he surprisingly neither narrates nor even mentions it. This can only mean that Luke wants to end the book without drawing attention to Paul's martyrdom. Why not? E. Haenchen suggests that Luke 'did not desire, in the manner of the Revelation of John, to equip the Christians for martyrdom, but rather to spare the church martyrdom so far as possible'.[66] That is, by emphasizing the leniency of the government's treatment of Paul the prisoner (ἀκωλύτως as his final word!), Luke sought to persuade the Roman authorities in his own day to live peaceably with the church. This suggestion will have to be judged in the wider context of the discussion, whether political apology was a significant part of Luke's purpose. It is more likely, I think, that Luke's purpose in deliberately suppressing the theme of martyrdom, except in the special case of Stephen (which we shall mention below), was to disparage a tendency, perhaps already making its appearance, to glamorize a martyr's death, as was to happen in the second century in Ignatius (especially in his epistle to the Romans) and in the *Martyrdom of Polycarp*. The Christian's business is not to play the hero, but to bear his witness in humility. The strange account which Luke gives of Paul's suffering fits in well with this idea. For Luke's account stands in sharp contrast with Paul's own account of his sufferings, for instance in 2 Cor. 4 and 11. According to the Epistles Paul often falls into real distress, in which only God's grace can encourage and strengthen him. But in Acts even the worst that happens to him cannot seriously weigh him down. To mention what is perhaps the most extreme example: in Acts 14:19f. we read, 'They stoned Paul and dragged him outside the city, thinking that he was dead. But when the disciples surrounded him he got up and went into the city. The next day he went off with Barnabas to Derbe' – about 100 kilometres away! It is also instructive that the story of Paul's escape over the wall of Damascus in a basket is told in Acts 9:25 as the bold exploit of a determined and resourceful man, but in 2 Cor. 11:32f. Paul, the ever hunted and oppressed apostle, cites it as the supreme example of his humiliation.[67] During his imprisonment as well as his mission in Acts we get the impression that Paul is in control of things.

Behind this picture we can, I think, perceive two things. First, it cannot be denied that in order to honour this great Christian leader of the previous generation Luke has been glad to use traditions about Paul which are in part already legendary (e.g., Acts 28:2–6). But second, Luke portrays Paul in his persecutions and long imprisonment in such a way as to warn and encourage his contemporary fellow-Christians. This is what the Christian life is like: 'through many afflictions must we enter into the Kingdom of God' – so Barnabas and Paul told the churches in Lystra, Iconium and Derbe (14:22). But through the Holy Spirit and the Word of God these afflictions are turned into mere annoyances, which a resolute Christian can easily endure. Even if it should come to the point of having to die for one's faith, that is no grim disaster, as the Lord Jesus had taught, Luke 12:4–7. But in fact that necessity is likely to arise in only a rare, exceptional case. In the whole of Acts only two Christians die a martyr's death: the death of Stephen is painted vividly on a big canvas (ch. 6–7), to show how a Christian behaves in extreme circumstances; on the other hand the beheading of James is mentioned only briefly and in passing 12:2, so as not to let this set-back be emphasized.

The church within which Luke writes is under pressure, through theological argument as well as through physical assault and judicial processes: all that cannot be avoided. But the Holy Spirit is working irresistibly on, and that can only give the Christian joy and confidence to take his share in the witness to Christ, to which the whole church is called. The truth of his doctrine is guaranteed by Holy Scripture and an unassailably genuine tradition of witnesses; his leaders have been proved blameless in relation to both Judaism and the Roman state; and the life of his fellowship in the church is marked by love, joy and peace. The cause of Jesus is God's great action in history, and its coming victory can already be perceived today. In order to demonstrate all this, Luke's picture of Paul was of the greatest significance to him.

Notes to ('The Picture of Paul in Acts') Chapter Three

1. Older studies, culminating in K. Lake and his colleagues in *Beginnings*, 1920–1933, thought mainly in terms of a series of written sources. But in 1923 M. Dibelius, following his pioneering work (alongside K. L. Schmidt and R. Bultmann) on the form-critical method in the study of the gospels, tried a new approach in which interest was centred on oral tradition as the chief means by which Luke obtained his material: 'Stilkritisches zur Apg' = ch. 1 in his *Aufsätze*. One of the *Beginnings*-team, *H. J. Cadbury,* also soon saw the need

to move in this direction: *Making*, 1927, ch. 3–5, 14. E. Haenchen's influential commentary, first published in 1956, was based on the assumption that in Acts Luke had very little oral tradition to go on, and almost no written sources: *Apg* 92–101, 125–129 (ET 81–90, 117–121). This view was rightly criticized by many reviewers, notably R. Bultmann, 'Zur Frage nach den Quellen der Apg', as excessively sceptical; cf. C. K. Barrett, *New Testament Essays*, 105ff. On the other hand, some recent scholars, e.g. those whose works are reviewed by C. Burchard, 'Paulus in der Apg', and Burchard himself, *Der dreizehnte Zeuge*, are certainly too confident about the possibility of identifying, behind the text of Acts, extensive traditions in fixed oral form. The major study of sources in Acts is J. Dupont, *Sources of Acts*. On the 'we'-sections, see below, n. 40. For more recent work, see W. G. Kümmel, *Einleitung*, 141ff. (ET, 174ff.).

2. See M. Dibelius, *Aufsätze*, especially ch. 9; U. Wilckens, *Missionsreden*, part III.
3. See the next two notes.
4. P. Vielhauer, 'Paulinismus'; E. Haenchen, *Apg*, 120–124, (ET, 112–116).
5. U. Wilckens, 'Interpreting Luke–Acts'; P. Borgen, 'From Paul to Luke', 168–182; C. K. Barrett, *New Testament Essays*, ch. 6.
6. See (e.g.) C. K. Barrett, *New Testament Essays*, 82f.
7. From the extensive literature on Acts 17:16–34 the following may be mentioned: E. Norden, *Agnostos Theos*; M. Dibelius, 'Paulus auf dem Areopag', = ch. 2 in his *Aufsätze*; B. Gärtner, *Areopagus Speech*; W. Nauck, 'Tradition und Komposition'; H. Conzelmann, *Apg*, 96–105; H. Conzelmann, 'The Address of Paul on the Areopagus', in *SLA*, 217–232; E. Haenchen, *Apg*, 495–510 (ET, 515–531); S. G. Wilson, *Gentiles*, ch. 8.

From the literature on Rom. 1:18–32: A. Feuillet, 'La connaissance naturelle', M. D. Hooker, 'Adam in Romans 1', E. Käsemann, *An die Römer*, 30–48; U. Wilckens, *Der Brief an die Römer*, 93–121.

Much discussion has been devoted to the question, how far the speech is Pauline and biblical (Gärtner) and how far it is inspired by Hellenistic philosophy (Dibelius). Many individual phrases are capable of explanation against either background, and it is likely that this reflects Luke's drawing here on a long tradition of Hellenistic Jewish mission-preaching (Nauck), with which indeed Paul himself was no doubt acquainted.

The chief differences between Acts 17:16–34 and Rom. 1:18ff. are, first, a difference in mood, in that the former looks hopefully on the possibility that human beings will, with the moral encouragement given by the warning of coming judgement (v. 30f.), at last find God, who has all the time been accessible to them (v. 27–29), whereas in Rom. 1:18ff. Paul looks on human society as in a desperate state, because of wilful ignorance of God (v. 19–21, cf. 3:22b–23). Second, in Acts 17:30 human sin seems to be treated rather lightly, being identified with the ignorance shown in worshipping cult-objects of human manufacture (v. 29, cf. v. 16, 22b–23), but in Rom. 1:23f., 25f., 28 idolatry is interpreted as a deep-seated perversion of the honour due to God, which leads to moral depravity. Third, Acts 17:28b-29a regards kinship with God as an innate characteristic of humanity, whereas in Romans human beings are by nature children of Adam (5:12) and divine sonship is the gift of election realized through faith in Christ (8:14). Fourth, the motives for repentance suggested in Acts 17:24–31 are gratitude for the providence of creation and fear of the coming judgement, whereas in Romans they are not only the coming judgement (2:12) but also the seriousness of the present human plight (1:18–32) and the power of God's salvation in the cross of Christ (1:16f.; 3:21–26).

By reason of space it is obviously unfair to compare the nineteen verses of Acts 17:16–34 with the whole of Romans. But Rom. 1:18–32 can only be interpreted in the context of the whole epistle. The themes touched on in the Areopagus-speech are not significantly developed elsewhere in Luke–Acts, though some of them are foreshadowed in Acts 14:15–17.

8. *People of God*, 173f.
9. Colossians and especially Ephesians give this impression through an ecumenical or even cosmic ecclesiology, but they contain little concrete information about the number and extent of Pauline congregations. The Pastoral Epistles have a quite different ecclesiology. Titus suggests that Paul was active in Crete, which is historically unlikely in the light of the genuine Pauline epistles and Acts. 1 and 2 Timothy add nothing geographically, except to suggest in very general terms a wider activity of Paul than is otherwise known.
10. Acts gives us almost no description of the internal life of the congregations, apart from Antioch and Jerusalem: but Paul is apparently welcomed without hesitation by the churches he has certainly not previously met (Puteoli, Rome) as well as many others not founded by him (Caesarea, Tyre, Sidon and of course Antioch). Luke represents the church-government of the Pauline churches as presbyterian (14:23; 20:17), but this is also on the way in Jerusalem itself (15:6, 22f.; 16:4; especially 21:18). In one case Paul seems to have re-founded a 'church' already existing on an inadequate basis (19:1–6); a similar, though perhaps not so extreme case, had had to be dealt with by Peter and John (8:14–17); see J. D. G. Dunn, *Baptism*, ch. 8.
11. For a full discussion of the variety of NT usage, including also 'false apostles', see C. K. Barrett, *The Signs of an Apostle*. See also C. K. Barrett, '*Shaliaḥ* and Apostle', 98ff.
12. Since the title of the Didache is original (see F. X. Funk/K. Bihlmeyer/W. Schneemelcher, *Die Apostolischen Väter*, I, XIII), this work contains the term 'apostle' in two different meanings: 1:1 and 11:3–6, as noted above. This suggests that 'the Twelve Apostles' did not completely or suddenly supplant all other meanings of 'apostle', and makes Luke's general consistency in using the title all the more striking.
13. G. Klein, *Die Zwölf Apostel*. Other studies on the term 'apostle' have concentrated on (a) the possible Greek or Hebrew antecedents of the Christian terminology, (b) Paul's and (c) Luke's concept of the qualifications and functions of apostles. An extensive bibliography is given by B. Rigaux, 'Die zwölf Apostel'.
14. See E. Haenchen's discussion, *Apg*, 130–134 (ET, 122–126).
15. *Apostel*, 76–79.
16. *Apostel*, 190f.
17. G. Schneider, 'Zeugen', 60–63, acknowledges that Luke did not invent the concept 'the Twelve Apostles' (following Haenchen, see n. 14, above, and others). But he credits him with first linking this concept with that of 'witness'. In 1 Cor. 15:15 Paul, having just linked himself with 'all the apostles', who have met the risen Christ (v. 7–10), speaks of the *testimony* he has given about the resurrection (ἐμαρτυρήσαμεν), and the risk that he would be a false *witness*

(ψευδομάρτυρες) if he declined to give it. Thus Luke may have received from tradition the criterion that an apostle was one who had met the risen Lord and witnessed to this experience.

This observation may provide us with a clue for a guess about the process by which 'apostles' came to be identified with, and reduced to, the Twelve. It may be that claims about resurrection-appearances were multiplying and causing confusion, through their contradictions and the many uses to which they were put, as we see later in docetic and Gnostic literature. Since those who claimed such experiences would (on this hypothesis) have linked them with their status as apostles, this may have provoked a reaction in the church, to reduce the number of apostles, and therewith the authoritative witness to the resurrection as the key to Christian faith, in a drastic way. Despite Paul's high status in Luke's eyes, his encounter with Jesus on the way to Damascus is not a resurrection-appearance of the Lord, since it comes long after the ascension. See below, p. 99f.

18. This seems to me more probable than the alternative suggestion, that the terminology is a sign of the deutero-Pauline perspective in which Paul is *the* apostle (C. K. Barrett, *New Testament Essays*, 81): for Barnabas here has equal standing with Paul. G. Klein, *Apostel*, 213, followed by G. Schneider, 'Zeugen', 52f., denies that Paul and Barnabas are meant in 14:4: 'with the apostles' means 'on the side of the Apostles', by which the Twelve are meant, as the heads of the cause represented by Paul and Barnabas; then 14:14 is removed (as an example of 'apostles') by following the Western text. Whatever may be the right reading in 14:14, the explanation offered of the former passage is made improbable by the fact that, though the Apostles for Luke have a distinctive function, the church's mission is not theirs but belongs to Jesus. A. Lindemann, *Paulus im ältesten Christentum*, 61f., objects to the view that Luke has let in a usage in contradiction to his general conception: Luke would not be so careless. Instead he supposes that for Luke ἀπόστολοι can mean either 'leaders of the church of Jerusalem' or 'missionaries to the Gentiles'; Luke however never uses the word in the singular, and so Paul's partnership with Barnabas provides the only setting in which it could refer to him. This view does not seem to me to take seriously enough either the usage in Luke's Gospel (esp. 6:13, cf. Acts 1:2ff.) or the tension of Acts 9:1–19 with such passages as Gal. 1:1–17; 1 Cor. 9:1f.; 15:1–11. No explanation is offered for Luke's alleged need to restrict ἀπόστολος to the plural. If Luke's usage were so general, we should expect some more examples of the sense 'missionaries to the Gentiles', e.g. in Acts 16:19–17:12; 18:5–17, where Paul travels in partnership with Silas.

19. In Gal. 1:11 'the gospel preached by me' is the same as 'the gospel which I preach among the Gentiles' in 2:2. Paul means not the Christian message in all details of its content, but the essential point that the coming of the Messiah means the end of the Law and salvation is only possible by faith (Gal. ch. 3–4) it is this insight which came directly to Paul by divine revelation, and with it the call to be apostle to the Gentiles. Elsewhere Paul acknowledges his dependence on oral tradition within the church for information about Jesus (e.g. 1 Cor. 11:23; 15:3; cf. 7:10, 12, 25). On this see D. Lührmann, *Offenbarungsverständnis*, 73–81 (especially 77f.) and 88–97 (especially 91f.). Cf. K. Wegenast, *Das Verständnis der Tradition*, 40–49, 52–70. In Acts 9:10–17 Ananias lays his hands on Paul to heal his blindness and impart the

Holy Spirit to him, but he says nothing about Paul's commission as a missionary. In 22:12–16 Ananias hints at the commission which Paul is going to receive but is not present when the commission itself is given (v. 17–21). In this speech, to Jews zealous for the Law (21:27–32) Luke's Paul emphasizes as much as he can his continuing contacts with Jewish orthodoxy through 'Ananias, a man pious in accordance with the Law, held in high regard by the Jews living at' Damascus (22:12).

20. C. Burchard, *Der dreizehnte Zeuge.*
21. Op. cit., 173ff.
22. Op. cit., ch. I, sections 4–6
23. Op. cit., 87f., 125–128.
24. Op. cit., 105–121, 124f., 128–136.
25. Op. cit., 111f., 130–136.
26. Op. cit., 136: 'Wenn Lukas . . . seine Berufung in Apg 22:14f. und 26:16–18 als Erwählung zum Zeugen dessen, "was er sah und hörte", interpretiert, dann legt er Paulus eine apostolische Eigenschaft bei, die das Amt der Zwölf in seiner Einmaligkeit und Fundamentalität stärker kennzeichnet als der Apósteltitel und die Teilnahme an der irdischen Wirksamkeit Jesu. Paulus ist nicht einer von ihnen, aber er ist dasselbe wie sie'. Similarly p. 174.
27. Op. cit., 176.
28. Op. cit., 174–176.
29. Op. cit., 176: Paul's activity represents an historical process, 'dessen Ende eine historische Zäsur bedeutet . . . Paulus' Reisen enden in Rom, wo er nach einer letzten Absage der Juden zwei Jahre frei predigt und dann offenbar stirbt'. The last sentence is no doubt true as an historical reconstruction, but is not what Luke says. Luke seems carefully to avoid, in ch. 28, marking a caesura with Paul's death. The case is different in 20:29f.: but by putting the prophecy of changed times after Paul's death there, rather than at the end of the book, and by leaving 28:30f. open-ended, Luke instead implies that the life and mission of the church will go on after Paul: there will be new dangers and challenges, but nevertheless an unbroken continuity.
30. Op. cit., 181–185. 'Es ist die Zeit des Bewahrens und der Geduld' (181); 'Geschichtsleere der Gegenwart' (182).
31. Op. cit., 17–19.
32. See n. 1, above.
33. Op. cit., 118–128.
34. Op. cit., 123f.
35. G. Lohfink, *Himmelfahrt*, especially 244–250.
36. See F. Hahn, 'Die Himmelfahrt Jesu', especially 424f.: '. . . Ob trotz einer starken Redaktionsdecke nicht doch hinter Apg 1:9–11 und partiell auch hinter Lk 24:50–53 eine vorlukanische Himmelfahrtsgeschichte steht' (425).
37. Burchard, op cit., 130–135, follows essentially the argument of N. Brox, *Zeuge und Märtyrer*, 43ff. Brox and Burchard argue that *μάρτυς* is used by Luke as a technical term, in the sense that it designates witnesses of the resurrection of Jesus: the Christian faith is based on their testimony to this event. The difficulty is that Luke uses the word in a quite general sense, or in other technical senses (e.g. Luke 11:48; Acts 6:13; 7:58). More important, when Paul in Acts 22:20 calls Stephen the *μάρτυς* of Jesus, it sounds rather like a title. Brox, 61–66, concludes that this is an 'exception' to Luke's technical usage. Burchard astonishingly ignores this reference to Stephen, both in his

detailed discussion of Acts 22:17–21, 161–168, and in his remark, 173f.: 'Für Paulus' historische Rolle ist seine Berufung zum Zeugen grundlegend. Er ist in Amt, Verküdigung und konkretem Handeln nach Lukas christusunmittelbar. Lukas stellt ihn, und ihn allein, in dieser Hinsicht neben die "zwölf Apostel".' He mentions Stephen only briefly, 130, n. 291: in Acts 22:20 μάρτυς is 'quasi-titular', but the lack of a specific election separates this witness from Paul and the apostles. 'Stephanus dürfte kraft seines Endes, nicht seiner Predigttätigkeit Zeuge heißen'. But why? By far the greatest part of the Stephen-story in Acts 6–7 is devoted to his speech, and it was the speech, and the other teaching-activity which preceded it (6:9–14) which led to his death. None of the more recent studies has disputed the conclusion of Brox, part 3, that the meaning of μάρτυς as one who dies for his faith begins only in the post-NT period.

K. Löning, *Saulustradition*, 137–144, accepts the same view in a modified form, that μάρτυς describes not an 'ecclesial office' but an 'evangelical function' (139): Paul shares with the apostles the same commission to preach. Brox, Burchard and Löning all see in Paul's experience near Damascus his equivalent of the apostles' seeing the risen Lord (Acts 1:22) which qualifies him to be a μάρτυς. This ignores the fact that it is Luke's own scheme, not known to us from any other part of the NT, which sets Paul's Damascus-experience *apart* from the resurrection-appearances: contrast 1 Cor. 15:(5–)8; cf. 9:1. It also ignores the fact that in Acts 13:31 (not discussed by Burchard!) Paul actually distinguishes the apostles, as witnesses from himself. Löning seeks to overcome the latter point by arguing that the qualifications for being a μάρτυς were two-fold for the apostles: (1) to have seen the risen Lord, and (2) to have seen his Palestinian mission (Acts 1:21f.; 10:39, 41; 13:31); and that they were two-fold for Paul: (1) to have seen the risen Lord (22:18; 26:16), and (2) to be a missionary to all people (22:15). But this is beginning to be elaborate, and weakens the argument that μάρτυς has a specific, technical force. After all, Stephen is called μάρτυς half as often as Paul is, though he appears in Acts very much less!

Luke's use of the μαρτυρ-group of words is conveniently summarized by G. Schneider, 'Zeugen', especially 43–55. Luke uses the noun μάρτυς in various connexions, but especially of being a witness for Jesus. He uses μαρτύριον and μαρτυρία, but only once each in the sense of testimony to Jesus. Of verbs he uses μαρτυρέω, but mostly in the sense of 'give a good reputation to' or 'support'; and μαρτύρομαι and διαμαρτύρομαι mostly of bearing witness to Jesus, but each once = 'solemnly declare' (Acts 20:26; 20:23, with the Holy Spirit as subject). μαρτυρέω and διαμαρτύρομαι are equated at Acts 23:11. The chief verb of 'witnessing' is διαμαρτύρομαι. Of 9 examples in Acts, the subject is 3 times the apostles and 5 times Paul. Conversely, when μάρτυς is used of a witness to Jesus, the reference is 8 times to the apostles, twice to Paul and once to Stephen. The usage of μάρτυς and διαμαρτύρομαι thus suggests a special link between the apostles and Paul as witnesses.

But there is enough variation in Luke's usage to warn us against using the vocabulary as proof of an *exclusive* link between the apostles and Paul. The latest full study of this question is that of E. Nellessen, *Zeugnis*. A major conclusion of this book is that the terminology of 'witness' in Luke–Acts cannot be restricted to the apostles plus Paul, but applies widely to the whole church and many individual members of it, providing continuity in the testimony to Jesus from the apostles down into Luke's own time. (See especially 278–280). This testimony by the church is actually continuous with God's own testimony to himself, Acts 14:17 (264–274); with that of the Holy Spirit, 5:32 (254f.); and with that of the prophets, 10:43 (257f.). An extensive review of literature is given by Nellessen, 1–41, and a bibliography by Schneider, 42f.

The other chief locus of 'witness'-language is the Gospel and Epistles of John. The only noun used is *μαρτυρία* and the only verb *μαρτυρέω,* but both are more frequent than in Luke–Acts. Here the witness borne is not to the specific fact of the resurrection, or to the whole story of Jesus, as in Acts, but to the fact that Jesus is the Son of God, sent by God for the salvation of the world. Though there are many who bear witness (John the Baptist, the disciples, the evangelist, the works of Jesus, the Holy Spirit, etc.) it is ultimately God himself who bears the chief testimony. For a recent, major study on the 'witness'-theme in John, with extensive reference to literature, see J. Beutler, *Martyria.* See also J. Painter, *John*; J. M. Boice, *Witness and Revelation.*

38. K. Löning, op. cit., 139–141.
39. C. Burchard, op. cit., 174–176, acknowledges the difference in the geographical scope of witnessing between the Apostles and Paul, but not the chronological.
40. See J. Dupont, *The Sources of Acts*, ch. 5 and 6; E. Haenchen, 'Das "Wir" in der Apg und das Itinerar'; W. Gasque, *Criticism*, 239–241.
41. So H. Conzelmann, 'Luke's Place', 305–307. G. Schneider, 'Zeugen', 51f., explains the paradox, that for Luke Paul is not an apostle, yet the terminology of 'witness', which chiefly is associated with the Apostles, applies also to Paul, by the suggestion that Paul has the special function of *mediating* the testimony between the time of the Apostles and Luke's time.
42. When Paul returned to Tarsus, Acts 9:30, he was not simply having a holiday or engaged in theological research, as is shown by 15:23 and 41. When he later came to Antioch, 11:26, it was apparently still before 41 AD, for in 11:28 it is prophesied that there will be a famine, and the famine took place in the reign of Claudius. But before he began his missionary journey from Antioch 13:1–4, the year 44 had already passed, for the death of Agrippa is reported in 12:23. How far Luke was aware of the dates of all these events is uncertain.
43. Paul was in Corinth for at least eighteen months, Acts 18:11f. (around 50–52 AD), after he had already travelled extensively on missionary work. Then, after further considerable travelling, he spent three years in Ephesus, 20:31.
44. Acts 24:27a is not quite clear, but apparently Paul spent two years in prison at Caesarea; then the journey to Rome took about six months; finally he was under detention in Rome for two years.
45. J. Jervell's essay, 'Paul – the Teacher of Israel' (= *People of God*, 153–183), began to rescue this section from the neglect in which it had lain. It has received a detailed treatment more recently in V. Stolle, *Zeuge*. (See below, p. 94.) C. Burchard, 'Paulus in der Apg', 890: 'Im Prozeß fehlt (die Verkündigung) fast ganz, niemand bekehrt sich.'
46. 'Paulus in der Apg', 889f., with n. 23.
47. *Der dreizehnte Zeuge*, 136–161.
48. Ps. Sal. 8:15 is sometimes cited to show that Rome is 'the end of the earth' and so that Acts 1:8 is already fulfilled in 28:30f. But this parallel does not

determine Luke's meaning. If he meant that the world-mission was now over, we might expect the ending of Acts to be more final, and not to show work still in progress. See G. Schneider, 'Zeugen', 50.

49. See E. Trocmé, *Le 'Livre des Actes'*, 35f., following K. Lake and H. J. Cadbury, *Beginnings* IV, 349 f.; W. Eltester, 'Israel', 99–107, shows that 1 Clem. 5:7, τὸ τέρμα τῆς δύσεως, means Rome, not Spain, and so is no evidence against Acts 28:31 as Luke's intended conclusion.
50. To whom he had written his most substantial epistle! Perhaps Luke did not know about the epistle. He does briefly show that Paul was given a royal welcome by the Roman Christians, 28:15 – see E. Peterson, *ἀπάντησις*, *ThW* I, 380 (where, however, this passage is not mentioned), but this only makes it the more striking that they are thereafter ignored.
51. For recent work, see G. Lohfink, *Paulus vor Jerusalem*; K. Löning, *Die Saulustradition*; C. Burchard, 'Paulus in der Apg'.
52. E.g. 17:3, 11; 18:5; 19:8. In Antioch-in-Pisidia Luke has Paul address the synagogue on another theme. In Thessalonica, Beroea, Corinth and Ephesus Paul is active in the synagogue but no major speech is reported.
53. In this respect, Acts agrees with the rest of the deutero-Pauline tradition, e.g. Col. 1:24; Eph. 3:1, 13; 2 Tim. 2:9f.; 4:6f. But Luke sees Paul's sufferings in a distinctive light, as we shall see in section 6, below.
54. E.g. NEB has no conjunction; TEV has 'and'!
55. *Der dreizehnte Zeuge*, 100f.
56. On the significance of suffering in Paul's own view of his apostleship, see C. K. Barrett, *The Signs of an Apostle*, 42–44; K. Stendahl, *Paul among Jews and Gentiles*, 40–52.
57. W. Radl, *Paulus und Jesus*.
58. See above, n. 45.
59. See M. Simon, *St. Stephen*, ch. 2; M. H. Scharlemann, *Stephen*, 86–90.
60. See P. Schubert, 'Structure', 177; and especially S. G. Wilson, *Gentiles*, 47f., 52–54.

60a. An interpretation along the same general lines as Radl and Stolle has recently been put forward by G. W. Trompf, *The Idea of Historical Recurrence in Western Thought*, Berkeley/Los Angeles/London 1979, 116–178, esp. 122–134. Approaching the question of 'recurrence' in Luke–Acts both more cautiously and more comprehensively than these writers, Trompf produces a more persuasive thesis. He notes many details in the trial and death of Stephen, the release of Peter from prison (Acts 12), Paul's speech at Miletus (Acts 20), Paul's journey to Jerusalem, Paul's trial, and several smaller incidents, which seem deliberately designed to echo elements in the life of Jesus. 'Luke hardly wished to deny that the deeds of the apostles formed fresh, distinctive episodes in history, but for him many of their acts only acquired their full meaning through crucial events which preceded them' (124). Trompf's interest, however, is not in examining how Luke showed continuity between Jesus and the church, but in arguing that Luke shares, along with Greek historians like Polybius, the Deuteronomist and Chronicler of the OT, and later historians down to Machiavelli, a philosophical conviction that 'history repeats itself', embracing ideas which 'were more than often protest ideas, used to affirm that desirable change had or should come, or was coming' (315).

61. 'Das Mittel der Zeit'.

62. *Der leidende Christus.*
63. Likewise E. Franklin, *Christ the Lord*, 9: 'The Gospel has spread from Jerusalem to Rome, but the Roman powers remain largely unconverted, the Jewish people have remained predominantly hostile, and the lives of Christians have by and large been subject to persecutions and disappointments which have resulted in a failure of nerve ([Luke] 18:8). It is this situation that Luke's history must embrace, and his theology justify.' As to the first point, Acts tells a confident and joyful story of Gentile conversions. We know almost nothing of the history of the Christian mission between 60 and 90 AD, but the evidence from the 90's on suggests that evangelism must have been astonishingly successful in the earlier period. The problem of Jewish unbelief is, however, an acute one for Luke, as we have seen in the previous chapter.
64. Op. cit., ch. 1.
65. Op. cit., 122–128, 131f.
66. *Apg*, 700 (ET, 732).
67. See C. K. Barrett, *NT Essays*, 95f.

4. Christians in the Roman Empire

To what extent, and in what sense, can Luke's purpose be understood as a political apology for Christianity, directed towards the Roman authorities? Or are the features of Luke's work which have led to theories of this kind capable of being explained in some other way? Recent studies have sufficiently refuted the idea that Luke was indirectly pleading for the extension to Christianity of formal recognition as a *religio licita:*[1] but since it continues to have some currency, especially through the influence of E. Haenchen,[2] it may be useful, in the context of our investigation into Luke's purpose, to summarize the chief considerations bearing on this theory. Of greater importance is the wider argument, that Luke was seeking (without any reference to a 'religio licita'-idea) to persuade the Roman authorities of the political innocence of Christianity, in order to win a favourable attitude from the magistrates in case of need, for example when Christians were persecuted.[3]

In Chapter One it was argued that the address of Luke–Acts is internal to the church; and the discussion in Chapter Two and Three has borne this out. It may therefore seem redundant to turn at this stage to the consideration of an argument which supposes Luke to be addressing government-officials outside the church. Yet the factors which gave rise to the theory of political apology, whether in the specific form of 'religio licita' or in the broader form, are certainly present in Luke–Acts; and we shall have to see what significance they have for Luke's purpose, within the framework that we have seen developing.

1 'Religio licita'

Since the late nineteenth century it has been widely assumed that there was in Roman law of the first century a technical category of 'permitted' religions, with the corollary that all other religions were 'non-permitted'. Judaism, it has been argued, was such a 'permitted' religion. It was in the interests of the Christians to win a similar status, in order to gain the protection and tolerance of the Roman state. The simplest way to achieve this goal was to prove to the Roman authorities that Christianity was a genuine form of Judaism; and this, it is alleged, Luke undertook to do.

In this theory there are two problems: the legal presuppositions, and the way in which Luke's actual procedure can be seen to measure up to the hypothesis.

The legal history of Rome's dealings with religious groups in the first century is complicated.[4] It is true that Rome extended privileges and protection to Judaism, but there is no evidence that this was done in the framework of a doctrine of 'permission', or that there were other religions treated similarly to Judaism, over against others that were not; there is, however, much evidence to the contrary. The general situation may be summarized by quoting a few sentences from A. D. Nock's treatment of Roman religious policy in the first century, in the *Cambridge Ancient History*:[5]

> 'Criminal law had no wide category of *laesa religio* or *sacrilegium*. Apart from proceedings against Christians as described by their own writers, *sacrilegium* is applied only to overt acts of sacrilege in the modern sense . . .
>
> 'Tertullian's statement, "sed apud vos quodvis colere ius est praeter deum verum", represents a general rule to which there are only certain specific exceptions . . .
>
> 'The Romans indeed gave privileges to synagogues, but that was a measure necessitated in the main by the anti-Semitism of Alexandria and of other Greek cities and by the desirability of avoiding the disorders which might arise if it was not officially restrained . . .
>
> 'With the beliefs of subject races Augustus interfered very little. If he forbade Roman citizens to take part in Druidical worship, his purpose was political: to withdraw Gauls who had received the citizenship from a strongly nationalist influence. True, among foreign worships he had his preferences; . . . and praised Gaius Caesar for not going to the Temple at Jerusalem. But he left, for example, Jewish privileges untouched. Their places of worship were protected from robbery, their sacred books or moneys from theft, and they were given free right to send offerings to Jerusalem. When Rome interfered, it was in matters of mundane consequence.'

It is clear that the situation as thus described has neither need nor room for a category of 'religio licita'. The phrase itself occurs only once in ancient literature, in Tertullian's *Apology*, 21:1. Even there the meaning of the phrase is not completely certain: it does not seem to be meant as technical terminology.[6] Even if it was so meant, the date (about 197 AD) sets it so far from Luke's time of writing that its relevance for Luke would need to be substantiated by some more contemporary evidence. When Tertullian, earlier in the same work (4:4), quotes the pagan population of Carthage as saying to the Christians, 'you are not allowed to exist', his meaning is ironical rather than legal.[7] This work comes between 180, when some Christians from Scillium were martyred at Carthage, and a renewed persecution at Carthage in 202.[8] These were isolated crises, but they point (and so does the whole argument of the *Apology*) to a continuing resentment of the pagan majority against the rising Christian minority. It was popular anger, not legal enactment, which told the Christians, 'you have no right to exist'. Some early hints pointing to such a relationship between Christians and pagans may be detected here and there in Acts, but that is a different matter from the existence of an official list of permitted religions.[9]

The theory of a 'religio licita' as explaining the purpose of Luke–Acts may therefore be regarded as unfounded and now discredited. Its career as a piece of scholarly tradition in modern times is curious, but not of direct concern to us here.[10]

Apart, however, from the legal question, the theory of political apology as thus presented implies that it is Luke's design to emphasize as much as he can the institutional unity of Jews and Christians. But this, as we have seen in Chapter Two, is precisely what Luke does not do. Nor is it true, as H. Conzelmann has supposed, that Luke has two different lines of argument, one addressed to the church, emphasizing the church's continuity with Israel, and another addressed to the government, showing the distance between Christians and Jews.[11] To put the matter in this way is to take too static a view of Luke's composition. Both continuity and separation are indeed to be found in Luke–Acts: but Luke, being, as we have suggested, a 'theological historian', sets out to show how the ultimate institutional separation of Jews and Christians developed out of an original unity of cultural inheritance. The emphasis at the end of Acts (where we have to look for Luke's climax) is entirely on the separation. The leaders of the Jews in Rome say that all they know of Christianity is that 'it is everywhere spoken against'. For the third time, and now quite definitely, Paul, in defiance of the High Priest, the Sanhedrin and recognized Jewish leaders everywhere, breaks with institutional Judaism in order to go to the Gentiles.

2 The Appeal to the Romans for Toleration

We may now turn to the broader suggestion, that Luke's chief purpose is to make overtures to Roman officialdom, seeking a friendly attitude towards the Christians. As the explanation of Luke's chief purpose, this theory suffers the serious disability, as we have already noted, that Luke was far too subtle about his work, if that was really what he intended.[12] In the Gospel, very little outside ch. 23, concerning the trial and execution of Jesus, can be understood in this light;[13] in Acts, only certain portions of the Paul-story are relevant. The apology, if that is what it is, has been interwoven with a great deal of matter a government-official would find not only irrelevant but also often puzzling. In this respect, Luke–Acts stands in the sharpest contrast with the Apologies of the second century, from Justin onwards, where the apologetic aim is everywhere explicit, and carried through in a sustained manner.

The theory of a political apology in Luke–Acts rests on two contentions: first, that Luke emphasizes the political innocence of the Christians, from Jesus himself onwards; second, that Luke always portrays Roman officials in a favourable light, or as friendly to the Christians (and thus indirectly urges the officials of his own day to follow the example of their predecessors).

Of these, the first is rather more persuasive than the second. Even so, it has been objected by J. Jervell that the charges brought against Paul are religious rather than political, and they are laid by Jewish interests, not Roman. Claudius Lysias and Festus cannot even make out what the charges are, and Festus has to call in Agrippa II for expert advice. The question is not whether charges of sedition have been proved against Paul: rather, such charges have not even been raised: politics is not Luke's concern.[14] However, Jervell's argument is exaggerated. Paul is accused of civil disturbances by Jews (Acts 17:6, 24:5) and Romans (16:20); when he takes Paul into protective custody, the tribune Claudius Lysias suspects him of subversive activity (21:38). So there are after all doubts raised about Paul's political innocence, and the very fact that Luke so emphasizes the religious motives that led to his prosecution by the Jewish authorities may be part of his attempt to show that the political suspicions against him were groundless. And there is an unmistakable emphasis on Paul's innocence. His beating and imprisonment at Philippi were illegal and unjust (Acts 16:37). Gallio recognizes no case against him (18:14f.) Claudius Lysias holds him as a prisoner on charge only out of deference to the Sanhedrin (22:30; 23:10, 30), and Felix keeps him in prison for the same reason (24:27) as well as in the hope of a bribe (24:26); it is hinted that Felix knows that Paul is innocent (24:22). Festus declares him innocent in almost the same terms as Gallio did (25:18f.), but only after Paul has been forced to appeal to Caesar because Festus is inclined to favour the Jewish authorities, who have it in mind to destroy Paul illegally if they cannot manage it by legal process (25:3). Finally, Agrippa confirms his innocence too (26:32).

Similarly, there is a strong political concern in Luke's description of the trial and execution of Jesus, Luke ch. 23. The original readers, already presumably familiar with the Gospel of Mark (Luke 1:1, 3), will have been surprised to find the charge brought against Jesus before Pilate expressed in such explicitly and emphatically political terms (Luke 23:2). We must beware of attributing the difference between Mark 15:1–3 and Luke 23:1–3 simply to Luke's redactional initiative, for there is a similar political note in the trial of Jesus in John 19:12–15: we may have here one of those elements of tradition shared by Luke and John, with which we shall be concerned in Chapter Six. All the same, Luke so phrases the charge that, on the one hand, its political nature is frankly acknowledged (and this is no doubt historically correct, in view of the inscription on the cross and the mode of execution): but on the other hand its falsity is underlined, in that the accusation of opposing the payment of imperial taxes is a downright lie in the light of Luke 20:20–26. Then in the course of the trial and its outcome Jesus' innocence is emphasized far more often than in Mark. Pilate declares it three times (23:4, 14f., 22), and Antipas agrees (v. 15); the penitent criminal asserts it (v. 41), and so does the centurion, and apparently even the crowds (v. 48).

It can therefore be agreed that (for what reason, we have still to consider)

Luke found it important to emphasize that the great founders of the Christian movement were free of any guilt of subversion. The second point, that Luke always portrays the Roman officials in attractive colours, or takes a positive view of the Empire, is less clear. Of the officials, no doubt the tribune Claudius Lysias of Acts 21–23 comes out best. The proconsul Sergius Paulus of Cyprus is 'an intelligent man', who is converted (Acts 13:7, 12), but remains a shadowy figure. The military magistrates of the colony Philippi by no means treat Paul properly (16:22f., 35–39). Gallio's merit in refusing to countenance a charge against Paul is rather spoiled by his tolerating the disgraceful treatment of Sosthenes right in front of the tribunal (18:12–17). Felix wants a bribe from Paul (24:26). Festus is ready to sacrifice Paul so as to gain favour with the Jews (25:9–11). Pilate is at best a weakling who gives in to pressure, when he knows quite well that his prisoner is innocent (Luke 23:22–25); and in Acts 4:27 Luke makes no bones about naming Pilate as a conspirator in the murder of Jesus.

By far the strongest point in favour of the view that Luke puts the Roman government in a favourable light is the matter of Paul's appeal to 'Caesar'. Although Paul's appeal is, so to speak, the carrier of the narrative from Acts 25:11 to the end of the book, and therefore by no means an unimportant element in the whole story, Luke never admits that the Caesar appealed to is Nero. And this cannot be because Luke either knew too little or cared too little to distinguish the various emperors by name (Luke 2:1; 3:1; Acts 11:28; 18:2): and in the case of Nero his later reputation in the church is guarantee enough that Christians of Luke's time had a clear picture of his career.[15] We can only assume that Luke had his own reason for passing discreetly over the later deeds of Nero, without even a hint. He wishes to put the emphasis elsewhere: Paul had a clear conscience, and he was prepared to let the facts speak for themselves; and the imperial court was to be trusted rather than the Sanhedrin in Jerusalem (Acts 25:3, 11).

On the other hand, Luke does not yield to a romantic view of the nature of political power, even in the Empire. The wording of Luke 4:5f. is stronger than that of Matt. 4:8f.: all the power and glory of all the kingdoms of the world are in the gift of the devil! The fact that Luke retains, and perhaps intensifies, the expression of this statement in his source[15a] indicates that his endorsement of the authority of the Empire is less wholehearted than that of Paul in Rom. 13:1f.[16] The behaviour of the apostles and the church in Acts 4 and 5 shows that the church may on occasion need to defy the state out of obedience to God, and that God supports them when they do so. Although the authorities in this case are not Roman, the formulation of Peter's principle in 4:19 and 5:29 points beyond the immediate situation and indicates how Christians are to regard any authorities at all.

Thus the evidence relevant to the theory that Luke's chief purpose was an appeal on behalf of the church for the favour of the Roman government is not as clearly in its favour as has sometimes been supposed. On the one hand, the Christians are completely free of any subversive or conspiratorial design: rather, they have often been the victims of conspiracy. On the contrary, they respect the state and seek to collaborate with its constructive purposes, and indeed entrust their own safety to its justice. On the other hand, Christians offer the state no unquestioning docility: only God can command total obedience.

3 The Attitude of Christians to the State

We have now seen three reasons for doubting that Luke wrote his work as a political apology for the Christians. First, Luke–Acts in general makes much more sense as a work addressed internally to the church than as one addressed to imperial officials. Second, the elements alleged to be apologetic are not prominent enough in the whole scope and plan of the work to make this suggestion persuasive. Third, Luke's praise of the Empire and his promise that Christians will be obedient to it are not unqualified.

Therefore we must see whether the elements in question make sense on the understanding that it is the Christians themselves that Luke is addressing. In this case, it is Christians whom Luke is reassuring that the death of Jesus was due not to any fault on his part or that of his disciples, but to Jewish duplicity and the failure of Roman integrity. It is Christians to whom he is emphasizing that Paul, though accused of civil disruption by both Romans and Jews (Acts 16:20; 17:6; 24:5) and the object of violent jealousy on the part of Greeks (19:26–31), had always behaved with honour and respect towards the state.

Why does he need to do this? He seems to be saying to his fellow-Christians: Jews, Roman and Greeks have been making accusations against us from the beginning, but they have never been correct or fair. In the nature of things, Christians have to put up with false accusations as well as persecution (Acts 14:22). But their proper response is not resentment or retaliation. Here Luke's meaning may be illuminated by two famous passages in the Epistles, having to do with the relation of church and state: Rom. 13:1–7 and 1 Peter 2:11–17. Both these passages are written in the context of persecution (cf. Rom. 12:17–21; 1 Peter 1:6ff.; 4:12ff.). The respective authors are concerned to cultivate among the Christians a sober, inoffensive style of life and an attitude of respect towards the government. In Chapter Three, section 6, we have seen reason to doubt whether persecution was a severe problem for Luke's church. But it remained a possibility, especially if Christians should be tempted to become provocative towards the authorities. It may be surmised that the common element in the background of Romans, 1 Peter and Luke–Acts is anxiety lest some Christians should adopt an attitude, if not of revolutionary defiance, then of self-assertiveness. From the second century onwards, at least, there was among the Christians a strong ideology of martyrdom, largely inspired by the memory of the Maccabees and, of course, by the passion of Jesus. While many martyrs suffered heroically in circumstances which they had done nothing to bring on themselves, others were driven to a fanatical desire for martyrdom out of their hostility towards Rome, regarded as the centre of idolatry.[17] The fact that honour and submission to the Emperor have to be enjoined so firmly as in 1 Peter 2:13–17 suggests that tendencies in this direction may have begun to appear fairly early. It has been argued persuasively by E. Haenchen that Luke deliberately intended to draw attention away from martyrdom:[18] for the case of Stephen is a special exception; apart from Stephen, the only Christian mentioned by name as having died for his faith is James the son of Zebedee, and his death is passed over remarkably quickly, in a sentence of seven words (Acts 12:2).

This, I think, provides an adequate explanation of Luke's care to draw attention to the political innocence of the Christians, and to take on the whole an optimistic view of the imperial government. And it is an explanation which fits in harmoniously with what we have so far learned from the study of other aspects of Luke's purpose. Luke wishes to reveal to his fellow-Christians in his own day the nature of their life and calling in Christ. The proper business of Christians is to live at peace with the sovereign power, so far as possible, and not to play the hero.[19] In order to encourage such an attitude, it was necessary for Luke to hold up before his readers the example of their great leaders, especially Jesus and Paul, and (like Paul and the author of 1 Peter) to take the best possible view of the regime.

Notes to Chapter Four

1. This idea was especially argued by B. S. Easton, *Purpose* (see above, Chapter One, n. 78).
2. E. Haenchen, 'Judentum und Christentum', especially par. 24; *Apg*, 111–113 (ET, 100–102). Also *Apg* [4–6]1961–1968, 560 (ET, 630); in *Apg* [7]1977, the whole section of four pages in which this reference to *religio licita* occurred is one of the few sections which have been completely rewritten, and the use of this phrase is lacking; but the rewriting was not for this reason.
3. This, as we have seen, is the chief motive envisaged by H. J. Cadbury, *Making*, ch. 20. It plays an important part in the interpretations of scholars who hold such otherwise divergent views as F. F. Bruce, *The Book of Acts*, 17–24, and H. Conzelmann, *MdZ*, 128–135 (ET, 137–144); though both of these add other elements in their reconstruction of Luke's purpose.
4. See especially A. Wlosok, 'Rechtsgrundlagen'; cf. her *Rom und die Christen*. Also W. H. C. Frend, *Martyrdom*, ch. 4.
5. A. D. Nock, 'Religious Developments', 490–492.
6. See H. Conzelmann, *Apg*, 10. The text, with T. R. Glover's translation, is as follows: '. . . fortasse an hoc nomine de statu eius retractetur, quasi sub

umbraculo insignissimae religionis, certe licitae, aliquid propriae praesumptionis abscondat'. '. . . Perhaps some question may be raised as to the standing of the school (Christianity), on the ground that, under cover of a very famous religion (and one certainly permitted by law), the school insinuates quietly certain claims of its own.' Glover's note, ibid., shows that he accepts the theory that there was such a legal category as 'permitted religion', and that may explain the phrase 'by law' within the parentheses.

7. 'Non licet esse vos!' T. R. Glover, op. cit., renders 'Your existence is illegal': but this, again, may be coloured by his acceptance of the 'religio licita' theory.
8. See H. Chadwick, *Early Church*, 91.
9. That governmental edicts were from time to time, and in various places, directed against Christians, need not be disputed. This was in connexion with the regulation of *collegia* or private associations, where the state felt that there was a danger of either subversive or criminal tendencies. Thus Christianity was branded by Tacitus as a *religio prava* in connexion with the Neronian persecution in 64 AD. But Judaism itself did not escape such attention: Jews were banned from Rome on a number of occasions, including one that comes into the scope of Luke's story (49 AD: Acts 18:2). On this see W. H. C. Frend, *Martyrdom*, especially ch. 4 and 8.
10. H. J. Cadbury, 'Some Foibles', 215f., traces it as follows: 'I do not find the terms [*religio licita* and its opposite *religio illicita*] in Theodor Mommsen's *Römisches Strafrecht* (1899), but in his earlier famous essay, "Der Religionsfrevel nach römischem Recht", he used the phrase *religio licita* twice. (N.8: *Historische Zeitschrift* 64/1890, 408n., 425 (*Gesammelte Schriften* III, 1907, 405n., 419). E. G. Hardy, *Christianity and the Roman Government*, 1891, 31, evidently derived it from Mommsen. Similarly J. Juster, *Les Juifs dans l'empire romain*, 1914, i, 246, and later writers.)'
11. H. Conzelmann, 'Geschichte', 244.
12. See the reference to C. K. Barrett's remark on this, Chapter One, p. 20–21.
13. The ethical teaching of John the Baptist, given only by Luke, encourages generosity, honesty and, on the part of soldiers or police, 'being content with your wages', i.e. John discourages anything that may smack of disloyalty to established authority: Luke 3:10–14.
14. J. Jervell, *People of God*, 167f.
15. See above, Chapter One, p. 8, with n. 37.

15a. A critical attitude to political authority is not to be thought of as originating with Luke: in this he reflects the attitude of Jesus. Luke alone, however, reports Jesus' contemptuous disregard of Antipas' threats (Luke 13:32) and his ironic reference to the title 'Benefactor' affected by Hellenistic kings. See W. Schrage, *Die Christen und der Staat*, 45f.

16. This comparison points up the error in H. Conzelmann's view that Luke's attitude to the state is shaped by his alleged doctrine of the delay of the parousia: *MdZ*, 139 (ET, 149): 'We can be certain that Luke's apologetic does not represent a merely incidental element, a practical adjustment to the world. It is based on an examination of the principles from the angle of redemptive history. The fact that the End is no longer thought of as imminent, and the subsequent attempt to achieve a long-term agreement as to the church's relation to the world show how closely related this question is to the central motifs of Luke's whole plan.' For the sequence from Rom. 13.1f. to v.11 shows that acceptance of the divinely ordained function of the state is easier in

the setting of an imminent expectation of the End. Luke's church may or may not expect a further, long delay (see below, Chapter Five), but has in any case already lived long enough in the world to have some reservations about the extent to which civil obedience must be granted.

17. See W. H. C. Frend, *Martyrdom*, 13–15, 194.
18. E. Haenchen, *Apg*, 700 (ET, 732).
19. A similar view is taken by E. Plümacher, 'Lukas als griechischer Historiker', 260f.: it was Luke's aim to guard his readers 'vor der Tendenz zur Resignation oder zur totalen Konfrontation mit dem Staat' (261).

5. The Lucan Eschatology

1 The 'Classic Theory' Called in Question

Since P. Vielhauer's essay of 1950 on the 'Paulinism' of Acts[1] there has been no doubt among students of Luke that the interpretation of eschatology lies at the heart of Luke's purpose in writing his two-volume work. Following Vielhauer, H. Conzelmann propounded what has become the 'classic' theory of the eschatological doctrine intended by Luke and how it is related to his purpose.[2] Its essence is the teaching of the 'delay of the parousia'. According to this view, the church in Luke's day was in more or less serious embarrassment, because the eschatological consummation announced by Jesus as imminent (Mark 1:15; 9:1; etc.) and expected by the early church to arrive very soon (e.g. 1 Cor. 7:29; Rom. 13:11; 1 Thess. 4:15) had not occurred, and therefore the Christian message risked being no longer persuasive. Luke set out deliberately to solve this problem, and his effort constituted a major purpose, perhaps the decisive purpose, of his whole enterprise. His solution was to recast the prophecies of Jesus so that, while an End to world-history is still envisaged, it is now located in the indefinite future. The Holy Spirit is a substitute for the delayed eschatological fulfilment, and is not itself a part of that fulfilment. Therefore Luke, unlike Paul (in particular), views the life of the church in the present as having no eschatological quality. Sustained by its memory of God's action in Jesus in the past, Luke's church must learn to accommodate itself to peaceful relationships with the Roman Empire, and other institutions of this world, through a long continuation of history until eventually the parousia comes.

Although the early criticism of Conzelmann's *Die Mitte der Zeit* tended to concentrate on other aspects of his theory than eschatology,[3] there have been doubts about the 'classic' theory since the beginning:[4] and in recent years these have been growing stronger. There has been on the whole no going back on the conviction, due especially to Conzelmann, that Luke is a self-conscious, careful and independent theologian, and that eschatology is one of the dimensions of the gospel-story where his theological initiative has been strongly at work. But doubts have developed particularly at two crucial points. First, is it true that Luke has consistently removed the final consummation into the distant future? Are there not many passages in Luke–Acts which still speak, as the earlier tradition did, of an imminent End? Second, has this theory not overlooked the theme in Luke–Acts that eschatology has in part been fulfilled already?

There is no need here to review again the extensive discussion of Lucan eschatology, especially in its earlier stages.[5] We must however briefly summarize some of the main trends of research in the last ten years, which give some indication of the complexity of the problems, and help to indicate where the most critical issues lie.

1. In addition to the large number of scholars who have simply accepted the 'classic' theory, a number continue to affirm from their own detailed studies that Luke's purpose is to teach that the parousia will be long delayed. J. D. Kaestli argues that Luke has consistently eliminated all traces of the earlier teaching of an imminent End. E. Gräßer has criticized Kaestli for exaggerating the consistency with which Luke has rewritten his sources in this regard,[7] but himself continues to the present to maintain his earlier view in general agreement with Conzelmann.[8] G. Schneider slightly modifies the 'delay'-theory by stressing that for pastoral reasons Luke holds out the possibility that the End could come at any time: but essentially he believes that it will be far in the future.[9]

2. The view that, because of the delay of the End, Luke has turned towards 'individual eschatology', has been argued afresh by J. Dupont[10] and G. Schneider.[11] Luke, it is said, has reapplied some of the old eschatological language to the 'end' of each individual's life: judgement, and reception into heaven or hell, take place at death.

3. Some are no longer convinced that for Luke the End lies far ahead, but emphasize that Luke carefully separates the events of contemporary history, such as the persecutions suffered by the church, and the fall of Jerusalem, from any eschatological significance, since eschatology for Luke is a matter entirely of the future: so C. Burchard,[12] R. Geiger[13] and E. Kränkl[14]. For these scholars, Luke's own time can be said to be 'eschatological' only in the sense that people's present attitude to Jesus will determine their ultimate fate. Similarly, R. H. Hiers argues that for Luke the Kingdom of God is completely a matter of the future.[15]

4. S. G. Wilson, who accepts the supposition that there was a crisis in the church of Luke's day due to the delay of the parousia, has suggested that there are two strands in Luke's eschatology, one teaching a further delay and one imminence.[16] Luke was not concerned for systematic consistency but to appeal for constant faith, and retained (and even developed) the two strands so as to deal with two different responses in the church to the dilemma caused by the delay already experienced. The first supposed response was a renewal of apocalypticism; the second a denial that there would be any parousia at all. The 'delay'-strand was addressed to the neo-apocalypticists and the 'imminence'-strand to those who denied the parousia.

5. In a very long book, J. Zmijewski agrees with the 'classic' theory that Luke expects the parousia to be long delayed, but argues on the other hand that, though the parousia is still important, as the consummation of salvation, 'eschatology' is also a present reality since the coming of Jesus.[17]

6. E. E. Ellis denies that there is any evidence for a crisis in the church of Luke's day caused by the delay of the parousia: the 'delay'-theme in

Luke–Acts could equally well represent the evangelist's striving to oppose over-zealous expectations of the parousia.[18] Luke regarded it as wrong to place emphasis on the date of the future consummation: for him the church's mission was of vital importance, and a preoccupation with future eschatology was a hindrance to the mission. Ellis also emphasizes that there is in Luke a significant element of fulfilled eschatology, and this has the effect of somewhat reducing the prominence of the End in Luke's scheme.[18a] Essentially similar views are held by W. G. Kümmel[19] and F. O. Francis[20]. E. Franklin arrives at a somewhat similar outcome, but by means of a quasi-Platonic view of the Kingdom of God as a present but transcendent reality, which is to be 'revealed' by the parousia.[21] This group of scholars regards the 'delay'-theme, where it occurs, as an acknowledgement by Luke of the delay that has already taken place, not as teaching that a further long delay is to be expected.

From this summary it can be seen that we are very far from agreement. Luke's eschatology is not only more complex[22] than many assume, but also more problematic. The aim of this chapter is not to attempt a complete explanation of Luke's eschatology, for that would require another substantial monograph, even assuming that a complete explanation is indeed attainable, which may well not be the case. We may have to face the possibility that some essential clues to Luke's meaning were available to his first readers in their cultural setting, but are now lost for us. Or it may be that Luke was less neatly systematic in his conception of eschatology than our 'redaction-critical' method of study tends to require of him. A dozen years ago, the late W. C. van Unnik warned that in the enthusiastic new work being done on Lucan theology there was the danger of making too many general statements on the basis of inadequate exegesis.[23] That warning remains relevant, although in the meantime much fruitful exegetical work has been achieved. The aim of this chapter is to test, especially by detailed exegesis at a number of crucial points that do not seem to have been satisfactorily explained hitherto, the hypothesis that the 'delay'-theme in Luke–Acts has been greatly exaggerated in many modern interpretations, and that for Luke the most important point to emphasize about eschatology is the degree to which eschatological expectations have already been fulfilled in the experience of Jesus' disciples. This latter theme has a most important bearing on the identification of Luke's purpose in writing; and I believe it can be shown that Luke's emphasis on 'fulfilment' is more pervasive and important than has been shown so far.

It will be convenient to begin with a discussion of 'individual eschatology' because, though it is often seen as logically dependent on the delay of the parousia, it is in fact exegetically independent of it. That will leave us free to pursue the close connexion between those passages having to do with the 'delay'-theme and various other aspects of future eschatology in Luke–Acts, before we finally concentrate on the theme of fulfilment.

2 Individual Eschatology

The theory of 'individual eschatology' is that, since the ultimate parousia has failed to occur within the expected time, Luke has begun to reinterpret eschatology as referring to the reception of the individual's soul into heaven or hell at his death.[24] A preliminary question is whether the context of ideas in which Luke worked would allow such a shift. It is now clear that the simple alternative, that Greek thought envisaged immortality of the soul and biblical thought the resurrection of the dead, is inadequate. The later parts of the Old Testament, and much Jewish thought in the post-OT period, within Palestine as well as abroad, embraced ideas which would make Luke's adoption of 'individual eschatology' perfectly conceivable.[25] The decisive question, then, is not the background but the exegesis of Luke's own text. The passages usually adduced in proof of Luke's individualizing of eschatology are Luke 12:20; 16:19–31; 23:43; Acts 7:55–60; 14:22. The first and the last of these need not detain us. In Luke 12:20 all that is actually mentioned is the rich man's death, not what happens to him thereafter.[26] In Acts 14:22, there are many other, and more likely, possibilities for interpreting 'we must enter the Kingdom of God' than that it refers to what happens immediately upon each individual's death.[27]

The parable of the rich man and Lazarus in Luke 16:19–31 is a different matter. Here an elaborate description of individual eschatology is given, pertaining to both consolation and punishment. It must however be remembered that this is a very rare case among the gospel-parables, in that it is a borrowing from a pre-Christian story.[28] Whether the borrowing was done by Jesus, by Luke or by some stage of the tradition in between is not for the moment important. At the level of the Lucan redaction the real point lies in the conclusion: 'If they will not listen to Moses and the prophets, neither will they be persuaded if someone should rise from the dead'. The irony of Luke's allusion to the failure of the Pharisees to believe that Jesus had risen from the dead is obvious. But, beyond that, this pre-existing tale offered the possibility of dramatizing pictorially the seriousness of each individual's responsibility for his conduct during his lifetime. It is no more necessary to believe that Luke took this eschatological description literally than it is to believe that every modern Christian who tells or retells a story about Saint Peter as gate-keeper of 'the pearly gates' has seriously conflated Rev. 21:10ff. with Matt. 16:19 to produce the eschatology which he really holds. To see Luke's own eschatological doctrine in Luke 16:19–31 involves two rather obvious difficulties: first, this imported story stands isolated over against the references in Luke–Acts to the future resurrection of the just (and of the unjust);[29] second, Jesus has no part in this eschatological action.

A stronger case can be made out for 'individual eschatology' in the case of the passage describing Stephen's death, Acts 7:55ff. C. K. Barrett sees here 'a private and personal parousia of the Son of man. That which was to happen in a universal sense at the last day, happened in individual terms when a Christian came to the last day of his life'.[30] We must weigh against this interpretation the objection of E. E. Ellis, that the real context of Stephen's vision is not his death but his speech: the Son of Man appears, not so much to receive a pious Christian at his death as to confirm the judgement declared by Stephen upon the Temple-cult and the Jewish nation.[31] The uniqueness of this reference to Jesus as 'Son of Man' outside the gospels remains a riddle: but if the fundamental significance of this title is the rôle of Jesus as judge,[32] then the explanation of the context by Ellis is quite appropriate. The wider context of ideas in Luke is not the parousia of the Son of Man but his active rôle in his heavenly enthronement. For parallel ideas in other gospels we may compare Matt. 16:19b and 18:18, and John 20:23, where heavenly ratification is promised for what is bound and loosed, or forgiven and retained, by the disciples of the Son of Man (Matt. 16:13ff.; Acts 7:56) when they are endowed with the Holy Spirit (John 20:22; Acts 7:55). It remains true, indeed, that Stephen as he dies calls on the Lord Jesus to receive his spirit (v. 59), just as in Luke 23:46 Jesus, as he dies, commits his spirit into the hands of the Father. It is at this point that we may detect in Luke's theology a tendency towards what might be called 'individual eschatology', in that the 'spirit' of a pious person is received by God at his death. Just how Luke combined this concept with that of the resurrection at the last day is not clear: but he does not seem to have adapted the traditional language about the Son of Man in this direction.

There remains Luke 23:42f.: the dying thief on the cross says, 'Jesus, remember me when you come into your kingdom', and Jesus answers, 'Truly I tell you, today you will be with me in Paradise'. Here we have a much stronger statement of the same idea expressed in Luke 23:46 and Acts 7:59b. It stands in tension not only with Luke's more usual concept of the resurrection of the dead at the last day but also, more glaringly, with the central tradition that Jesus died and was buried and only on the third day, not 'today', was raised; and with Luke's own concept that it was only on the fortieth day after that that Jesus ascended to heaven. On this, G. Lohfink makes the useful observation that Luke accepted from tradition a statement that strictly speaking jarred with his general scheme, because he valued its striking declaration of Jesus' prompt forgiveness of a penitent.[33]

We may therefore conclude that there is indeed a small element of 'individual eschatology' in Luke–Acts, represented especially by one saying taken up from tradition (Luke 23:43) and by two statements probably composed by Luke himself (Luke 23:46; Acts 7:59). But two observations are called for here. First, it is not a matter of Luke's having adapted traditional eschatological language in the direction of individual eschatology, but rather that he has accepted, to a quite small extent, an alternative way of thinking that is set beside his statement of the traditional, apocalyptic eschatology. Second, this phenomenon is not quite unique to Luke, and can certainly not be described as a distinctive theological innovation on his part. For it occurs in precisely the same form in Paul, as we see by comparing Phil. 1:23 with 1 Thess. 4:15–17 and 1 Cor. 15:51f. In this respect, Luke is not so different from the main stream of early Christian theology as has sometimes been alleged.

3 The Delay of the Parousia

At the outset, two things must be distinguished. On the one hand, it is obvious that the climactic eschatological event or events expected in the future had not occurred as early as some expected (e.g. 1 Thess. 4:15ff.; 1 Cor. 15:51): it was a plain historical fact which Luke had of course to acknowledge. This is perhaps most clearly seen by the way in which Luke goes beyond Mark in separating the eschatological phenomena chronologically from the destruction of Jerusalem. For the latter has become a prophetic theme in its own right, mentioned in solemn oracles without reference to eschatology (Luke 19:41–44; 23:27–32). Luke looks back on the destruction of Jerusalem as a past event and forward to other events in the unknown future.[34]

On the other hand, it is a different matter to assert that Luke taught his readers not to expect the eschatological climax in the near future. This interpretation is already called in question by E. E. Ellis's observation that the assertion of a crisis in the church in Luke's day, because of the delay, is only an unwarranted assumption:[35] but also, more importantly, by the argument of many other interpreters that Luke does in fact retain many expressions pointing to an imminently expected climax, so that at the least Luke cannot be said to argue *consistently* for a delay into the distant future.[36] How strong, after all, is the evidence for a studied doctrine of 'delay' in Luke–Acts?

It is noticeable, in all the synoptic gospels, that the question about the Kingdom of God is sometimes 'when?' but also often 'to whom?'. Mostly this is expressed in terms of discipleship: it is Jesus' followers who will inherit, or enter, or see the Kingdom. But the warning is sometimes given that the Jewish nation, viewed as a religious institution, will *not* receive the Kingdom. This comes perhaps most strikingly to expression in Matt. 21:43, where the point of the parable of the wicked tenants in the vineyard is made explicit: 'the Kingdom of God will be taken away from you and given to a nation that produces its fruits'. Mark and Luke see the same point in the parable but do not feel any need to make it so explicitly. But it is Luke who makes the same point about the Kingdom most frequently.

In Chapter Two, section 5, we considered some passages that have played a big part in the 'delay'-theory, especially the parabolic sayings about the narrow gate and exclusion from the Kingdom (Luke 13:22–30), the parable of the great feast (Luke 14:15–24) and that of the minae and the unpopular king (Luke 19:11–27), where in each case the key-expression is 'the Kingdom of God': it is this from which the Jews are likely to be excluded, because of their rejection of Jesus, and to which the believing Gentiles will be admitted. In these cases I argued that Luke's real concern is not *when* the Kingdom of God will come (as is generally assumed) but *who* will qualify to be admitted to it.

We have now to examine four more passages which are of decisive importance for this question: (a) Acts 1:6–8; (b) Luke 22:69; (c) Luke 9:27; (d) Luke 21:32. The first and second are passages where Luke seems to be avoiding the promise of an imminent consummation where it might well have been expected. In the last two cases it is a matter of determining whether any meaning is possible other than the one which presents itself prima facie, that according to Luke Jesus expected the Kingdom of God as a future event, but within the lifetime of his contemporaries.

(a) The interpretation given above of Luke 13:22–30; 14:15–24 and 19:11–27 opens up an important clue to the meaning of Acts 1:6–8. The evasive answer of the risen Jesus to the question, 'Lord, are you at this time restoring the Kingdom of Israel?', is usually taken simply as an indirect denial that the Kingdom will come 'at this time', and so as an expression of the delay of the parousia. But the other element in the question also deserves attention: Jesus' answer includes an indirect denial that it is Israel to whom the Kingdom will be given. We must not overlook the fact that v. 6 is not a completely new beginning. In v. 3–5 we are told that the content of Jesus' intercourse with the apostles during the forty days was that he spoke with them about the Kingdom *of God* and instructed them to look forward to the gift of the Spirit within a few days. Thus the Kingdom of God and the Spirit are very closely linked. The new note in v. 6 is the apostles' suggestion that the Kingdom is something that belongs to *Israel*. Luke has already amply shown that this is a false belief, and the present passage reinforces the point. God has determined 'times and seasons' (v. 7) for dealing with Israel. With this we can compare Luke 24:21, where the term 'redemption' occurs, which is used also in 21:28, in close proximity and parallelism to the 'the Kingdom of God' in 21:31: the disappointed Emmaus-disciples had been hoping that Jesus was the one who would redeem Israel. The hopeful intention of the birth-narratives for the redemption of Israel (1:68; 2:38) is not after all to be fulfilled, for Israel has rejected its opportunity (13:34; 19:44b; etc.).[37] Not the redemption of Israel (24:21), but the fulfilment of the Father's promise for Jesus' disciples (v. 49); not the Kingdom for Israel (Acts 1:6), but the power of the Holy Spirit for the church (v. 8). Thus the point is repeatedly made that the Kingdom has nothing to do with Israel, nor with Jerusalem (Luke 19:11ff.; and in 19:38, on Jesus' entry into the city, his disciples hail the coming King, but Luke drops the reference in Mark 11:10 to 'the coming Kingdom of our father David'). The Kingdom has instead been bestowed by the Father upon Jesus, who in turn bestows it on the apostles (Luke 22:28f.), presumably as representative of the whole church: for another saying preserved only in Luke says, 'Fear not, little flock! for your Father has decided to give you the Kingdom' (12:32). Thus both the Kingdom and the 'redemption', which seem to mean the same thing (Luke 2:38 = 23.51c; 21:28 = v. 31), belong not to Israel but to the body of Jesus' disciples: it is as if Matt. 21:43 had provided a text for extensive exposition in Luke.

But now the question arises, *when* does the gift of the Kingdom to the disciples become effective? The frequent contrast, 'not Israel but the disciples of Jesus', again makes the fall of Jerusalem suggestive. This event looms so large in the Gospel of Luke, and is so constantly linked with the passing of God's judgement,[38] that it seems to mark for Luke the final seal of Israel's exclusion from the Kingdom: and so, therefore, the alternative heirs come into their inheritance. However, it is remarkable that the fall of Jerusalem is never mentioned in Acts; and the Kingdom of God is referred to in Acts only (with one exception, 14:22)[39] as that which is taught or proclaimed. We shall consider later what is meant by the 'proclaiming' of the Kingdom.[40] The absence of reference to the fall of Jerusalem in Acts can be explained by the new geographical focus. The church's mission must begin from Jerusalem (Luke 24:47–49; Acts 1:8): but it is a city whose doom has already been adequately emphasized. Luke's concern is now mainly with the Jews of the Dispersion. But the city is still shown as contributing to her own 'desolation' from the point of view of the gospel of Jesus: the Seven and their followers are driven out from Jerusalem, and this leads to the rapid extension of the mission in other places (Acts 6:9–8:4); Paul is denied justice in Jerusalem, and this leads to his preaching in Rome (21:27 – 28:31). Eventually, as Luke has hinted (Luke 21:21), the church will move out of Jerusalem altogether. But it is in the Dispersion that the alternative 'Israel' or 'church' is now threshed out, and here the keyword tends to be 'salvation' (Acts 13:26; 28:28; also 'eternal life', 13:46f.) rather than 'Kingdom of God'. The latter can serve as a summary of the message proclaimed by the risen Jesus (1:3), Philip (8:12) and Paul (19:8; 20:25; 28:23, 31), but even here controversy as to whether Israel will inherit the Kingdom occasionally shines through (19:8f.; 28:23ff.; 28:31 after v. 28). The confrontation of Paul with the Jews of the Dispersion is a counterpart to that of Jesus with Jerusalem: and since the fall of Jerusalem does not occur until well after the story of Acts is concluded, it can be passed over, to allow the point with respect to the Dispersion to be made in its own right and in its own terms.

So Jesus' words in Acts 1:7, 'It is not for you to know times and seasons . . .', cannot mean that one day the Father *will* 'restore the Kingdom to Israel'. The question is asked in v. 6 in the traditional, nationalistic sense, and in that sense is rejected. The Kingdom of God is another matter. The phrasing of Jesus' answer still leaves room for Israel to participate in that, and the story of Acts, especially of Paul's mission (as we have seen in Chapter Three), emphasizes repeatedly that the opportunity of a share in the Kingdom is offered to Israel. But it is a Kingdom where the Gentiles, too, have their rightful place, and is not Israel's private prerogative. The Kingdom in this new sense is closely linked with the gift of the Spirit (Acts 1:3f., 8). This passage in fact has nothing to do with the 'delay'-theme.

(b) Luke 22:69 is often taken to be among the clearest evidences of a doctrine of the delay of the parousia in Luke.[41] In the parallel passage in Mark, 14:62, Jesus warns the High Priest and his colleagues: 'You will see the Son of Man sitting at the right hand of the Power and coming with the clouds of heaven'. (The opening 'you will see' is particularly striking, coming after the wording 'they will see' in the similar prophecy in Mark 13:26.) In Luke this is modified in two ways: only the heavenly session of the Son of Man is mentioned, not his coming with the clouds; and it is not said that anyone will see him, only that 'from now on' he will be there. This verse undoubtedly represents a most important aspect of Luke's Christology and eschatology. It reflects the importance to Luke of the ascension of Jesus, which is the real climax of his incarnation and mission (Luke 9:51; 24:51). Luke does not think of the ascension and heavenly session merely as an answer to the question, where the risen Jesus is until the parousia, as might be thought from Acts 1:9–11 and a quick reading of 3:19–21. The ascension and heavenly session have a very active theological function, as can be seen from passages such as Acts 2:29–36; 3:13–16; 5:30–32; 7:55–60; 9:4–6; 16:7; etc.[42] The knowledge that the Son of Man is seated at the right hand of God is of enormous importance to the church for which Luke writes: it is from this knowledge, as well as from the working of the Holy Spirit, that the church draws its life. So the first effect of Luke's modification of Mark 14:62 is to underline this fact, and thereby to reinforce the confidence and faith of the church of his own day. The circumstances in which his fellow-Christians are living, and the resources available to them, are the focus of Luke's attention. The 'time of the church' is no mere time of waiting for something else:[43] it deserves full and positive appreciation in its own right. A second effect of Luke's redaction in 22:69 is implicitly to deny that the members of the Sanhedrin will see the Son of Man in his heavenly glory: they will not believe what Jesus tells them, nor answer his questions (v. 68) – they remain in ignorance of the great things God is about to do; but despite them the disciples of Jesus will know of his presence in heaven, and some of them will even see it (Acts 7:55f.).[44] So the enthronement of the Son of Man in heaven is like the Kingdom of God: it is God's powerful action on behalf of the disciples, from which however the unbelieving Jewish authorities are excluded. Does the modification have also a third effect, that of postponing the parousia into the distant future? That question cannot be answered directly. Luke 22:69 does not speak of an imminent parousia, but neither does it speak of a distant one. It may be that Luke is denying the parousia's imminence, but it is at least as likely that what he is denying is the parousia's importance, by comparison with that of the ascension and heavenly session.[45]

(c) In Luke 9:27, 'There are some of those standing here (αὐτοῦ) who will not taste death until they see the Kingdom of God', Luke has made two alterations from the wording of his source in Mark 9:1 which call for attention. First, why has he changed the adverb modifying 'standing' from ὧδε to αὐτοῦ? Since αὐτοῦ in Acts 18:19 and 21:4 means 'there' rather than 'here', it has been suggested by H. Conzelmann that Luke means not those standing where Jesus is delivering his teaching (i.e. his contemporaries, his actual hearers) but those standing at some unspecified place at some future time.[46] Lexicographically this is most unlikely: Luke is probably using a synonym.

In the NT αὐτοῦ (adv.) occurs only four times: Luke 9:27; Acts 18:19; 21:4; Matt. 26:36. In classical Greek it means 'here' more often than 'there' (LSJ s.v.). In LXX it occurs thirteen times, *always* = 'here'. This is also its meaning in Matt. 26:36, where it is actually contrasted with ἐκεῖ. Mark's ὧδε is a common NT word for 'here' (9 × Mark, 17 × Matthew, 15 × Luke, 2 × Acts). Until the 3rd century BC it meant not 'here' but 'hither', and this meaning also occurs fairly often in the NT, including 5 or 6 of the 17 examples in Luke–Acts, and 5 of the 17 examples in Matthew, but only 1 of 9 in Mark. Luke clearly maintained no consistency in this vocabulary-field, but he has a well-known tendency to vary the wording of his source with the use of synonyms.[47]

But in the context, the suggestion that Luke means 'there, where the Kingdom of God will take place at an unknown time in the future' is exegetically impossible, because the follow-words 'will not taste death until . . .' imply an expectation within a limited space of time. In Luke 2:26–32 Symeon is told by the Holy Spirit that he will not see death before he has seen the Lord's Messiah: then, having seen the infant Jesus, he is content to be 'released', because 'my eyes have seen your salvation'. A meaning such as 'those who are "there" when the Kingdom of God arrives will not die until they see the Kingdom of God' is hopelessly banal. The meaning can only be: Some (but not all) of Jesus' hearers will still be alive to see the Kingdom of God. There is no need for the phrase 'will not taste death until . . .' to mean (as some have supposed) that they *will* die *after* they see the Kingdom:[48] the idiom can be illustrated from Paul's expectation in 1 Thess. 4:15ff. and 1 Cor. 15:51: some will have died before the Kingdom comes, but some will still be alive.

More difficult is Luke's second variation from Mark, the omission of the phrase 'having come with power': this is presumably a deliberate change, and if we knew Luke's reason for it we should have advanced some way towards knowing what he understood by 'the Kingdom of God'. It is generally agreed that Luke's source, Mark 9:1, refers to the coming of the Kingdom of God as the great eschatological climax, probably identical with the coming of the Son of Man 'in the glory of his Father with the holy angels' (Mark 8:38).[49] Most modern exegetes regard Luke's alteration as intended to avoid this meaning: however, opinions differ as to what the new meaning is. Even the older exegetes, who were not so concerned about the comparison of Luke's wording with Mark's, differed greatly on the meaning of Luke 9:27b. A. Plummer (1896) lists seven possibilities proposed by his predecessors back to the patristic period:[50] the transfiguration; the resurrection and ascension; Pentecost; the spread of Christianity; the internal development of the gospel; the destruction of Jerusalem; the second advent. If one decides, with many modern commentators, that the new reference is to the coming of the Holy Spirit,[51] the dropping of 'with power' is surprising, for in Luke–Acts it is especially the Holy Spirit that is associated with 'power' (Luke 4:14; 24:49; Acts 1:8; 6:5, 8). E. E. Ellis regards the words omitted as redundant, since 'for Luke the presence of the kingdom is always "in power"', but nevertheless identifies the event predicted as the witnessing of the transfiguration, not the parousia.[52] This suggestion is still open to Plummer's objection:[53] it is odd for the time-reference 'will not taste death until . . .' to pertain to an event that will occur within eight days (Luke 9:28ff.). Moreover, the wording most naturally means that 'some' will see the Kingdom of God, not because of their faith, or because Jesus has taken them aside privately for the purpose, but because they will still be alive at the time when it may be seen. The order of the text makes it more likely that 'seeing the Kingdom of God' is connected with the coming of the Son of Man (v. 26) than with the following incident of the transfiguration, for (as is especially confirmed by a comparison of the flow of the text in Mark 8:38–9:2) Luke sets 9:28ff. apart from the preceding by a clear caesura, but v. 27 flows on from v. 26 without hesitation. H. Conzelmann vacillates between two views: that the nature of the Kingdom (though not the Kingdom itself) is to be perceived in the life of Jesus; and that the Kingdom will be seen from the parousia onwards:[54] but in either case he ignores the time-reference in the text. This diversity and uncertainty of opinion shows that it is by no means clear what Luke meant by 'the Kingdom of God' in this passage. A further problem arises from the word 'see'. Does the saying refer to witnessing the occurrence of an event, or to the perception of a reality that intrinsically was already available? The former is by far the more likely: for nothing outside the Johannine literature prepares us to expect a spiritual conception of the idea of 'seeing', and moreover the time-reference (once again) sounds as if a specific event is expected within a limited span of time, a matter of three or four decades: that is hardly relevant to spiritual perception, which depends on the receptivity of the observer and is not subject to predictable time-limits.[55]

So we cannot determine from the passage itself what is meant by 'the Kingdom of God' here. If any decision becomes possible at all, it will have to be indirectly, from wider considerations about Luke's usage elsewhere. But, whatever its nature, the Kingdom of God is an event expected within the lifetime of at least some of Jesus' hearers: that is quite clear in Luke, no less than in Mark. This passage cannot properly be used to support the theory that Luke taught his readers to expect a long delay of the parousia.

(d) Luke 21:31f., 'When you see these things happening, know that the Kingdom of God is near. Truly I tell you that this generation (ἡ γενεὰ αὕτη) will not pass away until all things happen'. This saying is crucial for the interpretation of the important but difficult discourse, Luke 21:5–36, which is to be examined in the next section. In the present context we are concerned only with the meaning of the phrase ἡ γενεὰ αὕτη.

Those who believe Luke to teach that the End will be indefinitely delayed cannot easily accept without modification the translation given above. And if we are to hold to the view that Luke is a careful, reflective theologian, writing towards the end of the first century, the saying is in any case difficult. Prima facie it means that 'all things', presumably those described in the preceding passage, including the celestial signs, earthly catastrophes and the coming of the Son of Man on a cloud (v. 25-27), will take place within the lifetime of Jesus' contemporaries. As long ago as 1957 E. Gräßer acknowledged that it could not mean anything else, and left it undecided, how the saying could be compatible with his view that Luke taught the doctrine of a long delay.[56] Supporters of the 'delay'-theory have therefore kept trying to get around the impasse by means of various alternative renderings of 'this γενεά', so as to avoid the narrow time-limit. Because of the persistence of these attempts, or of appeals to earlier ones, it is worth while going into some detail to show that Gräßer was on this point quite correct. Meanings that have been suggested include (i) the Jewish people, (ii) all humanity (alternatively: non-Christian humanity), (iii) Luke's generation, rather than Jesus', (iv) Jesus' generation, understood as extending, through the longevity of a few individuals, into Luke's time, (v) the last phase in the history of redemption, including several lifetimes.

(i) The most thorough attempt to establish another meaning than 'this generation', as far as I am aware, is that of M. Meinertz, who argues for the view, in itself an old one, that it means here 'the Jewish people'.[57] In classical Greek the chief meanings of γενεά are 'birth'; 'offspring, descendants'; 'race (those bound by common descent)'. But the common Hellenistic meaning, 'generation', occurs from the 5th century BC onwards: Herodotus II, 142: τρεῖς γενεαὶ ἀνδρων ἑκατὸν ἔτη εἰσίν; and there are several more pre-Hellenistic examples in LSJ s.v. Meinertz admits that in most cases in the NT (like the vast majority of LXX examples, of which there are over 200), γενεά can only mean 'generation'. But he considers the special phrase ἡ γενεὰ αὕτη to have a different, non-temporal meaning. The phrase occurs in just this form 16 times in the NT, of which 13 are in the synoptic gospels. Of the remaining 3, Hebr. 3:10 is a quotation of Psalm 94 (95):10 (but changing ἐκείνῃ of LXX to ταύτῃ); and Acts 2:40 and Phil. 2:15 are both allusions to Deut. 32:5. In fact our precise phrase occurs only twice in LXX (Gen. 7:1 and Psalm 11 (12):7), both times in a temporal meaning. In Blass-Debrunner-Rehkopf 292.2, n. 4, it is noted that the post-positive αὕτη in this stock-phrase points to Semitic influence. Since the phrase, even in the variant ἡ γενεὰ ἐκείνη, is not too common in the OT, it is likely that its occurrence in the synoptic gospels (where the OT is not quoted or directly alluded to) is due to contemporary Hebrew or Aramaic usage. The phrase itself does not occur often in Rabbinic literature, but the word דּוֹר (Hebrew, = דָּר Aramaic), which in LXX underlies the great majority of examples of γενεά, is very frequent, and always with the temporal meaning of 'generation'.[58]

We have thus a lexicographical likelihood that the phrase in the gospels is also intended temporally: but this needs to be verified by exegesis. In addition to the passage with which we are concerned and its parallels (Mark 13:30/Matt. 24:34/Luke 21:32), Meinertz pays detailed attention to Matt. 12:41f./Luke 11:31f. (the Ninevites/the queen of the south 'will arise at the judgement μετὰ τῆς γενεᾶς ταύτης') and Matt. 23:35f./Luke 11:50. (the violence 'from the blood of Abel to the blood of Zechariah . . .' will come upon/will be required of 'this generation'). In the former case it is argued that the point is to contrast the willing heathen with the hostile Jews; in the second example Meinertz asserts that the reference in Matthew (=Q?) cannot be to Jesus' contemporaries 'but to those who will see the parousia', because of the following saying, Matt. 23:37ff., and therefore the older, classical meaning of γενεά, 'race', must be called into play: 'this race' is the Jews. An argument similar to the latter is then applied to Mark 13:30/Matt. 24:34/Luke 21:32: the reference cannot be to Jesus' contemporaries, because 'no one knows about that day or hour'.

How well do these examples substantiate the argument? In the case of Matt. 12:41f./Luke 11:31f., it is true that a contrast between foreigners and Jews is intended: but this does not rule out an accompanying temporal reference. In fact the latter is explicitly indicated in the passage, because the reason why the Ninevites and the queen of the south will condemn this γενεά is that something greater than Solomon and Jonah *is here:* the judgement falls not on some unspecified Jews of the future, who will not witness the ministry of Jesus, but on the contemporary Jews who have witnessed it and have failed to perceive its significance. Exactly the same double theme occurs also in Luke 10:10–15: it will be more tolerable in the judgement for Sodom than for the towns which reject the preaching of the seventy disciples; because the Kingdom of God has drawn near; it will be more tolerable in the judgement for Tyre and Sidon than for Chorazin, Bethsaida and Capernaum, because the latter did not repent on seeing the miracles of Jesus: cf. Matt. 11:20–24. The meaning 'generation' is not only possible but actually required in Matt. 12:41f./Luke 11:31f.

In the next example, Matt. 23:35f./Luke 11:50f., there is no contrast between Jews and foreigners: the point is rather that the history of Israel has come to a crisis in the mission of Jesus, and the accumulated wrongs of the past are now due to be set right. The redactional significance of the following verses in Matthew is not that the judgement is deferred until a distant parousia (that in fact has to be read into the text) but that the desolation of Jerusalem is due to the rejection of *Jesus*, and it is only his contemporaries who are directly responsible for that. The same point is not underlined in the Lucan context, but it is made abundantly elsewhere in Luke, e.g. 3:9; 12:49ff.; 13:1–9; 13:22–35; etc. (see above, Chapter Two).

Finally in Mark 13:30/Matt. 24:34/Luke 21:32 the supposed contradiction in 'no one knows about that day or hour' is not enough to prove that it is something other than 'this generation' which will not pass away 'until (all) these things happen'. (Luke in any case omits the former statement, Mark 13:32.) Much more important is the consideration that the predicate 'will not pass away until . . .' becomes meaningless unless the subject is something intrinsically of fairly short duration. If the meaning of the saying (as understood by any of the synoptists) is that the fulfilment would come at some indefinitely delayed point in the future, and that the Jewish people would survive until that time, the original readers might well have wondered what point there was in the saying, since the destruction of Jerusalem, while it did not mark the end of Judaism, was clearly seen by the evangelists (and especially by Luke) as marking the end of the time when the disciples of Jesus needed to take the commonwealth of Judaism seriously.

There is thus neither lexicographical nor exegetical justification for taking ἡ γενεὰ αὕτη to mean 'the Jewish people'.

(ii) Much less is there any reason to take seriously the strange suggestion that it might mean 'the human race'. This seems to have been first proposed by H. Conzelmann. The brief sentence in which he put it forward, without argument or supporting evidence,[59] has continued for two decades to be appealed to as authoritative.[60] In the very rare examples in classical Greek literature where γενεά carries this meaning, it is made explicit by the adjective ἀνθρωπίνη and a contrast with non-human life, as Homer, *Iliad* 6, 146: see LSJ s.v. In Hellenistic Greek there is no evidence for it whatsoever. (The suggestion 'non-Christian humanity', put forward very tentatively by W. C. Robinson in 1964,[61] has in common with Conzelmann's only the conviction that the temporal meaning 'generation' is impossible. It is rather a variation of the argument of Meinertz discussed above under (i), based on Luke 11:29–31/Matt. 12:38–40 and Luke 11:50f./Matt. 23:35f.: but instead of seeing here 'the Jews', Robinson thought of the people who in the days of 'visitation' rejected the 'visitation', and suggested that in Luke 21:32 the reference is to such people, mentioned in v. 25b–26a. This is a very strained argument. There is nothing in v. 25f. to suggest that those events might take as long as a generation to happen. The more immediate connexion of v. 32 is with v. 31 and 28.)

Quite apart from the general lexicographical standing of γενεά its context in Luke 21:32 requires it to have a limited temporal meaning. Obviously the human race will not have passed away before the parousia, for there will be people to see the Son of Man's coming (v. 27). Conzelmann's exegesis makes Luke 21:32 as meaningless as it does 9:27 (see sub-section (c), above).

The three suggested meanings which remain to be considered have the advantage over those just discussed of recognizing the temporal meaning of γενεά.

(iii) The suggestion that 'this generation' is the generation of Luke and his readers rather than that of Jesus and his hearers has been revived recently by R. Geiger.[62] This is, as Geiger acknowledges, an expedient to deal with the puzzle thrown up by the fact that Luke seems to repeat the prophecy of Jesus that the End (v. 27) would come within a generation, yet when Luke wrote the generation of Jesus and his hearers was past, with perhaps the exception of very few individuals. But the text offers no support for assuming this adjustment in Luke's meaning. The setting is still the answer of Jesus to a question raised by some of his hearers in the temple. As Luke's procedure elsewhere often shows, he could easily have altered or omitted this saying if its plain meaning in its context was no longer what he wanted to affirm. It is true that in Luke a time-reference may occasionally be meant to be ambiguous: e.g. it is probable that Luke 4:21, 'Today this scripture has been fulfilled in your hearing', was meant by Luke not only as the fulfilment experienced by the congregation in the synagogue at Nazareth but also, in a secondary way, but the Christians of his own day. But that refers to a past event which has continuing significance, not to a future event which is expected to occur within a limited time.

It may be that ultimately the exegesis of Luke 21:5–36 will force us to take seriously some such suggestion as this, but it will only be at the cost of imposing great strain on the text.

(iv) An attempt to take seriously the most obvious meaning of 'this generation', and yet accommodate the fact that the parousia has still not occurred in Luke's time, can be made by extending the meaning of 'generation' through its last survivors. Thus R. H. Hiers argues that even as late as 95 AD there would have been still a few people alive who had been Jesus' contemporaries, and that Luke still expected the parousia to occur within their lifetime.[63] John 21 attests a belief among some Christians that the Lord's return would occur within the lifetime of his first disciples, even if that meant that only one of them was still alive.

But there are difficulties with this view, too. Hiers' argument depends on the idea that, while Luke's Jesus could teach that the parousia would come within the lifetime of his generation, Luke eliminated any passages in which Jesus says that it would come *soon*. Thus he has to interpret the mission of the seventy disciples in Luke 10 as an anachronistic reference to the Gentile-mission, since 'seventy' is a Jewish number for the Gentile nations: missionaries in the time well after Jesus' death might be able to declare that the Kingdom of God had 'come near' (Luke 10:9, 11), though Jesus himself could not, as is shown by Luke's dropping of Mark 1:15. Now, whatever may be the origin of the tradition lying behind Luke 10:1–20, at least at the level of Lucan redaction it is dangerous to see it as intended to refer to the Gentile-mission decades later than the lifetime of Jesus: for not only are the missionaries described as sent out by Jesus and returning to him while he is on the way to Jerusalem, but also their message of the near approach of the Kingdom of God is addressed not only to unspecified towns that receive the message but also to specific Galilaean towns like Chorazin, Bethsaida and Capernaum, that do not. Luke understands the seventy disciples as Galilaean missionaries during the lifetime of Jesus: and since they are twice instructed to say that the Kingdom of God had drawn near, we may have to seek elsewhere an explanation of Luke's dropping Mark 1:15 (see below).[64]

A variation of this interpretation has been proposed by E. Franklin, who says that Luke and his readers belong to the generation of Jesus because, as the exalted Lord, he is their contemporary as well as the contemporary of those who witnessed his mission.[65] But Luke 21:32 does not say 'my generation' but 'this generation', i.e. not the generation of Jesus personally but that of his contemporaries in general.

(v) E. E. Ellis suggests, on the analogy of two passages in the Habakkuk-Pesher (1QpHab II.7; VII.2), that 'generation' may indeed be meant, but in a very broad sense, including several lifetimes. Thus the Lucan Jesus predicted the End within 'the last phase in the history of redemption', whose extent is left quite indeterminate.[66]

It is not clear to me that the phrase 'the last generation' does have this extended meaning in the passages referred to in the Habakkuk-Pesher. In any case, this would provide too narrow and uncertain a linguistic base for interpreting this saying of Jesus. Moreover, this suggestion shares with (i) and (ii) above the difficulty that there is a temporal urgency in the predicate, 'will not pass away until . . .', which becomes meaningless if the subject loses any identifiable chronological significance.

We must thus conclude that all these suggestions are unconvincing expedients, due to the conviction that from Luke's chronological position the generation of Jesus was past but 'all things', including the End, had not yet arrived. However awkward it may be for the theories now widely accepted about Luke's eschatology, Luke 21:32 can only mean that the generation of Jesus' contemporaries will not completely die out before 'all things happen'. This conclusion is further established by the fact that Luke retains from Mark the second-person address in v. 31, 'when you see these things happening, know . . .'; cf. v. 28 (Luke alone), 'when these things begin to happen, look up and lift up your heads, for your redemption is drawing near'. The text does not suggest that those who will see indications that the Kingdom of God is near are different from those who asked the question about the destruction of the temple in v. 7, who are the audience of Jesus' teaching in Jerusalem.

In this section I have not dealt comprehensively with all the arguments for a doctrine of the delay of the parousia in Luke–Acts, but have examined in detail a number of passages that have proved to be crucial to that doctrine. They do not support it; and we can, I think, conclude with confidence that to teach his fellow-Christians that the parousia would be long delayed was neither the central issue nor a significant aspect of Luke's purpose.

4 Luke 21:5–36[67]

The most important eschatological passage in Luke–Acts is the discourse of Jesus in Luke 21:5–36. In its position in the gospel, and in much of its material, it corresponds to the eschatological discourse of Mark 13, and for our purpose it is useful to be able to compare the two. It differs from the other major eschatological discourse in Luke 17:20-37, partly in being more than twice as long, and partly in that it is not so much concentrated on the End, but also is concerned with intervening historical events.

We must begin by summarizing the structure of the whole discourse:

(1) V. 5–7: Jesus prophesies the destruction of the Temple, and people ask him what sign will show when 'these things' are going to happen.

(2) V. 8–9: False teachers will claim in Jesus' name that they are (the Christ), and that 'the time has drawn near'; and wars will occur. But 'the end' will not come immediately.

(3) V. 10–11: Unlike Mark (13:8), Luke here has a new paragraph, so to speak, setting these words apart from the preceding. Wars will be accompanied, or followed, by natural catastrophes and signs from heaven.

(4) V. 12–19: Persecutions to be expected by Jesus' followers are mentioned here, following the order of Mark 13; but chronologically this passage is bracketed out by Luke, and brought forward to the time before the beginning of the rest of the series.

(5) V. 20–24: Jerusalem will be besieged and destroyed as punishment (for her unbelief). Disciples of Jesus are to flee from Judaea.

(6) V. 25–27: Signs in the heavenly bodies and catastrophes on earth will lead up to the coming of the Son of Man on a cloud.

(7) V. 28: When 'these things' begin to happen, the 'redemption' of Jesus' disciples is near.

(8) V. 29–33: As the sprouting fig-tree foretells summer, so disciples will recognize the approach of the Kingdom of God when they see 'these things' happening; 'all things' will happen within the lifetime of the present generation. Jesus' words will surely be fulfilled.

(9) V. 34–36: Disciples must be watchful and disciplined, so as to escape from 'all these things which are going to happen', and 'stand' before the Son of Man.

First we must consider no. 4 in this series. As has often been observed, the effect of Luke's rewriting of Mark is to remove the persecutions to be suffered by the church from the immediate setting of eschatology. The persecutions are no longer, as in Mark, part of the anguish of the last days (Mark 13:9–13, following v. 8b, ἀρχὴ ὠδίνων ταῦτα, which Luke omits).

But it does not necessarily follow that Luke's intention here, as the 'delay'-theory holds, is to help the church of his own day to adjust itself to a long period of persecution, because the end is long delayed. *The passage may not be addressed directly to the situation of Luke's contemporaries at all.* Instead, Luke's reference in v. 12–19 seems to be to the period leading up to the Jewish War, which is more or less the same as the period covered by Acts. This is shown both by the opening words, 'but before all these things', which places the time of persecution before all that is described from v. 8 onwards, and by the new beginning in v. 20, 'but when you see Jerusalem surrounded by armed camps . . .'. At several points the wording anticipates phrases used in Acts. The persecution in v. 12 is prophesied in terms that recur in Acts 9:2; 12:1; 22:4f.; and 26:10f. In much of the passage Luke's alterations of Mark emphasize the assurance of God's protection and favour of faithful disciples. In v. 13, persecution faithfully endured becomes testimony for the disciple before God (not testimony that he will give when on trial).[68] Mark 13:10 is dropped, because persecution sets in well before the gospel has been preached to all nations. V. 14f. has much the same intention as Mark 13:11 (which Luke has already used in 12:11f.), but the wording looks forward to Acts 4:8–14, especially its last clause, οὐδὲν εἶχον ἀντειπεῖν. V. 16f. becomes not a general statement of divisions in families but is addressed more personally to disciples: they will be subject to hatred even from within their own families. V. 18 is literally inconsistent with v. 16, but provides reassurance of God's protection of faithful disciples: it is repeated by Paul in Acts 27:34. Then comes in v. 19 Luke's interesting variation of Mark 13:13b. It is usually stated that Luke's reason here is that he no longer thinks it possible for his readers (much less for Jesus' hearers) to 'endure to the end', because that End is far off.[69] But there is another, and I think more likely, possible interpretation: Luke regards 'salvation' not as something reserved for 'the end' but as a present reality for faithful believers (Luke 2:30; Acts 2:40f., 47; 11:14; 13:26, 46f.; 16:31; 28:28).

The terminology of 'salvation' (the verb σώζειν and the nouns σωτήρ, σωτηρία and σωτήριον; also the verb διασώζειν) occurs fairly strongly in all strands of the New Testament: the most conspicuous exception to this generalization is that none of the nouns occurs in Mark or Matthew.

In Paul, 'salvation' has primarily an eschatological reference (e.g. Rom. 5:9; 1 Cor. 5:5), but is also in part a present reality (2 Cor. 6:2; cf. Rom. 8:24; 1 Cor. 1:18). In the deutero-Pauline tradition the emphasis shifts in favour of present salvation (e.g. Eph. 2:5, 8; 2 Tim. 1:9; Tit. 3:5). As a present reality, salvation means especially release from the deadening power of sin.

In Mark, σώζειν has two quite separate references. As in general Greek usage, it means to rescue from physical danger: so of Jesus on the cross (15:30f., 49); similarly, it refers to the healing of physical illness (3:4; 5:23, 28, 34; 10:52). On the other hand, 'to be saved' means 'to be received into the Kingdom of God' at the End (10:26, cf. v. 23ff.; 8:35, cf. v. 37–9:1).

Luke takes up many of the Marcan examples, in both senses used by Mark. But he also adds passages in which, on the one hand, the Pauline and especially deutero-Pauline sense of present salvation through the forgiveness of sins is expressed; and, on the other hand, especially in the canticles of Luke 1–2, passages drawn from old Jewish-Christian tradition, in which God is the saviour of the nation Israel (Luke 1:47, 69, 71: perhaps also 2:11, 30; in 1:77 national salvation is linked with the forgiveness of sins). The theme of present salvation occurs in Luke 19:9f. and probably in Acts 2:21, 40, 47; 11:14; 15:1, 11. In some passages Luke hints at a connexion between physical and spiritual healing: e.g. Acts 4:9–12; in Luke 7:50 the same formula of 'salvation' is used for the forgiveness of sins as is used in Mark 5:34 pars. for physical healing. A similar link between physical and spiritual is hinted at in Acts 16:30f. In particular, for Luke salvation is a 'way' (Acts 16:17, cf. Luke 3:4–6) which may already be travelled by believers. Luke links Isa. 40:5 (LXX) with 42:6 at Luke 2:30–32 and Acts 28:28 to show that the present availability of salvation is extended to the Gentiles as well as Israel; and Isa. 49:6 is quoted to similar effect in Acts 13:46f. (cf. v. 26). It is curious that Jesus receives the title 'Saviour' in Luke–Acts only in the Jewish nationalistic sense: Luke 2:11; Acts 5:31; 13:23. This usage comes to Luke from old tradition, and he is able to use it to show how salvation was first offered to Israel (cf. John 4:22): all the same, from the outset of Luke's story it is made clear that salvation for Israel cannot be separated from salvation for the Gentiles (Luke 2:30–32; cf. John 4:42).

Matt. 1:21 is rather reminiscent of Luke 1:77. In Matt. 8:25 and 14:30 there is probably a deliberate ambiguity between physical and spiritual salvation. Otherwise the usage in Matthew is the same as in Mark.

Moreover, since Luke does not regard v. 12–19 as an exhortation addressed to all Christians generally, but is primarily concerned with the period before the siege of Jerusalem, Luke himself and his readers look back on the time to which the words apply. Whatever the tradition-history of these words may be, and whatever the meaning of such teachings may have been as spoken by Jesus, at the level of Luke's redaction the purpose of the passage is to make his readers, late in the first century, more aware of the divine favour which enabled the church to survive the difficulties of its earliest decades. Persecution had occurred, but by the favour and power of the risen Jesus (v. 15, 18) the church had not only survived but flourished and increased through that period before the Jewish War. This is meant to reinforce the readers' confidence that in their age, too, their faith in Jesus is no delusion but a proper and fruitful response to the action of God in history. Thus the passage Luke 21:12–19 is not eschatological, but nor on the other hand does it contribute to a doctrine of the delay of the End.

The question asked of Jesus in v. 7, to which the discourse is the answer, refers only to the destruction of Jerusalem. In Mark 13:4 there are two questions, one about the fulfilment of Jesus' prophecy of the destruction of the Temple, and a second about the End.[70] When Matthew takes up this verse, Matt. 24:3b, he clarifies and emphasizes the distinction between the two questions. But in Luke 21:7 the one question, about the destruction of the Temple, is repeated tautologously.[71] Why did Luke make this change (which does not improve, but rather spoils, his literary expression)? H. Conzelmann, followed by a number of others, seeks an explanation in Luke's desire to separate the fall of the Temple as sharply as possible from the End.[72] The destruction of Jerusalem and of the Temple is not part of the End, and the two chronologically quite distinct events must not be put side by side. However, Matthew, too, looks back on the destruction of the Temple as a past event, and therefore not part of the End, and his editing of the Marcan source goes in the opposite direction from Luke's. It may be asked whether Matthew's way does not achieve more clearly the desired result, of showing that the following discourse discusses two questions, not one. Later Luke does make the required distinction, but v. 7 does not prepare us to understand that the discourse will be dealing with two quite distinct matters: Luke's new wording here may be a sign of increased emphasis on the events leading up to and including the fall of Jerusalem, which, as we have emphasized in Chapter Two, were of special importance in his understanding of God's dealings with the world.

Where, if at all, is the question of v. 7 answered? It seems clear that in Mark 13 the question about the eschatological 'sign' in v. 4 is answered by the reference to the 'abomination of desolation' in v. 14.[73] In Luke 21:7, too, the questioners ask about the 'sign' (of the destruction of the temple). In v. 11 and 25 there is mention of 'signs' (plural) from heaven or in the heavenly bodies, but these do not seem to be the 'sign' (sigular) asked for in v. 7. The answer to the question seems to come in v. 20: '*When you see* Jerusalem surrounded by armed camps, *then know* that her desolation is near'. The destruction of Jerusalem, v. 20–24, is the climax to which the question in v. 7 points forward. What comes in between must be read in that context.

What is the significance of Luke's new 'paragraph' at v. 10 (contrast Mark 13:8)? And what light does it shed on the meaning of the prophecies in v. 8f. and v. 10f. respectively? As we have noted, v. 12–19 describe events chronologically prior to those of v. 8f. and v. 10f. and corresponding in a general way to the story told in Acts. The troubles forecast in v. 8 do not seem to be reflected in Acts, except that in Acts 20:29f. Paul predicts the emergence after his death of false teachers in the church. Luke seems to refer this prophecy of false Messiahs to the time before the Jewish War. From Gamaliel's anachronistic reference (Acts 5:36f.) to Theudas (after 44 AD) and 'after him' Judas the Galilaean (6 AD), it seems that Luke may have had a generalized impression of several 'messianic' pretenders in the period leading up to the War. Mark has prophecies of false teachers and false Messiahs twice in this passage, v. 5f. (before the messianic woes properly begin, cf. v. 8c) and v. 21f. (after the woes are over, v. 19f., and just before the cosmic signs heralding the parousia, v. 24ff.). Luke omits the latter. The wars and civil disturbances of Luke 21:9 must refer either to the civil unrest of the last few years before the War broke out in 66 AD or to the War itself.

J. Zmijewski and R. Geiger both seek an answer to this question by relating the 'signs' of v. 11 to the 'sign' asked for in v. 7. Zmijewski suggests that v. 10f. refers to the siege and fall of Jerusalem as a preliminary set of 'signs', with further signs of the End coming later, in v. 25ff.[74] In that case the 'wars and disturbances' of v. 9 must refer to preliminary troubles, of which there was much before the War broke out in earnest. This view has the advantage, at first sight, that v. 10 sounds like an intensification of warfare, which would suit the events of 66–70 AD; Luke otherwise does not describe the End in terms of international wars. But Geiger rightly observes that the pause in v. 10, coming straight after the words 'but the end will not (take place) immediately', implies that what follows does refer to the End.[75] Geiger's argument is further reinforced by the observation that Luke has strengthened the wording of Mark 13:7 by the addition of a motif from Mark 13:10, a verse which he then drops: it is not the preaching of the gospel to all the nations which 'must happen *first*', but the wars and disturbances of v. 9.[76] Thus, although one might have expected a reference to the War to be more strongly expressed than in the wording of v. 9a, it seems clear that Luke's rewording of Mark in v. 9b 10a is intended to distinguish events which belong immediately to the End (v. 10b–11) from those which do not. It is here that Luke makes the distinction which he failed to make in v. 7; and he prepares for it by inserting into the claims of the false teachers, v. 8, the words 'the time has drawn near': the fall of Jerusalem is not an immediate precursor of the End. Geiger argues that the hearers in v. 7 ask for 'a sign', which they relate to the destruction of the Temple, but Jesus answers about 'signs' only after the Temple has been destroyed (v. 11, 25), as a way of emphasizing that the destruction of the Temple is not itself part of the End.[77] Relating the answer about 'signs' to the question about 'a sign' in this way is confusing and improbable. It is better to understand, as suggested above, that the question of v. 7 is answered in v. 20ff., and that the mention of 'signs' in v. 11 and 25 belongs to a new theme.

V. 12–19 have already been discussed above. In v. 20–25 Luke has adapted the apocalyptic-sounding words of Mark 13:14–20 to make an unambiguous reference to the destruction of Jerusalem, seen not in an apocalyptic but a prophetic light, as punishment by God, presumably for the rejection of Jesus and his mission by the leading authorities and institutions of Judaism. The only problem for our present discussion is raised by the last clause, 'until the times of the Gentiles have been fulfilled' (v. 24c). It is not quite certain what is meant by these 'times of the Gentiles'. Some have thought, on the basis of certain Old Testament passages, that the meaning is that the Gentiles, viewed as a hostile power, will ultimately have their rule terminated by the return of the Jews.[78] But in the light of our discussion in Chapter Two that is most unlikely. Again, it has been suggested that the reference is to world-judgement: just as the Jews have been judged in the destruction of the Temple, so the Gentiles will have their turn for judgement.[79] But that, too, seems to me to miss Luke's point. In so far as Luke sees 'Jews' and 'Gentiles' as distinct groups, he contrasts them as respectively inclined to unbelief and to faith. The appropriate comparison with Paul's thought in Romans is not with ch. 1–3, where both groups have sinned and need God's grace, but with ch. 9–11, where the Gentiles are threatening to supersede Israel in the inheritance of Abraham. The most likely meaning is 'until the Gentile-mission has been completed'[80] (cf. Mark 13:10, which Luke omits).

It is clear from v. 24a–b that the fall of Jerusalem now lies in the past; it is also clear from Acts 28:30f. that the Gentile-mission is still actively in progress in Luke's time. Therefore v. 24c indicates the time in which Luke lives, the time of transition from the past event of the fall of Jerusalem to the future events of the End. It has sometimes been argued by proponents of the 'delay'-theory that Luke means by v. 24c that this gap is a long one, and that the End will be far removed from the fall of Jerusalem.[81] Yet the construction of this passage by Luke points in just the opposite direction. It is especially important that v. 25ff. flow on quite smoothly from the preceding paragraph. Luke does not use here any of the usual formulas of separation, such as 'and he said to them' or 'but when' (v. 10, 12, 20, 29).[82] There is indeed less of a pause marked by Luke 21:25 than by the corresponding verse Mark 13:24, and yet it is Luke, rather than Mark, who is usually said to emphasize the separation between the fall of Jerusalem and the End. From this it is at least clear that Luke does not emphasize the time-gap; and it is probably legitimate also to understand that Luke is indicating to his readers that there is a thematic connexion between what precedes and what follows. The End still lies ahead, but the fall of Jerusalem, as an act of divine judgement (v. 22), is an anticipation of it, and therefore has an eschatological dimension, despite the relatively un-apocalyptic language of v. 20–24 by comparison with Mark 13:14–20.

In the prophecy of the End, v. 25–28, Luke follows Mark closely only in v. 26b–27. In v. 27, Luke's alteration of Mark's 'clouds' to 'a cloud' is no doubt meant to point forward to the cloud of Jesus' ascension (Acts 1:9), but perhaps also to recall the cloud of the transfiguration, which is rather more emphasized in Luke 9:34f. than in Mark 9:7. But why does Luke in v. 25a so drastically abbreviate Mark 13:24–25a, and insert the new material of Luke 21:25b–26a? And why does he substitute his v. 28 for Mark's v. 27? It may be conjectured that Luke had a conception of the End differing from that found in Mark and other parts of early tradition, in that he retained a stronger interest in what would happen on the earth and did not locate all the important action in heaven. In v. 25, as in v. 11, he speaks of 'signs' in heaven (cf. the 'sign of the Son of Man' in Matt. 24:30; this seems to have been an important element to Luke, as he introduces the word 'signs' into the prophecy of heavenly portents in the quotation from Joel 3:3 LXX in Acts 2:19), but then goes on in v. 25b–26a to portray the confusion of the nations and the dismay of people at what was coming upon the οἰκουμένη.[83] In Mark 13:27, 'And then he will send out his angels and gather his elect from the four winds, from the end of earth to the end of heaven', the action described, by which believers are at the parousia rescued out of the world to be with Christ, the Son of Man, is an important part of the parousia-theme in the rest of the New Testament: e.g. 1 Thess. 4:16f.; 1 Cor. 15:50–54; Matt. 13:37–43; 24:31; 25:31–46. Neither here nor elsewhere is such a hope expressed in Luke. By writing instead, 'When these things begin to happen, look up and lift up your heads, because your redemption has drawn near', Luke seems to mean that the Son of Man at his coming will bring relief to his people where they are, on the earth: cf. Luke 18:7f.

This brings us to the question, what are 'these things' which will 'begin to happen'? It was shown by F. Hahn that in Mark 13:4a–b and 29f. a careful distinction is made between the expressions 'these things' and 'all these things': the former refers to the calamities leading up to and including the destruction of Jerusalem, and the latter extends the scope through to the parousia.[84] It is likely that Luke perceived the significance of this terminology, and retained it himself.[85] In v. 7 'these things' clearly means the destruction of the Temple. In v. 12, 'before all these things' comes immediately after the reference to the events of the End in v. 10f. In v. 32 and 36 'all (these) things' again refers to the consummation of the Kingdom of God and the judgement of the Son of Man respectively. So it seems that the expression 'these things' in v. 28 and 31 may well mean the events culminating in 70 AD.

If this is correct, we have in both v. 28 and v. 31 (for Luke seems to identify 'the Kingdom of God' with 'redemption')[86] a *denial* that there would be a long gap of time between the fall of Jerusalem and the End.

This is confirmed by v. 32. 'Truly I tell you, this generation will not pass away until all things take place'. In the previous section of this chapter (3(d)) we examined in detail a number of attempts that have been made to give ἡ γενεὰ αὕτη a sense other than the literal one, 'this generation', and found them all to be unjustified. The text means that Jesus prophesied that 'all things', including the coming of the Son of Man, the redemption of his disciples, and the Kingdom of God, would happen within the lifetime of his contemporaries. Now it cannot be escaped that there is a difficulty here: for we have seen in earlier chapters, e.g. in connexion with Luke's picture of Paul (Chapter Three, section 4) and with his preface (Chapter One, section 2) reason to believe that Luke saw himself as belonging to a later generation than that of Jesus' earthly life, and yet Luke still writes before the occurrence of the End. It may be that there is no neat solution to this problem. Many recent studies of Luke's eschatology have emphasized how important it is to Luke to maintain the force of the moral challenge in Jesus' eschatological teaching,[87] and it may be that this perspective made it less important for him than we think to set forth a pattern of eschatological expectations consistent with the chronological relation between Jesus' mission and Luke's own writing. And of course Luke does not use the word γενεά to describe his relationship to the time of Jesus' mission and that of the original eye-witnesses of it: he clearly reckons with overlapping generations, and gives a somewhat extended meaning to 'this generation' in Luke 21:32, so that it includes Luke's own time. But there is no warrant for giving it any further extension than that.

One more observation provides further confirmation. In Jesus' promise to his disciples, v. 28, in the parable of the fig-tree and its explanation, v. 29–31, and in the closing exhortation, v. 34–36, the address continues in the second person; by substituting v. 28 for Mark 13:27 Luke even adds to the emphasis on this. The text gives no hint that the 'you' being addressed are any different from the questioners of v. 7.

Nothing in our examination of Luke 21:5–36 has emerged to support the 'delay'-theory. Even if an extended meaning of 'this generation' in v. 32 is thought to be possible, that can only be by straining the phrase itself, and in any case imminence is intended by its predicate. Nor does any other part of the discourse support this theory: not v. 12–19, for example, nor v. 24c.

Elsewhere in Luke–Acts, as we shall see, there occur quite strong statements both of future eschatology, imminent rather than still long delayed from Luke's perspective, and of eschatology seen as already fulfilled. There is in Luke 21:5–36 also a hint of the latter. Although the fall of Jerusalem is predicted in prophetic rather than apocalyptic language, as in Mark 13:14–20, the smooth transition from Luke 21:20–24 to v. 25ff. suggests that that event is to be understood in an eschatological light. Some aspects of God's promise remain to be fulfilled: but equally, some important aspects have been fulfilled already. The time between the resurrection of Jesus and the End is not uneschatological in quality. The question asked of Jesus at the beginning of the passage, v. 7, refers only to the destruction of the Temple. The answer given by Jesus in the following discourse shows that the fall of Jerusalem is not identical with the End, but also that it is not far removed from the End, either in time or significance.

5 The Future Coming of the Kingdom of God

As we have just seen, the context requires that in Luke 21:31f. 'the Kingdom of God' is an eschatological term. It is what comes at the End, after the coming of the Son of Man on a cloud with much power and glory (v. 27). Luke expects it to come soon, within the lifetime of at least some who witnessed the mission of Jesus (v. 32).

That this is Luke's own conviction is shown by the fact that the expression 'the Kingdom of God' is introduced secondarily by him in v. 31. In the corresponding passage in Mark, 13:29, which Luke otherwise follows closely, the subject of 'is near' is left unexpressed, but it is presumably 'the Son of Man' in v. 26f.

This enables us to resume (from section 3 (c) of this chapter) the interpretation of the similar saying in Luke 9:27, 'Truly I tell you, there are some of those standing here who will not taste death until they see the Kingdom of God'. We still cannot determine Luke's reason for leaving out the phrase 'having come with power' (from Mark 9:1), but it is clearly not because he rejects the fully eschatological meaning of 'the Kingdom of God'. Both in 21:31f. and in 9:27, Luke reports, without embarrassment or modification of the essential meaning, the prophecy of Jesus, as contained in Mark, that the consummation of all things, expressed as the arrival of the Kingdom of God, would occur within the lifetime of some of Jesus' contemporaries.

The traditional saying of Jesus, 'the Kingdom of God has drawn near', occurs twice in the charge of the seventy missionaries, Luke 10:9, 11. This fact is of rather special interest, because in Mark 1:15 this formula is the foundation of Jesus' whole preaching. In Matthew the same formula is accepted as the beginning of Jesus' preaching (Matt. 4:17) but also extended to the preaching of John the Baptist (3:2) and that of the Twelve (10:7). But Luke passes over it for the beginning of Jesus' mission, and does not reapply it in either of Matthew's ways. Instead, the foundation of Jesus' mission in Luke is the announcement that the promise of 'the acceptable year of the Lord' has been fulfilled (Luke 4:18–21); and the Twelve are simply commanded 'to preach the Kingdom of God' (9:2). Luke's avoidance of this saying in two such important places has often been taken to show that he wants to eliminate the imminent expectation of the Kingdom of God from Jesus' teaching.[88] Yet, as we have seen in Luke 9:27 and 21:31f., this is clearly not the case. Luke's reason for choosing other formulations in 4:18ff. and 9:2 is quite different, as we shall argue in section

8, below. Therefore there is no reason either to regard the saying in Luke 10:9, 11 as a mere careless acceptance of the wording of Luke's source (cf. Matt. 10:7), which does not really accord with the evangelist's own theology,[89] (Luke has, after all, written the sentence twice in this passage, so that it is not unemphatic in its effect) or to resort to the extravagant theory that Luke understood the charge to apply to missionaries of his own day rather than those sent out by Jesus.

In other passages, too, Luke retains with their full force statements of Jesus looking forward to the Kingdom of God as a fully eschatological entity, especially under the figure of the messianic banquet. As we have seen elsewhere (Chapter Two, section 6) Luke 13:22–30 is a careful composition by Luke out of various pieces of tradition of the teaching of Jesus. Here Luke's main interest is in Jesus' appeal to those who heard his preaching, and in the threat that their place in the Kingdom of God will be taken by the Gentiles, who will join the patriarchs and prophets at the banquet of the Kingdom. But there is no reason to believe that Luke does not take the latter seriously in itself. Only at the last supper does Jesus say that he himself will be part of that banquet. Luke 22:15–18 is no doubt traditional, liturgical language, but it is a longer and more impressive variant of Mark 14:25, and the fact that Luke has preferred this form does not suggest that he was uninterested in the theme. In Luke 22:28–30 (cf. Matt. 19:28) the same imagery occurs in a more developed form: the Kingdom in which the banquet is held is the Kingdom of Jesus, bequeathed to him by the Father, and in turn shared by him with the apostles. In his version of the Lord's Prayer, 11:3, Luke seems unfamiliar with the understanding of ὁ ἄρτος ἡμῶν ὁ ἐπιούσιος as a reference to the messianic banquet: this can be recovered only from Matt. 6:11 in the context of 6:9–13.[91] But it may not be the case that Luke has consciously played down eschatological expectation in the prayer, but rather that in the translation from Aramaic to Greek (long before Matthew and Luke) the rare word ἐπιούσιος was chosen, and Luke and his circle could only interpret it in the sense of food provided one day at a time, perhaps with an echo of the manna once given thus to the Israelites in the desert. But even without an allusion to the banquet of the Kingdom in v. 3, there is no reason why the prayer for the Kingdom in v. 2 should not have been understood by Luke as a prayer for its eschatological fulfilment, as in the other passages mentioned in this paragraph.

In the remaining reference to the Kingdom of God in Luke–Acts, apart from those to be considered in section 8 below, the time-reference and the nature of the Kingdom are not clear. In Luke 6:20b, 'Blessed are you poor, for yours is the Kingdom of God', there may be overtones of the heavenly banquet, because of the following promises that the hungry will be satisfied, the weepers will laugh and the persecuted will have great reward in heaven. In 12:31 the disciples are urged to seek the Kingdom, but whether as already available or as a hope for the future is not clear. Other passages speak of those who qualify for admission to the Kingdom, but do not make it clear whether the Kingdom is being thought of as present or future: thus 7:28; 8:10; 9:62; 18:16f., 24f., 29; though the last of these is linked with a promise of eternal life in the age to come (18:30). The reference to the Kingdom in 19:11 is only a negative one: Jesus rejects a false assumption but says nothing positively about the Kingdom. In 14:15 a Pharisee makes a conventional allusion to the banquet of the Kingdom: Jesus accepts the figure, but the use he makes of it is the same as in 13:28f.: the banquet will indeed take place, but the guests will be other than the Pharisees suppose.

6 Other Expressions of Future Eschatology in Luke

No doubt the strongest and most sustained expression of the expectation of a future, eschatological consummation given in Luke–Acts is in Luke 17:22–37.[92] The Son of Man, on his 'day', will be like a lightning-flash across the sky (v. 24); the day of the Son of Man's apocalypse (ἀποκαλύπτεται) will be like the day when fire and brimstone rained to destroy all the inhabitants of Sodom (v. 30); people outwardly appearing to share the same life will be separated by swift execution of judgement in the night (v. 34f.). Most of the passage is Q-material, which here probably represents very closely the original teaching of Jesus. In the setting of Jesus' preaching it will have been an urgent appeal to his hearers not to let the apparent peace and prosperity of life (eating, drinking, marriage, commerce and industry) lull them into ignoring God's demand for radical righteousness: the contemporaries of Noah and Lot, too, thought there was nothing much wrong! In v. 26, 'so it will be in the days of the Son of Man' is an expression reminiscent of Luke 11:30: as Jonah was a sign to the Ninevites, so will the Son of Man be a sign to this generation. Elsewhere, too, Sodom is used by Jesus as a warning sign of judgement to his contemporaries (Luke 10:12/Matt. 10:15; Matt. 11:23f.). There is strong emphasis on moral challenge and warning. The consummation envisaged lies fully within the eschatological frame of reference, as is shown perhaps even more by v. 34f. ('one will be taken and the other left') than by the apocalyptic mode of the coming of the Son of Man.

But what happens to these teachings at the level of Luke's composition? First we have to note that several details in the speech are problematic. The 'days of the Son of Man' in v. 26 can no longer refer to the days of Jesus' mission, for they are now in the past: apparently they can only refer in general terms to the period leading up to the 'day' of v. 30. '*One of* the days of the Son of Man' in v. 22 is a unique expression, whose meaning is quite uncertain: it may look back to the days of Jesus' earthly life, but that is made difficult by the forward look in v. 23f.; it may look forward to the day of the Son of Man (v. 24), or to the period inaugurated by it, but that is awkward, because nowhere else in the tradition is there either any suggestion that there will be a series of 'parousias' or any interest in an extended period lying beyond the final coming of the Son of Man from heaven, and it is unclear what else 'one of the days' could mean.[93] Also quite uncertain is the meaning of the figure about the corpse and the vultures in v. 37. The question 'where?' suggests a connexion with v. 21 (the Kingdom is present because of its signs in Jesus' mission?) or with v. 23 (false teachers will always gather a flock of followers?), and there are many other possibilities.[94]

There is one more curious problem in the passage: in this case an examination may help us to penetrate Luke's eschatological understanding with a little more illumination. v. 31f. have been added by Luke to his source. V. 32, 'Remember Lot's wife', was no doubt suggested to Luke by the reference to Lot's flight from Sodom in v. 29; then Luke brought in v. 31, borrowed from Mark 13:15f., because of its warning against 'turning back', which is what Lot's wife did. As a vivid call to single-minded response to Jesus' message the passage is most effective. But the importation spoils the possibility of any consistent or clear portrayal of the expected course of events in the eschatological consummation. For the warning against going down from the roof into the house to collect one's belongings is out of place in the context of the day when the Son of Man is revealed, when one is taken and the other left from the bed or from the hand-mill. The warning has to do with flight from an earthly, historical disaster, and as such is quite appropriate in the context of Mark 13:15f., whence Luke got it, for there the reference is to flight from Jerusalem during the war: but when the parousia comes, there is nowhere to flee to, for the elect will be taken and the others left (v. 34f.) right across the world (v. 24).[95]

From these considerations we may draw the following conclusions: (1) Either Luke thought of the parousia in more earthly, less cosmic terms than Paul, Mark, Matthew and other NT writers (as was suggested above with reference to Luke 21:25–28/Mark 13:24–27), or his concentration on the spiritual challenge of eschatology led him to accept a telling phrase (v. 31f.) at the cost of consistency in his eschatological picture. (2) Luke has retained here the words of Jesus' eschatological preaching as transmitted through Q, because he understood the importance of their significance as spiritual challenge. Because of the passage of time, the chronological perspective of Jesus' eschatological teaching has been strained. Some parts of the discourse are no longer clearly comprehensible to us, and it is possible that Luke himself may not have been completely clear on the meaning of some of the material he received from the tradition (e.g. v. 37). But there is no reason to doubt that he expected an ultimate, eschatological climax at some time in the future, even if he was neither able nor particularly concerned to describe consistently how that would occur. (3) In this passage, nothing is said directly as to whether the End would be imminent or long delayed. There are some hints of delay, e.g. the 'longing' of v. 22, and the unexpected insertion into the eschatological context of v. 25, 'but first he must suffer many things and be rejected by this generation'. But from Luke's perspective that is hardly avoidable: a delay has indeed already taken place between Jesus' lifetime and Luke's; but that does not necessarily mean that Luke expected a further, extensive delay after his own time.

The eschatological teaching in Luke 17:22–37 is concerned much more to warn the unrepentant about the coming of judgement than it is to promise salvation to the faithful. The opposite is the emphasis in the following parable, Luke 18:2–8a. J. Jeremias has shown that the difficult Greek syntax in v. 7b is due to an underlying Aramaic expression; and this makes it certain that the whole of v. 2–8a is pre-Lucan,[96] though it may be doubted whether v. 6–8a was from the very beginning transmitted along with v. 2–5 as a unified piece of Jesus' teaching: more likely, v. 6–8a was a very early interpretation of the parable, made during the Aramaic stage of transmission (cf. Luke 16:8, where another shocking parable of Jesus is given an interpretation introduced by a similar formula). Luke's introduction in v. 1 looks as if the evangelist thought the parable was an encouragement to prayer: but actually the parable as received by Luke, enlarged by v. 6–8a, assumes that people *are* praying, and encourages continued hope: so the emphasis in v. 1 should be seen in *μὴ ἐγκακεῖν* not to lose heart in critical or desperate circumstances. For our present purpose we do not need to determine what the basic parable, v. 2–5, meant as originally spoken by Jesus: but the end of v. 1 agrees with v. 7 in seeing the setting of the larger piece in a time of severe persecution: it is rather reminiscent of Mark 13:20, 'If the Lord had not shortened the days, no flesh would have been saved: but, for the sake of the elect whom he has elected, he has shortened the days'. The Aramaic interpretation of the parable may have arisen in a time when Christians in Palestine were undergoing the sort of persecution mentioned in Luke 21:12–17, or rather in the more forceful parallels in Matt. 10:16–22, 24ff.; 24:9–13, 16–22. As we have seen elsewhere (Chapter Three, section 6, 'The Persecution of Christians according to Luke'; and the present chapter, section 4, p. 153–157, on Luke 21:12–19), Luke himself does not take too grim a view of the persecution suffered by Christians: so the note struck in Luke 18:1–8a is a little surprising. But then it is not at all surprising that a sudden switch comes in v. 8b, 'But will the Son of Man find faith on the earth, when he comes?' This is a typical Lucan note, and v. 8b is almost certainly to be ascribed to Luke's hand.[97] Faith as the means to salvation is a frequent theme in all the synoptic gospels and Acts, but it is especially in Luke–Acts that a concern is found about the *persistence* of believers in their faith: so Luke 17:5; 22:32; Acts 14:22f.; 16:5; cf. *πιστεύειν* in Luke 8:12f. (not in pars.) and *ἐν ὑπομονῇ* in v. 15 (not in pars.). This is not to deny that Luke 18:8b may have been a genuine saying of Jesus: it is its present location that is certainly due to Luke.

Once more, the effect is that a piece of traditional eschatological teaching is applied by Luke in the sense of spiritual challenge to faithful and persistent discipleship. But what can we learn from this passage about

Luke's concept of eschatology? The coming of the Son of Man, v. 8b, is no doubt to be understood with reference to the ultimate parousia, as in 17:24, 30. H. Conzelmann sees in Luke's introduction, v. 1, the expectation of a long period of time before that happens, since disciples are encouraged to pray 'always' and 'not to lose heart'.[98] Yet if this had been the point of Luke's concern it would have been simple for him to drop the phrase ἐν τάχει, which is emphatic where it stands. The editorial introduction certainly hints at a crisis of confidence, but the delay of the parousia is not the only possible reason for that. Even if the delay experienced up to Luke's time may have been of some concern to him, there is no hint in what follows that he expected the delay to continue much longer.

For our present purpose we can deal much more summarily with the eschatological parables in Luke 12:35–48.[99] No doubt as taught originally by Jesus these were 'crisis-parables' in which he called on his contemporaries for repentance and faith. At various stages of their transmission, no doubt already in the oral stage, and certainly in Q and by Luke, they received gradual modifications, in which the delay of the eschatological climax, already being experienced, is acknowledged: but the message remains essentially the same, that those who have heard Jesus' preaching and have begun to take it seriously must be prepared for the parousia of the Son of Man at any time. Luke acknowledges the delay that has already occurred, but in this passage does nothing to suggest that a further, long delay is to be expected. In this respect his editorial direction is quite similar to Matthew's, and his eschatology not markedly different from that of, say, Mark or Paul or the author of Hebrews. Like Matthew, Luke has gone beyond Q in the degree to which all this material is seen as addressed not in general to Jesus' original hearers but to his disciples and especially to the leaders of the church. Nevertheless, there is one tantalizing point to observe about Luke's arrangement. These parables about watchfulness, in which the church is called on to be prepared for the parousia at an unknown time in the future, are followed, without any interruption or pause, by a long section which Luke no doubt understood to have connotations of future eschatology, but which even in its present form deals with the crisis within Palestinian Judaism caused by the mission of Jesus, 12:49–13:9 (or even, with scarcely a break, to the end of chapter 16). This fact cannot be explained very clearly or precisely, but it suggests that Luke preserved, more consciously than Matthew, a connexion between the historical crisis of Jesus' mission and the ultimate crisis of the parousia and the last judgement. Here, too, we find Luke not concerned to distil a neat doctrine of eschatology, but to show how Jesus' warnings of judgement (and that, for Luke, is above all what eschatology means) have already been fulfilled in the case of Judaism and must still be heeded in the case of his disciples. The past and the future of eschatology are not essentially different.

7 Future Eschatology in Acts

As is well known, the material relevant to future eschatology in Acts is only slight, and can quickly be reviewed. There are no long discourses on eschatology at all. Of the short references to future eschatology, the most striking is in 3:20f., where Luke has taken up, and to some extent reworked in his own way, a very ancient tradition of Christian mission-preaching, marked by eschatological expressions almost obsolete in the rest of the New Testament.[100] Even here, v. 21 draws attention more to the ascension than to the consummation. For Luke, Jesus' heavenly session describes no more idle time of waiting, but is a very active theological concept. Correspondingly, the ascension has decisive theological importance. Nevertheless, Luke does not think of the heavenly session as lasting for ever, for it lasts only until 'the restoration of all things'. How long will that be? E. Gräßer sees a 'retarding factor' in the divine necessity (δεῖ) of the heavenly session, and so recruits this passage as evidence for his theory that Luke teaches a doctrine of further, indefinite delay of the parousia.[101] But he can do this only by unjustifiably ignoring the eschatological meaning of 'times of refreshment' in v. 20,[102] and taking the latter to mean merely the forgiveness following on repentance (v. 19). In fact v. 20 holds out the possibility that the eschatological consummation may come quite quickly. This is an unusual note in Luke–Acts; even more surprising is the suggestion that the coming of the consummation depends in some way on Israel's willingness to repent.[103] F. Hahn has shown that Luke is here using very ancient Christian tradition, which he has however edited and adapted in his characteristic way.[104] For our present purpose the important point is that Luke was willing to take up this ancient eschatological tradition, even though it does not represent the climax or indicate the main thrust of Peter's sermon in which it is set. (Acts 3:12–26). Subtle interpretation may detect a hint of 'delay' (v. 21) or a hint of 'imminence' (v. 20): but Luke in fact emphasizes no particular time-reference: he simply accepts the traditional Christian expectation that the parousia will come at some time.

The eschatological consummation is mentioned with direct reference to Jesus only three times more in Acts, and always very briefly. In 1:11 his future coming on a cloud is mentioned. At first sight this seems quite unimportant: the main emphasis of the context is on the ascension, and the future parousia seems to be made subordinate and almost incidental. From Acts 2:33 onwards it is explicitly taught by Luke that the importance of the ascension is the continuing relationship between Jesus in heaven and his disciples on earth, through the Holy Spirit. Acts 1:11 could have been formulated to point forward to this; but instead it mentions the ultimate parousia, apparently as a consolation for the apostles in the separation they are experiencing. The instruction not to keep looking into heaven may suggest a 'delay', but the real emphasis is to direct their attention to what is to happen imminently, in the gift of the Spirit.

In the other two examples the reference to the parousia has to do with the last judgement, a more typically Lucan emphasis. In 17:30f. Paul's hearers in the Areopagus-council are called on to repent now because of the coming judgement-day which God has fixed for Jesus to judge the world. Though brief, this statement forms the climax of Paul's speech, which otherwise has emphasized the accessibility of God to the genuine seeker. Similarly, Peter's address to Cornelius and his friends ends with the declaration that Jesus' resurrection points forward to his function as judge of the living and the dead, though forgiveness of sins is available to those who believe in him (Acts 10:41–43). In both of these examples, nothing is said about the ascension, the heavenly session or the Holy Spirit, but the line of thought runs straight from the resurrection to the judgement. In 10:41–43 nothing is said about the timing of the judgement, but in 17:30f. the hint is of imminence rather than delay. With these two passages may be mentioned 24:25, where Paul frightens Felix with a discussion 'about righteousness, self-control and the coming judgement' as implications of the story of Jesus (v. 24). Again, nothing is said about when this judgement is expected to happen, except that the prospect is realistic enough to cause Felix concern.[105]

There remain five examples, which perhaps stand somewhat on the margin of eschatological doctrine. They all occur in speeches of Paul in the various debates and formal hearings after his arrest, and all have to do with the hope of Israel (or, of the Pharisees) in the resurrection of the dead at the final consummation: Acts 23:6; 24:15, 21; 26:6–8; 28:20. But in each case the point is not really to look forward to what will happen at the end (as is the case with the similar terminology in Luke 14:14, cf. 18:30) but rather to argue from the general Pharisaic belief in the ultimate resurrection of all humanity to the reasonableness of the Christian belief in the resurrection of Jesus as the first instance of it (cf. 26:23). In a formal sense, this is rather like Paul's concept of Christ's resurrection as the 'first-fruits' of the future resurrection of those who are in him, 1 Cor. 15:20–23, cf. I Thess. 4:14. But the passages in Acts lack the Christological and soteriological thrust of Paul, and sound more like an academic debating-point. Nevertheless, when Luke claims the doctrine of a future, general resurrection as common ground between the Pharisees and the Christians, it at least means that he accepts it as a widely-agreed part of Christian doctrine, to which he himself also subscribes.

The sum of all this is that the eschatological hope directed towards the future is certainly present in Acts, though greatly reduced in prominence by comparison with the Gospel of Luke. How is this difference between Luke's two volumes to be explained?

One theory is that the two volumes were written a considerable time apart, and that Luke had in the meantime modified his views: that by the time he wrote Acts, long after the Gospel, the further experience of the non-arrival of the parousia led him to play down the significance of eschatology.[106] Our conclusion in Chapter One makes this theory unlikely. The author of the Gospel of Luke is already a mature, well-formed theologian. In his first volume, the ideas which characterize volume two are already strongly represented. There are clear signs of coordination in the composition of the two volumes, not only in the sense that Acts echoes themes established in the Gospel but also that the Gospel is written with an eye forward to matters that could only be developed in the second volume.

An alternative explanation may be sought by consideration of Luke's sources. The point here is not that Luke mechanically reproduced such sources as by chance happened to be available, so that the balance of eschatology between the Gospel and Acts depends on the accidental preservation of more eschatology in the teaching of Jesus and less in that of the apostles. The question is rather whether the Jesus-tradition was intrinsically more eschatological than the apostolic tradition. The Jesus-tradition had a strong element of futuristic eschatology, partly because Jesus cast his message largely in terms of the Kingdom of God and the Son of Man, and partly because both the death and the resurrection of Jesus were such immense experiences for his disciples that his whole life and work soon came to be interpreted in a heavily eschatological way (cf. Mark 15:37f./Matt. 27:51–53). On the other hand, the tradition about the apostles and their associates, as Luke received it, may well have had a much smaller emphasis on future eschatological expectations, except in so far as the various preachers appealed to and reproduced the teaching of Jesus. Similarly, Acts contains very little of Jesus' ethical teaching. It is not to be thought that the apostles were uninterested in Jesus' ethical teaching or did not pass it on in their own work. Luke mentions in Acts both eschatology and ethics just enough to make it clear that the teaching of Jesus was in fact adhered to and taught to others by the early teachers and missionaries. But that has been expounded at length in the Gospel. The subject-matter of Acts is the new, distinctive set of experiences and problems that arose from the church in the time after the death and resurrection of Jesus. These problems included the implications of all that had been experienced in connexion with Jesus for the relationship of his disciples to the Israel with which he had come into sharp conflict; the nature of the Christian community as fellowship and institution; and the possibility of relationships with the Roman state and the Gentile world. These concerns had been prominent in the church long before Luke's time, and remained so for his generation as well.

Many interpreters have subscribed to P. Vielhauer's well-known remark that the very existence of Acts indicates that Luke does not think eschatologically, since one does not write history if one expects the end of the world to come at any time.[107] Against this E. Franklin has pertinently observed 'that Mark, who believed in an imminent parousia, still thought it worth while to write a gospel, and one which is not unconscious of the problem of continuing history'.[108] Once it is granted, as I think it must be for Acts, that a 'history' is not necessarily intended to preserve ancient information for the benefit of future generations, but may be intended to serve a practical, immediate need, then the case of Acts is not in principle different from that of other carefully-composed works in the New Testament, such as the Epistles to the Romans and to the Hebrews. The authors of these epistles did not necessarily believe that history would go on much longer, but in the meantime there was work to be done which justified the effort of vigorous thought and careful argument. The writing of Acts, or rather of a gospel extending into the apostolic age instead of ending with the resurrection of Jesus, was apparently Luke's original idea: but it did not necessarily arise because Luke had a different eschatological perspective from that of his predecessors. (One might speculate why it was not John who wrote an 'Acts'!)

Again, the question has sometimes been asked, why Luke does not end Acts with a reference to future eschatology.[109] Certainly Luke leaves his readers with a look forward into the continuing mission of the church, rather than towards the final consummation. But almost exactly the same is true of the Gospel of Matthew, in the case of which there can be no doubt about the seriousness of eschatological expectation. Matthew ends with the risen Jesus referring to 'the end of the age' (the same phrase from which the eschatological discourse begins, Matt. 24:3): but all the same, the emphasis falls not on this but on the period of which it will be the terminus, that of the church's mission (Matt. 28:18–20).

8 The Presence of the Kingdom of God

In the Jesus-tradition we find a double proclamation about the Kingdom of God. On the one hand, the Kingdom is already present in Jesus' own mission. This is explicit in Matt. 12:28/Luke 11:20, and the same is probably meant in the narratives of the miracles of Jesus, especially as interpreted in the passage about John the Baptist's inquiry from prison (Matt. 11:2–11/Luke 7:18–28), and in Jesus' associating with sinners and forgiving sins. On the other hand, the Kingdom is said to be coming soon from the standpoint of Jesus' mission: e.g. in the initial proclamation of Jesus in Mark, 1:15, and the majority of statements about the coming of the Kingdom. In Jesus' teaching the main emphasis is on the imminent coming of the Kingdom: but this expectation is so intense, and the signs of it in Jesus' activity so strong, that the Kingdom can even occasionally be spoken of as present already.[110]

This same duality of reference to the Kingdom is to be found in Paul, and in Matthew (though Q). In Luke the same duality is maintained, but with a difference of emphasis both from the Jesus-tradition and from Paul and Matthew. Luke lets the accent fall more heavily on the presence of the Kingdom.

The most conspicuous means by which he has done this is, as O. Merk has shown, the expression 'to preach the Kingdom', and the like.[111] Such phrases amount to one quarter of the total references to the Kingdom of God in Luke–Acts, and are unique to Luke. The key to this special Lucan usage is Luke 4:43, where Jesus refuses to be held at Capernaum, because 'I must preach the Kingdom of God in the other cities also, for it is for this that I was sent'. No mention has been made in 4:31–41 of the content of Jesus' preaching, so it is implied that the place where Jesus has already 'preached the Kingdom of God' is in his sermon at Nazareth, 4:16–27. But the explicit content of that sermon is the assertion by Jesus that the scriptural promise of 'the acceptable year of the Lord' has been fulfilled in the beginning of his mission, because of his endowment with the Holy Spirit. This means that 'preaching the Kingdom of God' is the same as preaching the fulfilment of the 'year of the Lord': that is, the *presence* of the Kingdom in Jesus' mission is being proclaimed. Whatever else the difficult verse Luke 16:16 may mean, it at least means as Merk has rightly pointed out, that the preaching of the Kingdom of God dates from the time of John the Baptist: that is, in Lucan terms, from the moment when Jesus was baptized and received the Holy Spirit (Luke 3:21f.).[112] 'To proclaim the Kingdom of God' is the task not only of Jesus himself, but also of his disciples, including the Twelve (Luke 9:2) and even an anonymous, rather hesitant, isolated follower (Luke 9:60). Acts begins and ends on this note: in Acts 1:3 the risen Jesus tells the Apostles, during the forty days before the ascension, 'the things about the Kingdom of God'; in Acts 28:31 the very last thing Luke tells us is that Paul was freely and openly 'proclaiming the Kingdom of God and teaching the things about Lord Jesus Christ'. It is true that in Acts 'the Kingdom of God' has become more or less synonymous with 'the Christian message': but we should nor prejudge the significance of this with an adverb like 'merely': in the light of the Gospel of Luke we should take seriously the possibility that Luke seriously meant to say, the Kingdom of God is a present reality for the disciples of Jesus, which they seek to share with whoever will listen. H. Conzelmann repeatedly asserts that when Luke uses such expressions as 'to proclaim the Kingdom' he is replacing the proclamation of the 'nearness' of the Kingdom with 'timeless expressions of its nature'.[113] In fact, expressions about the *nature* of the Kingdom are imbedded in the earliest tradition of the teaching of Jesus, in the parabolic formula 'the Kingdom of Heaven is like this' (Mark 4:26, cf. v. 30). But it is Matthew who most frequently retains, and perhaps sometimes secondarily introduces, this formula or a variant of it; for he has it some ten times, but Luke has it only twice (13:18f., 20f.). It is more likely that 'to proclaim the Kingdom' means to announce its presence.

The most explicit statement of the presence of the Kingdom is the Q-saying, Matt. 12:28/Luke 11:20: the exorcisms of Jesus prove that the Kingdom of God ἔφθασεν ἐφ' ὑμᾶς. This expression almost certainly means 'has arrived upon you (suddenly, before you expected)'.[114] That Luke retains this saying shows that he (and of course Matthew likewise!) at least agrees with what it says.[115] Luke (alone) appears to have a similar saying in Luke 17:20f.: but this is a difficult passage, whose interpretation is disputed: we shall have to return to it for a more detailed discussion. Meanwhile, we can note that Luke has a number of features which seem to point in the same direction, although the phrase 'Kingdom of God' is not used. First, the familiar cliché that Luke has a special sympathy for sinners and outcasts may in fact be a hint of his special emphasis in eschatology. If Luke shows us, more often and more emphatically than Mark and Matthew, how Jesus associated with sinners, even sharing meals with them (e.g., in addition to Mark 2:1–12 pars., 13–17 pars., Luke 7:36–50 beside Mark 14:3–9/Matt. 26:6–13; Luke 15:1f.(f).; 18:9–14; 19:1–10), it may well be because he is especially convinced of, and especially wishes to announce the presence of the Kingdom of God in Jesus' mission. Jesus' vision of the fall of Satan, reported only by Luke (10:18), falls into this pattern. (See below, section 9 (c).) In this connexion we may also mention the figure of God's 'visitation' of his people: this is borrowed from the Old Testament, but in the New Testament is almost confined to Luke–Acts (Luke 1:68, 78; 7:16; 19:44; Acts 15:14; otherwise only 1 Peter 2:12). As in the Old Testament, so here 'visitation' can be for either blessing or judgement: the former is meant in five of the six Lucan passages; only in Luke 19:44 is it for judgement. It may be that Luke understood this term to mean the same as 'the Lord's acceptable year' in Luke 4:19, and if so this is another indirect way of referring to the presence of the Kingdom: in Jesus' birth, in his raising of the widow's son at Nain, and in his entry to Jerusalem with a spiritual challenge to Judaism, God has 'visited' Israel; in the gift of the Holy Spirit to Cornelius and his houehold, God has 'visited' the Gentiles also.

It is now time to turn to Luke 17:20f.: 'Asked by the Pharisees when the Kingdom of God was coming, he answered them and said, "The Kingdom of God is not coming with observation, nor will they say 'Lo here!' or 'there!' for lo, the Kingdom of God is among you" '.

We may regard the long debate over the meaning of ἐντός as finally settled.[116] It cannot mean 'within' in a spiritual sense, least of all in an answer of Jesus to the Pharisees. It most likely means 'among'; the meaning 'within your grasp' or 'available to you' is also possible, but the decision between this and 'among' does not in the long run make too much difference to the sense. Recent exegesis has been much more concerned with another problem, that of the temporal force of ἐστίν. Is Jesus saying, '(Now, already) the Kingdom of God is among you', or something like '(When the day of the Son of Man comes, then suddenly) the Kingdom of God is among you'? It is this question which makes it uncertain whether we should add Luke 17:21 to the evidence in favour of the view that Luke emphasizes the presence of the Kingdom of God rather than its future coming. The scholars who take ἐστίν as having a future reference, despite its grammatical tense, are numerous:[117] and there are good reasons in the context for this view. For one thing, the following discourse about the coming of the Son of Man certainly refers to the future. Although Luke elsewhere can speak of both the Kingdom of God and the Son of Man as being either present or future, it is odd if in such close connexion he should have Jesus say that the one is present but the other is future, especially if (as is generally assumed) the terms are virtually synonymous. If ἐστίν has a future sense, that difficulty is removed. Secondly, what sense is there in saying 'they *will* say "Lo here!" or "there" 'about something that is already present, though either unrecognized or only recognized in faith? But if the Kingdom of God is to come like a flash of lightning on the day of the Son of Man, an unknown day in the future, then at that time they will *not* say 'Lo here' or 'there', because there will be no point in it: in contrast, they *will* say 'Lo, there, lo here' (v. 23) in the period of waiting that is to be endured before the day of the Son of Man (v. 24). In v. 23 the subject of 'they will say' is easily supplied: it is false teachers, apocalyptic enthusiasts; in v. 21 it is vaguer: 'people'. If ἐστίν has a future reference, then there is a contrast intended between v. 21 and 23: on the day of the Son of Man 'they' will no longer be able to say what they will be saying in the interval; and so it is implied that the apparently vague 'they' of v. 21 are the same people as the 'they' of v. 23.[118] But that means that the sense of v. 21a can only be gathered retrospectively, from v. 23, which is rather awkward. Indeed, on either interpretation of ἐστίν, v. 21a reads awkwardly in its context. We must also consider the principal objection to taking ἐστίν as future. Coming after πότε ἔρχεται in v. 20a and ἐροῦσιν in v. 21a, the present tense is striking: it would have been more natural for Luke to write ἔσται if that is what he meant; it may well be that the present is written deliberately, to emphasize the unacknowledged and unexpected presence of the Kingdom of God in the very midst of the community where Jesus' questioners were.

It may be possible to shed some more light on these problems by considering the literary composition of the whole section, 17:20–37. As a starting-point we can take the detailed analysis provided by R. Schnackenburg.[119] By means of arguments based on language, style and tradition-criticism, Schnackenburg concludes that the greatest part of the section was taken over by Luke from Q. To Luke's own composition are to be attributed the question of the Pharisees in v. 20, the address to the disciples in v. 22a, the rest of v. 22 except for 'days will come' (which links directly on to v. 23), v. 25, v. 32, and the insertion of v. 31 (borrowed from Mark 13:15f.). Schnackenburg leaves unresolved, because the arguments seemed to him to be evenly balanced, the question whether v. 21b, 'for lo, the Kingdom of God is among you', was in Q or was added by Luke. He suggests that v. 20b–21(a) was attached to the following discourse in Q, but originally was a separate saying, joined on in Q by key-word-association through 'lo here or there'.

I believe we can with profit take Schnackenburg's analysis a little further. It seems unlikely that v. 20b–21a existed as a separate saying without 21b (or something like it): for then we could have only two negative statements, which seem to desiderate a positive antithesis, and that is what 21b provides. On the other hand, as we have seen, v. 21a sits awkwardly in its context, whereas its near-twin, v. 23a, fits naturally in its setting. It may be suggested, therefore, that the original saying consisted of v. 20b and 21b, 'The Kingdom of God is not coming with observation, for lo, the Kingdom of God is among you'. A detached saying in this form would not only agree with 11:20 concerning the presence of the Kingdom of God, but also be a quite close parallel to 11:29–32 and 12:54–56. These three passages are all polemical, and criticize Jesus' contemporaries for demanding apocalyptic or messianic signs while failing to notice the eschatological character of the events taking place before their eyes. So although Schnackenburg is probably correct in assigning v. 20a (the question of the Pharisees and the formulation of v. 20bf. as Jesus' answer to it) to Luke's composition, Luke has nevertheless appropriately understood the thrust of the saying by giving it such a setting. Schnackenburg's analysis of v. 22–37 may be accepted without reservation. We may, however, be more hesitant as to whether the core of v. 20f. was already attached to it before Luke. For the separation between v. 20f. and 22ff. is marked by more than the change of address (which, as Schnackenburg says, can easily be explained as Lucan edition dividing up an originally unified whole): for we must still take account of the troublesome v. 21a. I suggest this can best be explained as having been inserted by Luke precisely for the purpose of linking the saying v. 20b, 21b on to the discourse, v. 22ff. The point then is: people may indeed say, with regard to the day of the Son of Man, which has not yet arrived, 'Lo there! lo here!': but with regard to the Kingdom of God they cannot say that, because the Kingdom is here already. The future tense, 'they will not say', in v. 21a, is certainly awkward, as R. H. Hiers has well pointed out: but it is copied from v. 23a, and the point is precisely to contrast the two statements. If this is correct, the conclusion from this passage regarding Luke's view of eschatology is that the 'day' of the Son of Man lies in the future, but the Kingdom of God is already present.

In view of the abundant evidence we have found that in Luke–Acts the Kingdom of God is regarded as a present reality as well as a hope for the future, we should consider the possibility that Acts 14:22, too, should be considered in this light. On their return-journey through Lystra, Iconium and Antioch-in-Pisidia, Paul and Barnabas exhort the new disciples to remain in the faith, and explain to them 'that we must enter the Kingdom of God through many afflictions'. Some explain this as a reference to individual eschatology, but the arguments for this are not strong.[120] Others think this may be a genuine Pauline reminiscence (cf. 1 Thess. 3:2–5), in which case the reference to 'entering the Kingdom of God' will no doubt be to what happens after the parousia.[121] But while, as we have seen, Luke did not think of the parousia as long delayed, the context here suggests that he thought of 'entering the Kingdom of God' as something still more immediate. The 'afflictions' are referred to just after it has been mentioned

(v. 19) that at Lystra Paul was stoned until apparently dead, at the instigation of Jews who came from Antioch and Iconium. The context does not have any obvious reference to eschatology. It is therefore quite likely that the meaning is that persecution is an attendant circumstance of entering the Kingdom, i.e. of entering now, by faith, the Kingdom which is a present reality. The fact that the pioneer missionaries and their earliest converts were rejected and sometimes very roughly treated by 'official' Judaism is no argument against the reality of the Kingdom of God, which came with their message.

9 Eschatology Already Fulfilled

It is a general characteristic of early Christian theology that 'eschatology' is no longer entirely a matter of the future, as it was in contemporary Jewish theology.[121a] For it was evident to all Christians that the whole phenomenon they had experienced in Jesus' life and work and death and resurrection was somehow a fulfilment of God's promises concerning the consummation of his intention for the world. Everywhere there is tension between the concepts that 'salvation', God's ultimate gift, is something already present and that it is something still awaited. This is as much true for those writers for whom the future consummation is a prominent and lively hope, such as Paul, Mark and Matthew, as it is for someone like John, who emphasizes the eschatological quality of the present. We now have to ask where Luke stands in relation to this matter.

We have already noted the importance to Luke of the theme that the Kingdom of God is already a present reality. We hope now to see how Luke understands the fulfilment of eschatological hopes, from a number of other perspectives: the Holy Spirit, the terminology of 'fulfilment', and the present experience of judgement and salvation.

(a) Luke clearly regards the coming of the Holy Spirit upon the disciples of Jesus at Pentecost as an 'eschatological' event.[122] In the Old Testament and post-OT Judaism the renewal of the Spirit was part of the expectation associated with the age to come, and Luke's long quotation from Joel in Acts 2:17–21 explicitly draws the connexion between this ancient hope and the fulfilment of it in the experience of the apostles and their associates. One of the few modifications Luke has made to the LXX text of Joel 3:1–6 in his quotation is to substitute in the first clause *ἐν ταῖς ἐσχάταις ἡμέραις* for LXX's *μετὰ ταῦτα* so it is Luke's own initiative which emphasizes that this event points to the arrival of the 'last' days. But what is meant by the 'last' days? The phrase can mean either that the consummation is imminent, for there are not many days to run before it comes, or else that the expected new age, the age when the fulfilment of God's promises is actually experienced, has already arrived.[123] In the light of his eschatological statements elsewhere, Luke may actually intend both meanings: but the emphasis clearly falls on the fulfilment rather than on the imminent expectation. This is evident from his description of the coming of the Spirit and its effect on the apostles and those who hear them. The language about the wind, fire, nations and languages echoes the eschatological description in Isa. 66:15f. (LXX). Test. Judah 25:3 speaks of 'one tongue' as part of the eschatological fulfilment. There are some hints in Acts 2 of the eschatological theme of the new covenant. The Jewish celebration of Pentecost as a commemoration of the giving of the Law at Sinai does not become explicit in our sources until after 70 AD,[124] and Luke does not use here language connected with 'law' or 'covenant': but Philo, in a midrash on Exod. 19 (preceding the giving the Law at Sinai) speaks of a marvellous, heavenly sound which was changed into 'flaming fire like πνευμα and of a voice coming out of the stream of fire from heaven and speaking in the language customary for the hearers.[125] Rabbinic tradition held that God's voice was divided into the seventy languages of the world when the Law was offered at Sinai.[126] All this suggests an interpretation of the Pentecost-event as a re-enactment of God's coming to Israel to establish the Sinai-covenant, so that the new covenant of the end-time is hinted at.[127] The quotation from Joel also shows how Luke understood the fulfilment of the 'last days'. Luke does not explicitly quote the Old Testament remarkably often: but his quotations sometimes mark a decisive new turn in the story, and are sometimes quite long. The length of the quotation may serve to underline the importance of the point being made, but more importantly, it is Luke's habit not to abbreviate his quotations (as John notably does) but to keep on until he has reached a further significant statement, even at the cost of including some unimportant material in between. Thus, in Luke 3:4–6 he continues the quotation from Isa. 40:3ff. at much greater length than the other three evangelists, so that he can include the words 'and all flesh will see God's salvation' in 3:6; but all the details in 3:5 are unnecessary. Similarly, in Acts 2:17–21 the first and most important point is the outpouring of the Spirit upon 'all flesh', which Luke interprets, by his insertion of v. 18c into the Joel-text, as causing prophecy. Then he wants to go on to the words 'and it shall be that whoever calls on the name of the Lord will be saved' in v. 21, which makes the same point as Luke 3:6. There is no need to regard the heavenly and earthly portents in v. 19f. as having any great significance for Luke at this point, though in the light of Luke 21:25f. he presumably also felt no need to do away with them. At any rate, in the further course of Acts Luke pays no more regard to heavenly portents and little to the apocalyptic consummation, whereas the gift of the Spirit to 'all flesh', people of all races, and the 'salvation' of 'all who call on the name of the Lord', become the real theme of the book. He understands the 'last days' as the age of the Holy Spirit and of salvation.

It is important here not to be misled by over-subtle quibbling over definitions. Sometimes it is said that Luke postpones the eschatological consummation into the remote and indefinite future, and accepts the doctrine of the Spirit as a consolation for the delayed 'parousia' and the absence of Jesus, and therefore 'thinks uneschatologically'. It is implied by this interpretation that Luke has withdrawn from the sharp distinctiveness of Christian faith, experience and doctrine represented by earlier theologians, most notably Paul, and has substituted for it a low-keyed, undemanding unexciting piety which can accommodate itself easily to the prevailing culture of the Roman world.[128] It is the point of our present discussion of Acts 2 that Luke is in fact saying just the opposite. The ultimate, apocalyptic consummation of eschatology has for him somewhat receded in importance, if not in time. But what he emphasizes instead is not a long-extended time of waiting, with a rather low voltage of religious experience, but a most joyful and confident statement that the essential expectations of the end-time have already been realized. Jesus is by no means absent. The conceptual model Luke uses to describe the relationship between Jesus and his disciples, after the ascension, is different from that of 'indwelling', shared by Paul and John: instead he mostly thinks of a vertical communication between Jesus, enthroned at the right hand of the Father, and his disciples on earth, mediated by the Spirit.[129] Though different, that model does not imply a weaker relationship. In fact, for Luke the time of the church is a period charged with eschatology: the powers of the new age are at work wherever people respond to the message and 'name' of Jesus in faith.

(b) The concept of 'fulfilment' of God's promises is associated with Jesus in many parts of the New Testament. In the case of Luke this takes a distinctive form, which is instructive for the interpretation of his eschatology.[130] This applies not only to the fulfilment of scripture or of prophecy[131] but in a more general way to the fulfilment of God's intentions for the world through Jesus. The most striking example is Luke 4:21, where Jesus declares the fulfilment in his own person of the 'passage' he has just read to the synagogue-congregation, from Isa. 61:1f. and 58:6. This incident makes a different impact from the famous formula-quotations in Matthew. The latter have the form of reflection by the evangelist on the connexion between the prophecies of scripture and the mission of Jesus, on which he looks back over the gap of many years. Of course the incident in Luke 4:16–21 arises in the same way, but dramatically it has the effect of confronting Jesus' audience, to their astonishment, with the fulfilment of their ancient hopes of salvation. But does Luke intend the word 'today' to be heard by his readers as applying by extension also to their own time? This is denied by P. Vielhauer,[132] H. Conzelmann[133] and E. Gräßer[134], who contrast Luke 4:21 with 2 Cor. 6:2, 'Lo, now is the acceptable time; lo, now is the day of salvation', on the ground that Luke puts the 'time of salvation' back in the past, in the time of Jesus, which is different from his own time. But against this, it must be borne in mind that Luke's gospel and Paul's epistle cannot be directly compared without taking account of the difference of medium: Paul can address his readers directly; Luke prefers to do so only indirectly, through the drama of his narrative.[135] Luke nowhere retracts the assertion that God's promises have been fulfilled, or suggests that the 'fulfilment' was somehow only temporary.[136] On the contrary, Luke's whole style of writing emphasizes the fulfilment that is not merely given and then withdrawn again in the life and mission of Jesus, but continues to be effective in the experience of the apostolic church. As for Luke 4:16–30 itself, there are no doubt several reasons why Luke preferred to describe the beginning of Jesus' mission in this way rather than in the brief form of Mark 1:14f., 'After John was arrested, Jesus came into Galilee, proclaiming the gospel of God saying, "The time has been fulfilled and the Kingdom of God has drawn near: repent and believe in the gospel"'. From the purely narrative point of view, it gave a specific and graphic setting for the beginning of Jesus' work. As we argued above in Chapter Two, it also gave Luke the opportunity of drawing to the very outset of the mission Jesus' confrontation with the Jewish nation and his promise to the Gentiles, so that the incident becomes 'programmatic' of Luke's understanding of the whole story of Jesus. With respect to eschatology, the formulation in Mark makes two statements: the time has been fulfilled; and the Kingdom of God has drawn near. In Mark here 'fulfilled' apparently means 'almost to the brim', so that the overflowing with the cataclysm of the Kingdom can be expected from moment to moment. In Luke the tension between presence and futurity has been resolved in favour of presence. But that which is present is no mere anticipatory sign: it is the actual fulfilment of God's promises. Luke emphasizes this by greatly expanding the references to the presence and work of the Holy Spirit. In Mark we have so far had only two references to the Spirit: Jesus sees the Spirit descending upon him like a dove at his baptism (1:10), and the Spirit sends him out into the desert for his encounter with Satan (1:12). In Luke the descent of the Spirit at Jesus' baptism is described as an objective, physical fact, rather than a vision (3:21f.). In Luke 4:1 Jesus is not sent into the desert by the Spirit as an external force, but, 'filled with the Spirit', he is 'led in the Spirit in the desert', so that the Spirit is understood as being in the closest personal association with Jesus: then, at the end of the temptations, 'Jesus returned in the power of the Spirit into Galilee', (4:14). This has the effect of building up expectation for the opening words of Jesus' preaching: 'The Spirit of the Lord is upon me' (v. 18). It is this, above all, which 'has been fulfilled today' (v. 21). And in view of the significance of the Holy Spirit in Jewish theology, this is a truly eschatological proclamation: it is equivalent to saying 'the Kingdom of God has arrived', as is indeed retrospectively made explicit in 4:43, which looks back to this initial sermon.[137] Not only so, but the emphasis on the Spirit as the token of fulfilment is prepared for in the Lucan birth-narratives. That the birth of Jesus is due to conception by the Holy Spirit (1:35) is nothing new in Luke, for this is also stated in Matt. 1:18, 20. But in the Matthaean birth-stories these are the only two references to the Spirit. In Luke the whole environment of Jesus' conception and birth is marked by an outbreak of Spirit-activity. John the

Baptist will be filled with the Holy Spirit from his birth (1:15); at the conception of Jesus, Elisabeth (1:41), and at the birth of John, Zechariah (1:67) are filled with the Spirit. The Holy Spirit is mentioned three times in relation to Symeon (2:25, 26, 27), who, having seen the infant Jesus in the Temple, bears witness to the arrival of God's salvation. The references to the aged Anna as a prophetess, without further explanation (2:36), may seem to imply that Luke was unaware of the Jewish tradition that prophecy had been dormant for some centuries: but the emphasis in Acts 2:7–16 on the novelty of the phenomenon of the Spirit, and in v. 17f. (including Luke's own underlining, v. 18c) on prophecy as the consequence of Spirit-endowment, makes this improbable. Anna, too, is part of the new surge of the Spirit attending the birth of the Christ. There is of course a formal inconsistency between the report on the one hand that the Spirit was so active in the circumstances around the birth of Jesus, and the declaration on the other hand that the Spirit would be given only after Jesus' ascension (Luke 24:49; Acts 1:5, 8; 2:33). But this is of the same order as the inconsistency, shared also by Matthew, between the conception of Jesus by the Spirit and his reception of the Spirit at his baptism. Strict logic is not what concerns the evangelists at this point, any more than in the various statements about the presence and futurity of the Kingdom. Luke's point is that the Spirit marks both Jesus' birth and his mission as fulfilling the hopes of the new age: after his ascension the same mark of fulfilled eschatology is shared by all who remain, or become, his disciples. It is interesting that, if we disregard the first four chapters of each gospel, Luke actually refers to the Holy Spirit less often than Matthew: four times against seven; whereas in the first four chapters Matthew has five and Luke thirteen or fourteen examples. Luke thus respects the tradition of the gospel-material, which is restrained about speaking of the Holy Spirit in connexion with the course of Jesus' mission. But first he has established firmly in his readers minds that the advent of Jesus marks the advent of the Spirit, and thus of the fulfilment of salvation. In Acts, on the other hand, the Spirit is mentioned sixty-two times. Now, without any question, the disciples, too, live in the time of fulfilment. 'Today this scripture has been fulfilled in your hearing' applies even more to the time of the church than to the time of Jesus' mission.[138]

This perspective of Luke's explains the strange use of various verbs meaning 'to fulfil' in certain places in Luke–Acts. Luke describes the subject of his whole work as 'the things which have been fulfilled among us (*περὶ τῶν πεπληροφορημένων ἐν ἡμῖν πραγμάτων*) (Luke 1:1). The use of the long word *πληροφορεῖν* instead of the more usual *πληροῦν* is no doubt due to the desire for sonorous rhetoric in the preface.[139] But why a word meaning 'fulfil' at all, rather than some word meaning 'happen'?[140] At the very beginning, Luke hints that the story he is to narrate has the significance of the fulfilment of ancient expectations, or of divine promises. This becomes explicit in Acts 13:32f., where Paul says, 'We proclaim to you that the promise God made to the Fathers he has fulfilled to us their children'. This promise is then identified specifically with the resurrection of Jesus, and located in a specific Old Testament text, Psalm 2:7. Unlike Matthew and John, who frequently identify details of the life of Jesus (sometimes even quite trivial ones) as the fulfilment of particular OT texts, Luke usually relates 'promise' and 'fulfilment' in a much more sweeping way. The only specific events seen as fulfilment are the high points of the story: Jesus' mission, death, resurrection and ascension, the gift of the holy spirit, the Gentile mission and the destruction of Jerusalem.[141] In many of these passages Luke cites a particular Old Testament passage. But he also frequently uses a broad formula as 'all the things written by the prophets' (Luke 18:31 cf. Acts 3:18; 13:27), 'all the things that are written' (Luke 21:22), 'the scriptures' or 'all the scriptures' (24:27, 32, 45), and even the Old Testament divided into the three categories of its canon (24:44).

It is mainly in this broad sense that Luke thinks of fulfilment. The whole Christian story – the story of Jesus and of the church – is the fulfilment of the whole purpose of God as set forth in the whole of the Old Testament. From this it is only a short step to thinking of the Christian story as 'fulfilment' without any explicit reference to the Old Testament at all, as in Luke 1:1. It is doubtless against this background that we must understand the strange expression in Luke 9:31, where Moses and Elijah at the transfiguration discuss with Jesus his 'exodus' which he is going to 'fulfil' in Jerusalem.[142] In Luke 9:51 the expression 'when the days were being fulfilled' is a biblicism, cf. Gen. 25:24; Lev. 8:33; Jer. 25:12; also Luke 1:57; 2:6; 2:22; and it only sounds strange in the context because it is the days 'of his ascension' which are already said to be being fulfilled when Jesus is about to start his long journey to Jerusalem.[143] But in Acts 2:1 the related expression 'while the day of Pentecost was being fulfilled' is even stranger,[144] for the LXX and other NT examples all refer to the fulfilment of an extended period of time, but this one only to the arrival of a particular day.[145] We may suspect here an overtone of Luke's general theme of the fulfilment of God's promises;[146] and the same may well be true of Luke 9:51. The phrasing at the beginning of the Pentecost-story and of Jesus' journey to Jerusalem, like that of the whole work, prepares us indirectly to see eschatological fulfilment in the matter to be narrated.

(c) In all the synoptic gospels it is clearly stated that, in the mission of Jesus, judgement, salvation and the overthrow of Satan have become a present reality. Luke differs from Mark and Matthew only by giving more emphasis to this theme. But that difference of emphasis helps to reinforce the point that for Luke the fulfilment of eschatological expectations is a dearly held conviction.

In all three synoptic gospels, Jesus' practice of exorcism is interpreted as marking the overthrow of Satan (Mark 3:22–27/Matt. 12:22–29/Luke 11:13–22). But in Luke (alone) this is only confirmation of a point already established: in 10:17–20 the seventy disciples joyfully report to Jesus that they, too, have been able to perform exorcisms in Jesus' name, and Jesus tells them that he has seen Satan fall like lightning from heaven. The latter is an emphatic declaration that the eschatological hope of Satan's downfall has been fulfilled,[147] and is something of an embarrassment for the 'delay' theory.

H. Conzelmann[148] asserts a priori that this can only be a 'picture' of the future Kingdom, which can only be brought by the parousia. He suggests tentatively that the reason why the disciples are told not to rejoice in their victory over the demons is that this experience is not equivalent to the ultimate consummation, and they have much conflict still to undergo.[149] But this contradicts the plain meaning of the text: 'Do not rejoice in this, that the demons are subject to you: but rejoice because your names have been written in heaven'. The contrast is not between present victory and future distress (which, as we have seen, is not at all what Acts describes). The saying warns the disciples against claiming as their own achievement what is only the outcome of their obedience to God (cf. Simon Magus, Acts 8:18ff.!), and has nothing to do with the timing of the eschatological consummation. The text does not say that the victory over Satan is either limited or temporary, or only foreseen for the distant future, but rather stresses the actuality of Satan's defeat, both on earth and in heaven. As with other aspects of his eschatology, so with the defeat of Satan, Luke does not aim for strict chronological consistency, for Satan is not herewith eliminated from his story. In Luke 22:3 Satan 'enters' Judas to inspire his betrayal of Jesus. This appears to be a traditional theme to explain the enormity of Judas' behaviour (cf. John 13:2, 27), which Luke has not thought it necessary to revise. When Jesus says at the last supper that Satan has asked for the disciples to sift them like wheat (Luke 22:31) the imagery does not seem to derive from the usual post-Old Testament concept of Satan as the independent enemy of God, which also lies behind the other references to Satan (or 'the devil') in Luke–Acts,[150] but from the older view (Job 1–2) that Satan is the heavenly tester who can only act with God's permission: but Jesus' prayer (v.32) prevails against him, except in the case of Judas, whose defection was in any case foreseen in Scripture (Acts 1:16–20 cf. Luke 22:21f.; Acts 2:23). Luke 8:12 envisages that Satan will continue to be able to stop some people being saved by faith after they have heard the Word. Ananias in Acts 5:3 provides an example of this, in addition to Judas. But on the whole this is not where the balance lies for Luke. The Kingdom has come, though it must be consummated in the future; similarly Satan has fallen, though he still has some residual nuisance-power. Essentially, the time of the church is no less a 'Satan-free time' than that of the mission of Jesus.[151] The mood in Acts is one of spiritual confidence,[152] because with respect to Satan, too, the promises have been fulfilled.

Likewise, we find in Luke the balance somewhat shifted towards the present in the activity of the Son of Man as judge and deliverer. This theme is to be found in all the synoptic gospels, and is most forcefully evident in the pericope shared by all three, Mark 2:1–12/Matt. 9:1–8/Luke 5:17–26: Jesus defends his right to forgive the sins of the paralytic who has been let down through the roof, on the ground that 'the Son of Man has authority on earth to forgive sins'.[153] In Luke (alone) there seems to be an echo of this incident in the story about the woman who anointed Jesus' feet as he sat at table (Luke 7:36–50; contrast Mark 14:3–9/Matt. 26:6–13/John 12:1–8). Jesus declares to the woman that her sins have been forgiven, in virtually the same words used to the paralytic (7:48; 5:20b). In both stories Jesus is criticised by Pharisees for the blasphemy of claiming God's prerogative of forgiving sins (5:21 and 7:49); in 7:39 also for tolerating the ministrations of a sinner. In both stories, faith leads to salvation (5:20; 7:50). Although the title 'Son of Man' does not occur directly in this passage, it does occur immediately before it, in Jesus' saying about the Son of Man who 'came eating and drinking' (7:34), and it is very likely this which suggested to Luke the location of the passage about Jesus' forgiving a sinner while he was at a meal.[154] It is only Luke who includes the story of Jesus' encounter with Zacchaeus (Luke 19:1–10) and with it the saying that 'the Son of Man came to seek and to save the lost'. Here, too, the eschatological function of the Son of Man is seen as already at work in the mission of Jesus.[155] In the passage just mentioned, the present activity of the Son of Man is expressed in the positive aspect of forgiveness and salvation. That in Jesus the Son of Man is also present for judgement is probably the intention of the saying about the sign of Jonah in its Lucan form, Luke 11:29–32: the Son of Man will be a sign to this generation as Jonah was a sign to the Ninevites (v. 30), which refers to his preaching, calling on his contemporaries to repent (v. 32). The condemnation of those who fail to repent will be confirmed in the future judgement, (v. 32), but the verdict is already being determined, because it is the Son of Man (v. 30) who is confronting 'this generation' with 'something greater than Jonah'.[156] Finally, something of the same shift of emphasis is to be found in Luke's use of the terminology of 'salvation'. (On this, see above, p. 117f.) In Mark and Matthew the verb *σώζειν* mostly refers to physical healing or rescue from physical danger, and this meaning also occurs in Luke and Acts. It can also refer to salvation from sin, or in the last judgement: but in this sense it is always future in Mark and Matthew (Mark 8:35 pars.; Mark 13:13/Matt. 24:13/Matt. 10:22; Matt. 1:21; Mark 10:26 pars.); we have just seen two examples in Luke where such salvation has already been bestowed by Jesus during his mission (Luke 7:50; 19:10), and in Acts there are many examples (2:21, 40, 47; 11:14; 15:1, 11; 16:30f.; probably 4:12 as distinct from v. 9). The related nouns *σωτήρ, σωτηρία* and *σωτήριον* occur several times each in Luke–Acts but never in Mark or Matthew. In Luke–Acts they mostly refer to the present experience or possibility of salvation brought to Israel and to the world by Jesus. At his birth Jesus is described as saviour (Luke 2:11), and Symeon declares that, having seen the infant Jesus, he has seen God's salvation; at the other end of Luke's story, Paul affirms that God's salvation has been sent to the Gentiles.

From these various perspectives we confirm the conclusion that, though Luke shared with the whole apostolic and sub-apostolic church the expectation of a great future consummation of universal history, in which Jesus would come as Son of Man from heaven as judge and saviour, it is clear that his own emphasis lies on the reality of the present fulfilment of eschatological hopes.

Notes to Chapter Five

1. See above, Chapter Three, n. 4.
2. H. Conzelmann, *MdZ*, Part II.
3. A list of reviews of Conzelmann's *MdZ* until 1962 is given by H. H. Oliver, 'Birth Stories', 202. The length of the list gives a quick indication of the great impact made by this book.
4. E.g. H. E. Turlington's review, *JBL* 76, 1957, 321; and H. J. Cadbury's of the English translation, *JBL* 80, 1961, 305, though Cadbury had earlier expressed interest in Conzelmann's ideas on Luke's eschatology: 'Acts and Eschatology', 320.
5. See J. Zmijewski, *Eschatologiereden*, 8–37; J. Rohde, *Methode*, ch. 5, esp. sections (a) (Conzelmann), (c) (Lohse), (e) (Bartsch) and, in the English version, sections (k) (Flender), and (l) (Robinson).
6. J.-D. Kaestli, *Eschatologie*.
7. E. Gräßer, 'Acta Forschung', *ThR* 42, p. 63.
8. E. Gräßer, *Parusieverzögerung*; and 'Parusieerwartung'.
9. G. Schneider, *Parusiegleichnisse*.
10. J. Dupont, 'Die individuelle Eschatologie', 37–47.
11. G. Schneider, *Parusiegleichnisse*, 78–84; 89f.; 94–98.
12. C. Burchard, *Der dreizehnte Zeuge*, 181f.
13. R. Geiger, *Endzeitreden*.
14. E. Kränkl, *Jesus*, 204f.
15. R. H. Hiers, 'Why Will They Not Say, "Lo, here!" Or "There!"?'; 'Delay.'
16. S. G. Wilson, 'Eschatology'; also *Gentiles*, ch. 3.
17. J. Zmijewski, *Eschatologiereden*; the argument of the book is summarized in 'Die Eschatologiereden Lk 21 und Lk 17', 30–40 (cited here after the latter).
18. E. E. Ellis, 'Eschatologie' (ET, *Eschatology in Luke*). Ellis says (396, ET, 19) that the presence of apocalyptic fever in the second half of the first century is documented by both Christian and non-Christian sources. On closer inspection, it turns out that the non-Christian sources meant (Josephus, Tacitus and Suetonius) are all referring to messianic prophecies associated with the Jewish War of 66–70 AD.

18a. Ellis shows that the person of Jesus is what for Luke holds the present and future aspects of eschatology together. This insight, according to the most recent publication on Lucan eschatology, represents a significant breakthrough. See J. Ernst, *Herr der Geschichte. Perspektiven der lukanischen Eschatologie*, Stuttgart 1978 (SBS 88), 107, cf. 50f. Ernst's monograph consists largely of a criticism, in now rather familiar terms, of the 'classic' theory (23–88) followed by a briefer criticism of Flender's 'two-level' interpretation (88–107) and some very brief critical notes on Ellis's essay, which, however, also receives warm praise (107–111).

19. W. G. Kümmel, 'Anklage', 425–428; 431–435. Cf. his *Einleitung*, 111–114 (ET, 142–145).
20. Fred O. Francis, 'Eschatology'.
21. E. Franklin, 'Ascension'; *Christ the Lord*, ch. 1.
22. See especially Fred O. Francis, op. cit., 62.
23. W. C. van Unnik, 'Luke–Acts', 28.
24. For a review of earlier studies on this theme, see E. E. Ellis, 'Eschatologie', 382–387 (ET, 5–10).
25. See G. W. E. Nickelsburg, *Resurrection*, especially the Appendix, 177–180, refuting O. Cullman's well-known study, 'Immortality of the soul or Resurrection of the Dead'.
26. J. Dupont, 'Die individuelle Eschatologie', 38f., finds in v. 21 and 33f. a concern for what happens to the rich fool after his death. But it does not seem to me to follow necessarily that being 'wealthy towards God' and having 'inexhaustible treasure in the heavens' refer to provision for heavenly life immediately after death. Nor is Dupont's exegesis of Luke 16:9 as teaching individual eschatology compelling (op. cit., 42f.).
27. See above, section 5, pages 123–5.
28. See J. M. Creed, *St Luke*, 209f., following H. Greßmann, 'Vom reichen Mann und armen Lazarus'.
29. Luke 14:14; Acts 24:15; cf. Luke 20:27ff. Acts 4:2; 17:18, 32; 23:6ff.; 24:21; 26:23.
30. C. K. Barrett, 'Stephen', 35f.
31. E. E. Ellis, 'Eschatologie', 382f. (ET, 6).
32. See R. Maddox, 'Function'.
33. G. Lohfink, *Himelfahrt*, 237: 'Lukas folgt hier einfach einer Tradition, die ihm wertvoll war wegen der Zusage des sofortigen Erbarmens gegenüber dem, der umkehrt. Daß sich die Eschatologie dieser Tradition mit seinen eigenen Anschauungen nicht deckte, nahm Lukas in Kauf. Eine Redaktion des Jesuswortes war ihm nicht möglich, denn es steht und fällt mit dem "Heute noch", das die Bitte des Schächers radikal überbietet.'
34. But this point must not be exaggerated. It is not true, for example, as has often been alleged, that in Luke 21:20–24 and 25–27 the evangelist drives a wedge between the fall of Jerusalem and the earthly and cosmic catastrophes leading up to the coming of the Son of Man on a cloud. (On this see further below, section 4 of this chapter.) He at least maintains, from the earlier tradition, an 'essential' or 'material' connexion between them: so J. Zmijewski, *Bibel und Leben*, 37: 'ein sachlicher Zusammenhang'. H. Flender, *Heil*, 103f. (ET, 113), observes that by Luke's time the *chronological* separation between the past events of the fall of Jerusalem and the future consummation was so obvious as not to need any comment: but *theologically* speaking the destruction of Jerusalem *is* part of the last judgement.
35. E. E. Ellis, 'Eschatologie', 395 (ET, 17f.).
36. E.g. H. W. Bartsch, 'Parusieverzögerung', 116–131; also *Wachet aber*, 123; R.

Schnackenburg, 'Lk 17:20–37', 233f.; R. Geiger, *Endzeitreden*, 267; S. G. Wilson, *Gentiles*, 72ff.

37. These expressions in Luke 1:68 and 2:38 doubtless come from old Jewish–Christian tradition. Luke was able to take them up and turn them to good account in the dramatic structure of his work.
38. Luke 19:41–44; 21:5f., 20–24; 23:28–31; cf. 13:1–5 (–9), 34f.
39. See section 8, p. 132.
40. See section 8, p. 132.
41. H. Conzelmann, *MdZ* 77, n. 2 (ET, 84f., n. 3); E. Gräßer, *Parusieverzögerung*, 176f.; S. G. Wilson, *Gentiles*, 67f.
42. The significance of the ascension in Luke's understanding of eschatology has been emphasized by G. Lohfink, *Himmelfahrt*, 251–275; and E. Franklin, *Christ the Lord*, 29–41; cf. H. Flender, *Heil*, 87 (ET, 93f.).
43. Against the conclusion of C. Burchard, *Der dreizehnte Zeuge*, 185: 'Es geht Lukas nicht darum, eine unbewältigte Gegenwart zu verarbeiten, sondern eine als Zeit des Wartens und der Geduld durchschaute Gegenwart überstehen zu helfen.'
44. It might even be suggested (see R. Pesch, *Vision*, 19) that, as the Son of Man is standing rather than sitting, he is preparing for the parousia, which is imminent. It is certainly surprising that Acts 7:56 differs from Luke 22:69 in this detail. Although the latter is formed by adaptation of Mark 14:62, Luke presumably knew quite well that it was an allusion to Psalm 110:1, which is quoted in Luke 20:42f. and Acts 2:34f. However, we do not know how far Luke may also have been influenced by extra-canonical 'Son of Man' traditions: in 1 Enoch, the Son of Man/Elect One usually sits but also sometimes stands for judgement: cf. 1 Enoch 45:3; 61:8; 62:1–3; and 69:26–29 with 49:2. We cannot be sure what nuance Luke intended by this change. R. Pesch, op. cit., makes the fact that the Son of Man is standing rather than sitting the key to his whole discussion. He concludes that the decisive clues from the background are Ass. Mos. 10:3 and Isa. 3:13, and that this is indeed a vision of judgement, but in the sense that the divine verdict is now that the gospel should go forth from the Jews to the Gentiles. As we have seen in Chapter Two, the latter theme has a much wider basis in Luke–Acts than this one passage.
45. So E. Franklin, *Christ the Lord*, 28f.
46. H. Conzelmann, *MdZ* 96 (ET, 104f., renders Conzelmann's 'dort' with 'at the time'). Conzelmann refers also to Acts 15:34, but this verse is textually doubtful.
47. See H. J. Cadbury, *Style*, 131–205.
48. So A. Plummer, *St Luke*, 250; Ellis, *Luke*, 141.
49. This is made explicit in Matt. 16:28. I. H. Marshall, *Gospel of Luke*, 378, argues that Mark's 'use of the perfect participle here indicates that the reference is not to experiencing the coming of the kingdom as an event but to seeing that it is already present'. Grammatically, that is sound enough; but does Mark indicate elsewhere that he regards the Kingdom of God as already present in his own time?
50. A. Plummer, *St Luke*, 249f.
51. J. M. Creed, *St Luke*, 132; I. H. Marshall, *Gospel of Luke*, 378.
52. E. E. Ellis, 'Present', 32ff,; *Luke*, 141; cf. A. R. C. Leany, *St Luke*, 166.
53. *St Luke*, 250.

54. H. Conzelmann, *MdZ*, 96 (ET, 105), 'The coming of the Kingdom can only be proclaimed as a future fact, without any reference to when it will happen, but the nature of it can be seen now'; *MdZ*, 105, n. 3 (ET, 114, n. 3), 'From his parousia onwards the Kingdom will be "seen" (Luke 9:27, contrast Mark 9:1)'.
55. Another possibility is to see here a suggestion of a proleptic 'seeing' of the Kingdom as a heavenly reality, in some sense like Stephen's seeing of the Son of Man in heaven in Acts 7:55f. Two considerations seem to me to weigh against this view. First, whereas Luke repeatedly emphasizes the ascension of *Jesus* to a position with the Father in heaven, he does not (and here I disagree with E. Franklin, *Christ the Lord*, 24f.) speak of the Kingdom of God as being transcendent in heaven, waiting to be revealed later on earth. As we shall see in subsequent sections of this chapter, Luke has two ways of speaking of the Kingdom: either it is a present reality since the mission of Jesus, or it will come as the fully eschatological consummation at the End. Second, Luke has not modified Mark's expression that 'there are some . . . who will not taste death until . . .', which seems to me inescapably to point forward to an *event* which will occur in the lifetime of some of Jesus' hearers, as it were overtaking them, regardless of their own attitude or capacity for perception.
56. E. Gräßer, *Parusieverzögerung*, 128–130, cf. 166.
57. M. Meinertz, '"Dieses Geschlecht",' 283–289.
58. J. Levy, *Wörterbuch*, I, 386, 422; M. Jastrow, *Dictionary*, 289, 320.
59. H. Conzelmann, *MdZ*, 122 (ET, 131).
60. E.g. J. Zmijewski, *Eschatologiereden*, 1972, 281f.; G. Schneider, *Parusiegleichnisse*, 1975, 60; O. Merk, 'Das Reich Gottes', 218.
61. W. C. Robinson, *Weg*, 65.
62. R. Geiger, *Endzeitreden*, 237.
63. R. H. Hiers, 'Delay', 146; so too S. G. Wilson, *Gentiles*, 77.
64. Section 9 (b), p. 196–199.
65. E. Franklin, *Christ the Lord*, 14.
66. E. E. Ellis, *Luke*, 246f.
67. For this section I am particularly grateful to Professor Ferdinand Hahn for his detailed and stimulating criticism. We discussed this passage at length on three occasions, and my indebtedness to his ideas goes well beyond the specific points that are acknowledged in one or two cases below.
68. So rightly I. H. Marshall, *Gospel of Luke*, 767, against the (harmonizing?) rendering of most of the current English versions (RSV, NEB, TEV) and many commentators (Klostermann, Creed, Manson, Rengstorf, Grundmann, Leaney, Schneider), cf. Phil. 1:19.
69. H. Conzelmann, *MdZ*, 102f. (ET, 129), followed by many.
70. See F. Hahn, 'Parusie', 252f.
71. So R. Geiger, *Endzeitreden*, 168. J. Zmijewski, *Eschatologiereden*, 93–95, thinks a reference to the End is implied by the plural ταῦτα following ἐλεύσονται ἡμέραι in v. 6, which he takes to mean 'the eschatological time'. But this is contradicted by the use of ἥξουσιν ἡμέραι in a quite uneschatological context in 19:43. Nor does it explain why Luke has altered Mark's wording here.
72. H. Conzelmann, *MdZ*, 117f. (ET, 126f.).
73. See F. Hahn, 'Markus 13', 253–256.
74. J. Zmijewski, *Eschatologiereden*, 241.
75. R. Geiger, *Endzeitreden*, 169–172.

76. F. Hahn, verbally.
77. R. Geiger, loc. cit.
78. See A. Plummer, *St Luke*, 483; J. M. Creed, *St Luke*, 257; E. E. Ellis, *Luke*, 245.
79. See A. Plummer, loc. cit.; H. Flender, *Heil*, 104 (ET, 113).
80. Cf. I. H. Marshall, *Gospel of Luke*, 770, 773f.
81. So H. Conzelmann, *MdZ*, 121 (ET, 130: but the passage is enlarged and the point emphasized in [4]*MdZ*).
82. R. Geiger, *Endzeitreden*, 216, cf. 208f., tries to explain this by the suggestion that the transition from past to future, from Luke's point of view, comes in verse 23f., and so Luke sees no need to retain the time-break of Mark 13:24 at Luke 21:25. I cannot follow this reasoning. All of v. 20–24 until 24 c has to do with the fall of Jerusalem. J. Zmijewski, *Eschatologiereden*, 240f., passes over the problem of the time-relation between v. 20–24 and 25ff. by emphasizing (following H. Flender, *Heil*, 104; ET, 113) the substantive *connexion* between the judgement of Jerusalem and the final judgement. These conflicting views show that there is a real problem here. See also S. G. Wilson, *Gentiles*, 71, n. 5.
83. R. Geiger, *Endzeitreden*, 215ff., 256, interestingly suggests that Luke avoids Mark's LXX-allusions, prophesying disasters in the heavenly bodies, because they include eclipses of the sun and moon, which the Greek world knew were predictable (since Thales predicted the eclipse of 585 BC), and did not signify the End: instead Luke preferred an allusion to Psalm 65:8f. LXX, because the language is vaguer, but can still describe how all nature will be rocked by the events of the End. Despite Geiger's suggestion, Mark's wording is quite naturally taken to refer to a permanent rather than a temporary eclipse, especially with v. 25 to follow. It is more important to observe that Luke's new wording shifts the emphasis from the heavenly catastrophes to their effect in human society on earth.
84. See F. Hahn, 'Markus 13', 252–256.
85. F. Hahn, verbally.
86. In Mark 14:43/Luke 23:51 Joseph of Arimathaea is described as προσδεχόμενος τὴν βασιλείαν τοῦ θεοῦ. (Matt. 27:57 and John 19:38 say instead that Joseph was a disciple of Jesus: is this because, from their more Jewish point of view, all Jews could be described as expecting the Kingdom of God?) This is reminiscent of Luke 2:38, where Anna finds a receptive hearing about the birth of Jesus among people προσδεχόμενοι λύτρωσιν Ἰερουσαλήμ.' Ἀπολύτρωσις is used several times in the epistles of the New Testament to mean either release from sin (Rom. 3:24; 1 Cor. 1:30; Eph. 1:7, 14; Col. 1:14; Hebr. 9:15) or ultimate salvation from all suffering and evil at the parousia (Rom. 8:23; Eph. 4:30). Only the former of these senses is conveyed, outside Luke–Acts, by λύτρωσις (Hebr. 9:12), λυτροῦσθαι (Tit. 2:14; 1 Pet. 1:18) and λύτρον (Mark 10:45/Matt. 20:28). In Luke 21:28 the sense 'release from sin' is not in place, so the reference here is to the ultimate salvation at the parousia. But there may be an additional n ıance. In Luke–Acts this group of words is used of national salvation from oppression. In Acts 7:35 Moses is the λυτρωτής of Israel from Egypt. In Luke 24:21 the Emmaus-disciples hoped that Jesus was ὁ μέλλων λυτροῦσθαι τὸν Ἰσραήλ. Luke 2:38 mentions people looking forward to the λύτρωσις of Jerusalem. In Luke 1:68 God is praised for having made λύτρωσις for his people, in the sense of national salvation. Similarly, in Hebr. 11:35 ἀπολύτρωσις refers to release from torture and execution. It is therefore likely

that in Luke 21:28 the 'release' of Jesus' disciples has a corporate connotation: the 'people of God' will be rescued by the Son of Man from the disasters which are going to overtake the rest of humanity: cf. v. 36.

87. See especially R. Schnackenburg, 'Lk 17:20–37', 232ff.
88. E.g., H. Conzelmann, *MdZ*, 105 (ET, 114); E. Gräßer, *Parusieverzögerung*, 188f.
89. In the earlier editions of *MdZ*, H. Conzelmann had no other explanation than this (see ET, 107). In the later editions, 98, he follows E. Gräßer, *Parusieverzögerung*, 140f., in regarding the insertion of *ἐφ' ὑμᾶς* in Luke 10:9 (cf. Matt. 10:7 and Matt. 12:28/Luke 11:20) as having the effect of turning the sentence into a reference to the nature of the Kingdom rather than to its imminence. Neither Conzelmann nor Gräßer explains why the insertion makes the alleged difference. And in Luke 10:11 the sentence from Mark 1:15 is repeated without alteration.
90. So R. H. Hiers, 'Delay', 150f.
91. Assuming that an eschatological reference is actually present here, as argued by J. Jeremias, *Das Vaterunser*, 22–24 (ET, 99–102). This interpretation is accepted by a number of recent commentators on Matthew, e.g. D. Hill (The New Century Bible) and (cautiously) P. Bonnard (Commentaire du NT) ad loc; but firmly rejected by E. Schweizer (NTD; ET). Schweizer argues that bread is not the usual food of the messianic banquet, despite Luke 14:15ff., and that an eschatological reference is unlikely in view of the following petition for forgiveness. The latest full discussion, by P. Grelot, 'La quatrième demande du "Pater" et son arrière-plan sémitique', also rejects the eschatological reference, but for other reasons. Exod. 16:4 must be seen as significant background to the bread-petition (following J. Carmignac and J. Starcky), and its primary reference must be to the provision of daily sustenance. The forms of this petition in Matthew and Luke can be explained as going back to a common Aramaic text, which justifies the rendering (Tertullian onwards) of *ἐπιούσιος* by *cottidianus*. The setting of the prayer in Matt. 6 (cf. v. 25ff.) supports this view. Grelot does not, however, discuss the form of the petition in the Gospel of the Nazarenes, on which Jeremias' interpretation largely rests; or the eschatological significance of the first half of the Lord's Prayer as affecting the interpretation of the bread-petition. In the absence of clear Greek evidence for *ἐπιούσιος*, the point must remain doubtful.
92. On this passage, see especially R. Schnackenburg's essay (note 36, above). Schnackenburg thinks the whole section Luke 17:20–37 was derived as a unit by Luke from Q, though Luke made a few small additions and alterations. In section 8, below, reasons will be given for the view that v. 20f. and 22–37 were brought together by Luke himself.
93. R. Schnackenburg, 'Lk 17:20–37', 227: In v. 26 'the days' are the days to which the Son of Man makes an end: the phrase is formed by analogy with 'the days of Noah'. 'The days' is a common Lucan expression: in 9:51 'the days of his ascension' refers to a *series* of events (death, resurrection, ascension) and in 17:22 'the days of the Son of Man' may refer to the series, the judgement of Jerusalem, the 'times of the Gentiles', and the end-events culminating in the coming of the Son of Man. 'Für ein solches Denken ist es nicht schwer, von den "Tagen des Menschensohnes" in einem doppelten Sinn zu sprechen, also sowohl die Tage vor der Parusie als auch nach der Parusie damit zu bezeichnen.'

94. See R. Schnackenburg, op. cit., 226.
95. Some interpreters explain that v. 31, like v. 33, calls on Jesus' disciples to abandon worldly security in favour of dedication to their Lord: but the words 'on that day' coming after v. 30, make such a meaning inappropriate. So J. Zmijewski, *Eschatologiereden*, 482–489.
96. J. Jeremias, *Gleichnisse Jesu*, 154f. (ET, 154f.).
97. Against J. Jeremias, op. cit., 155f. (ET, 155f.), though in agreement with his judgement in the earlier editions.

    Recently another analysis has been proposed by H. Weder, *Gleichnisse Jesu*, 267ff. Weder regards v. 2–7 (all but the last phrase) as a unity, v. 6f. being an explanation by 'the original narrator' (=Jesus), made necessary by the potentially offensive image of God as an unjust judge (cf. Luke 16:8a, also regarded as original). V. 7 (end) introduces a new question: 'Is he being tardy about them?' [Und zieht er es lange hin bei Ihnen?'], which is answered in v. 8. Weder follows Jeremias in regarding this addition as pre-Lucan. The original parable has no interest in the theme of 'delay', but expresses the certainty of God's gift of the Kingdom. The church-addition, v. 7 end–8, expresses the same certainty, with the addition of a reassurance about the imminence of the coming of God's salvation in the form of the coming of the Son of Man; and of a warning to remain faithful. Luke's addition (v. 1) is to emphasize the need for persistence in prayer (thus emphasizing in the widow the quality of persistence), which is justified by the certainty of God's coming salvation.
98. H. Conzelmann, *MdZ*, 103. (ET, 112, does not make the same point. Here again ET seems to be in some confusion, as the short paragraph dealing with Luke 18:1ff. is slipped in under the discussion of 18:30.) Cf. E. Gräßer, *Parusieverzögerung*, 38, who says, following H. Sahlin and K. Bornhäuser, that ἐν τάχει can mean 'suddenly' rather than 'soon'. But both the context and the normal Greek usage speak against this. I can see no justification in the text for Gräßer's view (37f.) that v. 8b means that the parousia is delayed *because of* the unfaithfulness of Christians. Rather, v. 8b warns wavering Christians that the parousia *will* come soon.
99. See G. Schneider, *Parusiegleichnisse*, Part I, ch. 1–3.
100. 'Times of refreshment' and 'times of the restoration of all things' are certainly primitive Christian eschatological terms: see F. Hahn, 'Überlieferungen,' 11–16. I can see no basis for the assertion of E. Gräßer in his lecture at the same Coloquium (see n. 8 above), 15, that the 'times of the restoration of all things' are to be identified with the time of the Gentile-mission. H. Flender, *Heil*, 89–91 (ET, 96–98), thinks the promise of times of refreshment refers to the meeting of the penitent hearers with the exalted Christ: but his assertion, in this connexion, that Luke reapplies to Jesus' exaltation theological statements that previously referred to his parousia, is too sweeping. The expression is reminiscent of 'the rebirth', in the Matthaean form of the saying about the twelve thrones (Matt. 19:28): the Lucan equivalent, Luke 22:28–30, has been assimilated to later eschatological terminology, in that it speaks of the 'kingdom' which Jesus has received from the Father to share with his disciples.
101. E. Gräßer, 'Parusieerwartung in der Apg', 16.
102. See F. Hahn, 'Act 3, 19–21', 13.
103. On this see F. Hahn, 'Act 3, 19–21', 11f.
104. Op. cit., especially section VI.
105. Is it significant that, in all three of these examples where the consummation is mentioned under the aspect of judgement, the audience is a Gentile one?

106. So S. G. Wilson, *Gentiles*, 86.
107. P. Vielhauer, 'Paulinismus', 13 (ET, 47), followed by H. Conzelmann, *MdZ*, 6 (ET, 14); E. Gräßer, *Parusieverzögerung*, 204; cf. E. Haenchen, *Apg*, 106f. (ET, 95f.); S. G. Wilson, *Gentiles*, 77. Cf. also E. Käsemann's similar remark, 'Das Problem des historischen Jesus' (ET, 28).
108. E. Franklin, *Christ the Lord*, 26. Another aspect of this question is taken up by E. Güttgemanns, *Offene Fragen*, 95–105. He criticizes the sociological assumption, widely accepted by later scholars from M. Dibelius, that 'literature' was incompatible with the character of an eschatological movement, because such a movement had its eyes fixed on an imminent, catastrophic event, and not on the 'world'. This assumption led Dibelius to play down the significance of the gospels as 'literature', a judgement that now looks odd in the light of the fruits of redaction-criticism. The analogy of Jewish apocalyptic, a thoroughly bookish phenomenon, should have warned Dibelius off this false trail.
109. So, most recently, E. Gräßer, 'Parusierwartung in der Apg', 22.
110. See especially W. G. Kümmel, *Verheißung* (ET, *Promise*).
111. O. Merk, 'Reich Gottes', 204–211.
112. Op. cit., 207f.
113. H. Conzelmann, *MdZ*, 105f., cf. 95f., 98 (ET, 114f., cf. 104f., 107).
114. Linguistically this is beyond dispute: see C. H. Dodd, *Parables*, 36. But it has sometimes been suggested that *ἔφθασεν* is a 'prophetic aorist' reflecting the future use of the Hebrew perfect, as in the OT prophets (so R. H. Fuller, 26). This, however, is not demonstrable as an idiom in Koine Greek; and the suggestion is not persuasive when weighed against the evidence presented in W. G. Kümmel, *Verheißung*, ch. 3.
115. Which statements in Luke–Acts express Lucan theology? Sometimes it is suggested that we can safely look for Luke's view of things only in his editorial modifications or the editorial framework in which he sets his material, or in the material which he alone preserves. Thus, with respect to the Kingdom of God, E. Franklin says that Luke always understands the Kingdom as present, and that he retains future references to the Kingdom only in liturgical language, which does not reflect Luke's own convictions (*Christ the Lord*, 23). On the other hand, R. H. Hiers, declaring that for Luke the Kingdom is always future, minimizes the importance of the explicit statement to the contrary ('Delay', 145, 153f.; 'Lo, here!', 384). The warning of E. E. Ellis is pertinent and sound: only with hesitation and great care should we conclude in any particular case that Luke has accepted from tradition something with which he is not in sympathy ('Eschatologie', 378–380; ET, 2f.). Certainly, the special Lucan material and Luke's distinctive editorial touches are the first and clearest guide to his convictions. But since Luke does not hesitate to alter the wording of his one known written source, even at theologically very sensitive points (e.g., apart from several examples already mentioned concerning eschatology, Luke 24:6/Mark 16:7), and since he presumably exercised similar freedom with his oral and other written sources, we must consider it likely that he in general subscribes to what he has accepted. We cannot, however, make this an absolute rule. There may be rare cases where Luke has accepted a saying because of his appreciation of one aspect of it, despite the fact that another aspect is in tension with his general view. This may be the case, for example, in Luke 23:43, which will be discussed below.

116. See B. Noack, *Gottesreich*, 3–50. A. Rüstow, 'ENTOC YMWN ECTIN', gathers interesting linguistic material, and argues, as does C. H. Roberts, 'The Kingdom of Heaven', 1–8, for the meaning 'within your reach'. But whereas Roberts regards the saying as meaning that the Kingdom is already available to those who want it, Rüstow, beginning from the assumption that the Kingdom of God is *never* said to be present in any other passage (209–212), thinks that its meaning here is that any person who wishes to enter the Kingdom, when it comes, has it in his power to qualify himself for entry, through repentance and good deeds. But the evidence for the idea that the Kingdom is present is much stronger than Rüstow allows, especially in Luke.
117. See R. Schnackenburg, 'Lk 17:20–37', 217f.; R. H. Hiers, 'Lo, here!', 379f.; B. Noack, *Gottesreich*, 37.
118. So R. H. Hiers, 'Lo, here!', esp. 382f.
119. R. Schnackenburg, op. cit. (see n. 36, above).
120. In his discussion of Acts 14:22, 'Die individuelle Eschatologie', 39f., J. Dupont does not mention the possibility that for Luke the Kingdom of God is a present reality which may be entered now. (See below, section 8 of this chapter.) He thinks v. 22b has a parallel in Luke 24:26: but the latter speaks of the Messiah's 'entry into his glory' after his suffering: and that refers to his ascension, and for Luke the ascension is personal and peculiar to Jesus: disciples do not have their own ascension. Nor does the second suggested parallel, Acts 20:32b ('to give you your inheritance among all those who have been sanctified'), seem to me necessarily to refer specifically to what happens to individual Christians at their death.
121. So G. Stählin, *Apg.*, 196.
121a. This is generally true for the Rabbinic, apocalyptic and apocryphal literature. According to H.-W. Kuhn, *Enderwartung und Gegenwärtiges Heil*, a partial exception must now be made in the case of the Qumran community. In a group of hymns (but not those attributable to the Teacher of Righteousness) there occurs the consciousness of present salvation, alongside the expectation of a future, eschatological consummation. Kuhn attributes the former element to the Qumran community's understanding of itself as already serving the spiritual or heavenly Temple. He draws the distinction between this view occurring at Qumran and the eschatology of early Christianity, that for the Christians an historical event belonging to the End has already taken place (in the Christ-event), whereas for the people of Qumran the future End simply reaches into the present as a 'sphere of salvation' (204).
122. On the significance in this respect of Acts 2:1, see below, p. 200.
123. E. Kränkl, *Jesus der Knecht Gottes*, 190ff., says Luke has altered LXX here because *μετὰ ταῦτα* would not make sense out of Joel's context, and *ἐν ταῖς ἐσχάταις ἡμέραις* does not necessarily have a fully eschatological sense, either in LXX or NT or early Christian writings; it appears from Acts 1:6–8 that Luke sees no temporal connexion between the outpouring of the Spirit and the establishment of the future eschatological Kingdom, and it is better to follow Gräßer in understanding the 'last days' here as 'the last historical epoch before the End'. Nevertheless, it seems to me that, despite Acts 1:6–8, the considerations mentioned below point in the opposite direction. The attempt of E. Haenchen, *Apg.*, 181 (ET, 179), to defend the B-reading, *μετὰ ταῦτα*, in Acts 2:17 has rightly been rejected by almost all who have discussed the point subsequently. Here is a clear case where the principle of the priority of the

more difficult reading should be applied. That Haenchen strove rather hard to prove so thin a textual case is a hint of the importance of Acts 2:17 as evidence against a doctrine of the indefinite delay of the parousia as Luke's main purpose. The B-reading can easily be explained as assimilation to LXX. E. J. Epp, *Tendency of Codex Bezae*, 67, describes the reading 'in the last days', in spite of its considerable non-Western support, as an 'alteration' by D. In this judgement he seems to be influenced by Haenchen, and perhaps also by the fact that for the convenience of organization in his whole work B is taken as the constant standard against which D is compared. Epp does not of course invest B with absolute authority, but his procedure opens the way to some confusion in a case like this where it is B and not D that departs from the consensus of the early codices. In the fourth edition (1962) of *MdZ* (87, n. 2) H. Conzelmann was briefly tempted to follow Haenchen here, but in his Acts-commentary of 1963, 28f., he supports the majority-reading. There is in any case no support in the text for Conzelmann's assertion, *MdZ*, 87 (ET, 95), that 'the Spirit Himself is no longer the eschatological gift, but the substitute in the meantime for the possession of ultimate salvation'.

124. See E. Lohse, *Πεντηκοστή*, ThW 6, 1959, 48. Lohse observes, however, that there is in Jubilees an anticipation of the later doctrine.
125. Philo, *Decal*, 33, 46.
126. Billerbeck, II, 1924, 604f.
127. That Luke was familiar with the idea of Jesus as bringer of 'the new covenant' is shown by Luke 22:20 (if, as seems increasingly agreed, the longer text in Luke 22:15–20 is genuine: see B. M. Metzger, *Textual Commentary*, 173–177).
128. See especially the various pronouncements on Luke by E. Käsemann (bibliography listed by E. Haenchen, *Apg*, 62, n. 2 (ET, 48, n. 3) and by W. G. Kümmel, 'Anklage', 418, n. 5 and 6). A reply to Käsemann and others who share his low evaluation of Luke's theology is offered by W. G. Kümmel, 'Anklage', and U. Wilckens, 'Interpreting L–A'.
129. It is no new observation, that Conzelmann and others who see in Luke an emphasis on the delay of the parousia also tend to underestimate the significance of the Holy Spirit in Luke's theology. There is a brief discussion of the Holy Spirit in *MdZ* (167–172; ET, 179–184) in the context of Christology, but there is none in association with eschatology. In the (very detailed) index locorum of *MdZ*, Acts 2:1–13 is not mentioned!
130. This was rightly emphasized by E. Lohse, 'Lukas als Theologe der Heilsgeschichte', 261–270.
131. See P. Schubert, 'The Structure and Significance of Luke 24'.
132. 'Paulinismus', 13 (ET, 47).
133. *MdZ*, 30f. (ET, 36f.).
134. 'Pausieerwartung in der Apg', 5.
135. H. Flender, *Heil*, 135–137 (ET, 150–152), says the contrast alleged between Paul and Luke here depends on denying to Luke any character as testimony; he compares the ambiguous use of 'today' in the OT, especially Psalms and Deuteronomy.
136. The chief evidence appealed to by Conzelmann to argue that Luke marks a hiatus between the mission of Jesus and the time of the church is the passage about the two swords, Luke 22:35–38. He suggests that the time between the temptation of Jesus, Luke 4:1–13, and his passion, is a 'Satan-free' time, which comes to an end with the passion, and introduces a time of danger and distress

for the disciples: *MdZ*, 5, 9, 30, 44, 73ff., 94, 97f., 158, 174, 186, 218f. (ET, 13, 16, 36, 50, 80ff., 103, 106f., 170, 187, 199, 232ff.). But the narrative of Acts spectacularly fails to bear out this interpretation: as we have seen in Chapter Three, section 6, Acts contrasts with Paul's epistles in showing how the disciples of Jesus are protected and strengthened by the Spirit: they do not look back on the time of Jesus' life as a better time which they have lost. In fact Luke 22:35–38 is an obscure and difficult passage, and in our present state of knowledge cannot by any means carry the heavy weight put on it by Conzelmann. See also below, n. 151.

137. So O. Merk, 'Reich Gottes', 205–208.

138. For a similar conclusion about Luke 4:21, but reached in a different way, see H. Flender, *Heil*, 135f. (ET, 150f.).

139. H. J. Cadbury, 'Commentary on the Preface of Luke', *Beginnings*, II, 1922, 496.

140. A. Denaux, 'L'Hypocrisie des Pharisiens', 278, draws attention to the importance of τελ-words (τελεῖν and τελειοῦν) in Luke–Acts, in much the same sense as πληρ-words. It is, however, to be noted that τελεῖν is still more characteristic of Revelation and τελειοῦν of John, 1 John and Hebrews.

At Mark 13:4/Luke 2:17 *Mark* has συντελεῖσθαι and Luke replaces it with γίνεσθαι. The point here may be that for Mark the events prophesied in the following discourse culminate in the parousia as the final eschatological consummation, but for Luke 'fulfilment' is not confined to the specific events prophesied here, but takes place in the whole story of Jesus.

The phrase ταῦτα συντελεῖσθαι πάντα is an echo of the apocalyptic language of Daniel 12:6f. (R. Pesch, *Markusevangelium*, 2, 276).

141. Luke 3:4–6; 4:18f.; 22:37; 24:44ff.; Acts 3:18; 2:25–31, 34f.; 2:17–21; 15:15–18; Luke 21:22. An exception to this concentration on the main lines of the story of Jesus is Acts 1:16–20 (the betrayal and death of Judas). These passages pointing to the fulfilment of *prophecies* in Scripture are different from those where *commands* of Scripture are deliberately obeyed: Luke 2:22–24; 10:26f.; Acts 23:5; and from those where theological argument is supported by reference to Scripture: Luke 19:46; 20:17, 28, 37, 42.

On Luke's use of the OT, see T. Holtz, *Untersuchungen*, and M. Rese, *Alttestamentliche Motive*. Holtz argues that Luke used the LXX of the Minor Prophets, Isaiah and Psalms. In his quotations from these books Luke is always true to his text. The much less frequent quotations from other parts of the OT were not made by Luke directly, but came to him from church-tradition. Rese, however, shows, against Holtz, that Luke on occasion did handle his LXX-text freely, in the interest of his theological message. But his use of the OT is in any case much more straight-forward than that of Matthew and John.

142. *Ἔξοδος* may here be only a solemn way of saying 'death', as in 2 Peter 1:15 and occasionally in classical Greek, see LSJ s.v.: but in the only remaining NT example, Hebr. 11:22, it refers to the exodus from Egypt led by Moses. In Matt. 2:13–18 the infant Jesus is set in parallel to the infant Moses, and in John 1:21; 6:14; 7:40 it is hinted that Jesus is the prophet (like Moses) of Deut. 18:15, 18. But it is only in Acts 3:22f.; 7:37 that this passage of Deuteronomy is actually quoted; and, if the longer text of the institution of the Lord's Supper in Luke 22:19f. is authentic, as seems increasingly likely, then Luke shares with Matthew and Mark (and Paul) the terminology of a 'new covenant' in

Jesus. And the association of ἔξοδος with Moses in Luke 9:30f. makes it hard to see in the former only a grandiloquism for 'death'.

143. G. Friedrich, 'Lukas 9:51 und die Entrückungschristologie des Lukas', argues that, although Luke draws extensively on traditions of 'assumption' in both Graeco-Roman and Jewish religious history, the meaning of ἀνάλημψις in Luke 9:51 is 'death' rather than 'ascension'. His reasons are two: (a) Lexicographically, ἀνάλημψις and ἀναλαμβάνειν can refer to 'death' as well as to 'assumption' or 'ascension' (49f.); (b) 'Die Entrückung ist nicht ein Kernpunkt der lukanischen Theologie, sondern ein geeignetes Schema, um die Trennung Jesu von seinen Jüngern zu beschreiben und den Einschnitt zwischen dem Wirken des irdischen Jesus und der von ihm beauftragten Boten in der Zeit der Kirche bis zur Parusie zu charakterisieren' (52). But the latter is clearly wrong, as is shown by such important passages as Luke 22:69; Acts 2:33; and 7:55f. It is in fact *central* to Luke's theology in Acts that Jesus is enthroned in the presence of God in heaven: see above, section 3(b) of this chapter. As to the first point, Friedrich himself does not deny that ἀναλαμβάνειν refers to 'ascension' in Acts 1:2, 11, 22. Since ἀνάλημψις in Luke 9:51 is hapax legomenon in the NT, it is hard to see why Luke would have used such a rare word unless he was making an allusion to the theme that later was to become so important in his book.

144. As can be seen from the vain attempts of versions into ancient as well as modern languages to turn it into some acceptable idiom.

145. G. Lohfink, *Himmelfahrt*, 214: 'Dem eigenwilligen Gebrauch von συμπληροῦσθαι in Lk 9:51 und Apg 2:1 liegt ein für Lukas typisches Mißverständnis einer biblischen Wendung zugrunde': e.g. in Luke 2:6 ἐπλήσθησαν αἱ ἡμέραι τοῦ τεκεῖν αὐτήν makes no sense literally: the Hebrew for what he means would be וַיִּמָּלְאוּ יָמֶיהָ לָלֶדֶת. 'Die Wendung [ἐν] τῷ συμπληροῦσθαι τὰς ἡμέρας τῆς ἀναλήμψεως ist also von der biblischen Sprache her ein Unding.' 'When the days were fulfilled' is a good OT phrase which suited Luke, especially at this turning-point of his story (Luke 9:51). But by the plural ἡμέραι he must have meant more than one 'day' (cf. Acts 2:1!): viz., the whole series of death, resurrection and ascension.

It may be that Luke has 'misunderstood' a biblical idiom. But he is too good a Greek stylist to commit himself to such an 'Unding' without good reason. In both cases, and especially the quite impossible Greek of Acts 2:1, it must have been most important for him to bring in the theme of 'fulfilment', not just as a clumsy way to give his story a biblical flavour, but so as to hint at a theological affirmation.

146. So E. Lohse, *Πεντηκοστή*, 50.

147. Jewish evidence for this hope: T. Levi 18:12; T. Judah 25:3; T. Asher 7:3; T. Dan 5:10f.; Ass. Mos. 10:1; Jub. 23:29: cited by I. H. Marshall, *Gospel of Luke*, 429.

148. *MdZ*, 98 (ET, 107f.).

149. There is confusion in the English version of *MdZ* at this point: n. 2 on p. 107 appears to relate to a discussion of Luke 11:19f. which appears in *MdZ* 99 but has fallen out of the text of ET.

150. In addition to the passages referred to above, Luke 4:1–13; 8:12; 13:16; Acts 5:3; 10:38; 13:10; 26:18.

151. For a critique of Conzelmann's theory of a 'Satan-free time' between Jesus' temptation and his passion, see S. Brown, *Apostasy and Perseverance*, especially 6–12.

152. Acts 28:3–6 provides specific confirmation of Luke 10:19; cf. Luke 21:18.
153. See R. Maddox, 'Son of Man in Synoptics', 57.
154. Op. cit., 66.
155. Op. cit., 62f. I would now interpret v. 9, 'today salvation has come to this house, since he too is a son of Abraham', differently. According to Luke, as we have seen in Chapter Two, above, it is right and proper that salvation should be offered to the Jews and accepted by them. That this did happen in some cases is a cause for joy, which sets the tragedy of the more general failure of Israel to respond to Jesus into sharper relief. Like the tax-collector in Luke 18:9–14 and the sinners of 15:1f., Zacchaeus represents the outcasts within the Israelite community hinted at in the parable of the great banquet, 14:21.
156. In the Matthaean parallel, 12:38–42, the same sort of point lies behind v. 39, 41: but the comparison between Jonah and the Son of Man is developed in a midrashic kind of way in v. 40, where the distinctive point about Jonah is no longer his preaching but his emergence from the belly of the whale after three days and nights, prefiguring the resurrection of Jesus. It is, however, doubtful whether v. 40 stood in the original text of Matthew, despite its solid support in the MS tradition: see K. Stendahl, *The School of St Matthew*, 132f.

6. The Special Affinities of Luke and John

In the many studies that have been devoted to the relationship between the Gospels of Luke and John, attention has been concentrated upon literary or source-relationships. The question mainly discussed has been whether the special similarities between these two gospels are due to the use of one gospel by the other evangelist as a source, or whether the two evangelists had sources in common. Our concern here is with Luke's purpose, and to ask whether comparison of Luke's work with the Gospel of John can help to illuminate this. But some attention to the source-question cannot be avoided, as a starting-point for our investigation. Nor can we avoid, in the first instance, a certain concentration on John, because of the fact that in its character and much of its material John stands over against the synoptic gospels as a group.

1 John and the Synoptics: Written Sources and Oral Traditions

Is there a direct literary relationship between Luke and John? Is Luke, as has often been suggested, a source for the composition of John? This is part of the wider, and complex, question of John's relation to all three synoptic gospels. Why does John differ so much in both substance and style from the other three gospels in telling the story of Jesus' mission? The answers that have been offered to this question are essentially along two lines: 1. John knew the other three gospels but drastically rewrote their story so as to open up on it a new insight, gained by John and the church to which he belonged through decades of meditation, argument and teaching about Jesus and living in obedience to him as their risen Lord. 2. John drew on information conveyed by oral tradition independently of the material used by the synoptists: where he overlaps with the other evangelists it is because of a common memory of the same incidents, and not because he knew the other gospels in written form. Many modifications of these basic answers have been proposed: that John knew only one or two of the synoptics (either Mark only, or Mark and Luke); that John used a now lost book which was a source of Mark; that John had read the synoptic gospels or had heard them read, or parts of them, but did not have copies of them on his desk as he wrote; that John used the other gospels, or some of them, but supplemented or corrected them from other sources; that the particular connexions of Luke and John are on the contrary due to Luke's having read and used John; etc.

A valuable survey of research on these questions over the last century or so was published in 1965 by J. Blinzler.[1] Blinzler shows that for the seventy years from H. J. Holtzmann in 1869 to P. Gardner-Smith in 1938 almost everyone agreed (with only various minor qualifications) that Clement of Alexandria had been right in regarding John as a supplementary gospel, intended to show the 'spiritual' meaning of the 'physical' story of Jesus told in the synoptics. But Gardner-Smith's little book wrought a remarkable change.[2] Gardner-Smith protested against two methodological errors which he found universally present in the work of those who discussed the question: first, that not enough account was taken of oral tradition, by which partly similar and partly variant information could be passed on, and it was too readily assumed that even partial agreement must be due to literary dependence; second, that people emphasized the points of correspondence between John and the synoptics and tended to take no account of the differences: a proper judgement about literary dependence would have to balance agreement against divergence. Gardner-Smith then went through John section by section and built up an impressive case that John draws partly on the same streams of oral tradition as the synoptics and partly on different ones.

There were two practical consequences that might be drawn from Gardner-Smith's conclusions, both having to do with evaluating the historical reliability of John.[3] One is that, if John is to be seen as drawing on oral tradition for most of his material, the degree of allegorization or free composition might be substantially less than would be required by thinking of him as a reinterpreter of the synoptic gospels; the other is that, if John is not dependent on the synoptic gospels, the reason for dating his work later than them is partly removed. In either case, the historicity of John's narrative seemed to be enhanced. Blinzler regards this as an important psychological reason why Gardner-Smith's argument was so widely persuasive, to the point where D. M. Smith in the 1960's spoke of a new consensus in its favour.[4]

But there was another reason, probably much more important: namely, the development in the period between the two world wars of the form-critical method, which opened people's eyes to the likelihood of oral tradition as the main vehicle for perhaps several decades by which the gospel material was preserved and communicated. However, Blinzler himself is not convinced of the Gardner-Smith solution, and he is able to name such leading Johannine commentators as C. K. Barrett and R. H. Lightfoot, as well as many other scholars, as witnesses with him against the consensus claimed by D. M. Smith.[5]

Blinzler holds that Mark was used as a written source by John, and for this he cites three main arguments:[6] 1. John in several passages mentions a person or event without explanation, as if his readers are already familiar with it, implying that he assumes in his readers a knowledge of Mark which he also possesses. 2. Many incidents occur in the same order in John and Mark, suggesting that John has followed Mark's order. 3. There are eight passages in which identical or very similar Greek phrases occur, suggesting that John is copying Mark's text.

None of these arguments really carries much weight. As for the assumption of familiarity, this is not confined to persons or events mentioned in Mark. For example, neither Nicodemus nor Nathanael occurs in Mark. Though Nicodemus is introduced with a brief explanation in John 3:1, Nathanael in 1:45ff. lacks any such explanation. Nor is John the only evangelist to write in this way. In Acts 12:17 Luke mentions James for the first time, but without any explanation of who he is: the Gospel of Luke even lacks a parallel to the brief mention of him in Mark 6:3. Similarly, the 'elders' of the Jerusalem-church are mentioned for the first time in Acts 11:30, but without explanation. We have no reason to think Luke was assuming in his readers knowledge of some other book in which James and the elders were introduced: oral tradition is explanation enough; and so is it in the Johannine cases mentioned by Blinzler.

The other two arguments perhaps are a little stronger. It may be argued that when John brings the cleansing of the Temple forward to ch. 2 (from Mark 11) this is for a particular theological purpose, but that on the other hand it is impressive that John agrees with Mark in putting Jesus' walking on the water immediately after the feeding of the five thousand (Mark 6:33–52/John 6:1–21). Yet in the passion-story John diverges widely from Mark's order (in many cases agreeing with Luke against Mark),[7] and not all the divergences can be seen to have a theological or artistic purpose.[8] Gardner-Smith and his followers regard oral tradition as again able to account for the linking of some incidents.

What about the cases where Mark and John share identical or almost identical Greek phrases of up to half a dozen words? Probably the most striking is in the story of the anointing of Jesus' head (Mark) or his feet (John) with 'myrrh of pistic nard, very costly' (Mark 14:3/John 12:3). Can such phrases be explained as having been handed on in oral tradition, or do they require the supposition of a link in writing? In the example cited, remarkable coincidence in wording is linked with divergence, as to whether it was Jesus' head or feet which the woman anointed. If it be argued that John altered this detail (out of reverence, or for some other reason), the matter becomes complicated by the need to bring into account the similar story in Luke 7:36–50, with which both Mark's and John's stories have some connexions, yet which also goes its own way in some important respects: for in Luke, too, it is Jesus' feet which are anointed. To the comparison of Luke and John in this story we shall need to return.[9] A complication of a different kind is presented by the identical command, 'Arise, take up your bed and walk', which in Mark 2:11 is addressed to a paralytic in Capernaum and in John 5:8 to a lame man at the pool of Bethesda in Jerusalem. It would be a most remarkable way to use a literary source, to lift just one such phrase from a story otherwise omitted and to insert it into a quite different story. Different memories in the oral retelling of Jesus' healings give a more natural explanation of the different settings given to a surprising command.[10]

The question of the literary relationship of John and Mark is not our main concern, and this is not the place to explore it in detail. But it is a relevant preliminary question to our discussion of the relationship of John and Luke, and we should try to estimate the method needed to resolve it. If John has used Mark as a source, he has clearly used it very freely indeed. Now the question is: *how far* would an evangelist feel free to depart from or correct the statements of a predecessor whose work he is using as a source and with which he presumes his readers to be familiar? Luke can quite clearly be seen to be departing from Mark and on occasions even correcting him (e.g. Mark 16:7/Luke 24:6, 49). But are the divergences of John from Mark similar enough to Luke's divergences from Mark to be consistent with the theory of literary dependence? J. Blinzler, C. K. Barrett and others stress that John's 'use' of his source or sources is quite different from Luke's or Matthew's.[11] But Gardner-Smith contended that John's alleged departures from Mark are in some cases pointless, and therefore the idea of any literary dependence at all is made implausible. When in John 1:21 John the Baptist denies that he is Elijah, this may be due to a different view of eschatology or 'the history of salvation' from that lying behind Mark 9:11–13. And there may be a theological reason for shifting the whole theme of the eucharist from the last supper to the context of the feeding of the five thousand. But why has the call of the first disciples in John 1:35ff. been told in a way without the slightest connexion with the story of the call of the four fishermen in Mark 1:16–20?[12] Why are the Twelve disciples as a group so much less prominent, though still present? Why does the mission of John the Baptist overlap in time with that of Jesus (John 3:22–4:3), especially since John the Evangelist is in general concerned to minimize the independent significance of John the Baptist (John 3:25–30; cf. 1:6f., 15, 19–34)? To get John the Baptist's activity over with before Jesus' begins would have fitted in well with John 1:30, 'After me there is coming a man who was before me'!

Again, while there are some stories which are obviously the same incidents in the respective gospels, though with varying details (such as the anointing of Jesus, and his entry into Jerusalem on a colt), and there are also stories in each gospel which are not in the other in any form, there are also one or two cases where we cannot be sure whether it is the same story. Thus, is the *παῖς* or *υἱός* of the *βασιλικός* at Capernaum whom Jesus healed by a command from a distance in John 4:46–53 the same as the *παῖς* or *δοῦλος* of the *ἑκατόνταρχος* or *ἑκατοντάρχης* at Capernaum whom Jesus healed in the same way in Matt. 8:5–13/Luke 7:1–10?[13] This very striking example of course relates to Matthew and Luke and not to Mark. But is the confession of Peter in John 6:66–69 the same as that in Mark 8:27–33? Why is the saying that a prophet is not without honour except in his own country applied in Mark 6:4 to Jesus' rejection by Nazareth in Galilee but in John

4:43–45 to his rejection by Judaea as distinct from Galilee (cf. John 4:54)?

In the light of these considerations, I believe the probability lies with Gardner-Smith's argument. John obviously has access not only to traditions about Jesus independent of those used in the synoptics, but also in some cases to different forms of the same traditions, where the differences are not attributable to John's acknowledged tendency to draw out the symbolic significance of the story.

The relationship between John and Luke is different in some interesting respects from that between John and Mark. Blinzler decided that John used Mark as a source, and that he did not use Matthew, but about Luke he could not make up his mind.[14] There are no cases of exact verbal correspondence between John and Luke like the eight between John and Mark. On the other hand, there is a surprisingly large number of cases where John and Luke share common stories or pieces of information or points of view, sometimes independently of the other two gospels and sometimes over against them. For convenience, let us distinguish three categories. First, a general category of common material. This can be further divided into small coincidences in matters of fact or imagery, and larger narratives with similar content or ideas. Second, a common historical and especially geographical perspective. Third, a common theological perspective.

2 Material Common to Luke and John

(a) In the first, intrinsically least important group, of small coincidences of fact or imagery, we note the following examples:

In Luke 12:37, in a parable, Jesus speaks of a grateful master who will gird himself, make his slaves recline at the dinner-table and come and serve them. It is rather like what Jesus himself does at the last supper in John 13:4.

According to Luke 22:43, an angel appears to Jesus in the garden of Gethsemane, strengthening him.[15] In John 12:28f., in Jesus' last public appearance before the last supper and arrest, a voice comes from heaven after Jesus says, 'Now is my soul troubled, and what am I to say? Father, save me from this hour?', which is the nearest we come in John to an incident like that in Gethsemane in the synoptics.

Luke 22:45 (alone) mentions the grief of the disciples as the reason for their sleep in Gethsemane. In John 16:6, 20ff., Jesus predicts the grief which the disciples will feel at his departure.

In Acts 1:21f., the qualification of a person to replace Judas among the Twelve Apostles is that he must be able to become a witness with the Eleven of the whole time in which the Lord Jesus 'went in and out among us, beginning from the baptism of John until the day he was taken up from us'. In John 15:27, at the last supper, Jesus, having said that the Holy Spirit will bear witness about him, says to the disciples, 'And you too are to bear witness, because you have been with me from the beginning'.

In these examples the degree of resemblance varies. In no case is it a matter of verbal identity: but nothing corresponding occurs in Mark or Matthew. Here we seem to have traces of a common line of oral tradition behind Luke and John.

(b) Much more important is the fairly long list of larger narratives with similar contents or ideas. These passages have been extensively studied, and there is no need for another detailed examination of them here. The classic study remains that of J. Schniewind published in 1914.[16] Schniewind's list of the relevant passages is as follows:

1.	Luke 3:3–20	John 1:19f., 26, 28; 3:22–4:3
2.	Luke 5:1–11	John 21:1–19
3.	Luke 7:1–10	John 4:46–54
4.	Luke 7:36–50	John 12:3–8
5.	Luke 19:28–40	John 12:12–19
6.	Luke 22:31–34	John 13:36–38
7.	Luke 22:39, 47–53	John 18:1–11
8.	Luke 22:54–71	John 18:12–27 (10:24; 3:12; 8:45)
9.	Luke 23:1–25	John 18:28–19:16
10.	Luke 23:26–56	John 19:16–42
11.	Luke 24	John 20

More recently, a study of similar scope was made by J. A. Bailey (1963).[17] The list shows how important the passion-narrative is with respect to the common materials of Luke and John: and a still more recent study has been devoted to this part of the material by H. Klein (1976).[18]

Only in a very few cases do the items in this list represent special Lucan-Johannine narratives. In most cases the narratives are shared by Mark or Matthew or both of them, but there are distinctive elements in the Lucan and Johannine forms of the stories. The most prominent example of a distinctive Lucan-Johannine story is the miraculous catch of fish (no. 2 in the list). This links Luke with the epilogue of John, but within the main body of John there is a brief resurrection-story shared with Luke: Luke 24:36–41, 47–49/John 20:19–22.

In addition to sharing a good deal of distinctive matter, Luke and John sometimes agree over against Mark and Matthew as to the order in which events are narrated. Again, this is most prominent in the passion-story, where for example Peter's denial of Jesus is predicted at the supper in Luke 22:31–34/John 13:36–38 but on the way to Gethsemane in Mark 14:26–31/Matt. 26:30–35; in Luke 22:21–23 Judas' betrayal is predicted after the institution of the eucharist, and in John 13:21–30 after the foot-washing, but in Mark 14:18–21/Matt. 26:21–25 before the institution of the sacrament; etc. Elsewhere, a striking example occurs in Luke 9:10–22/John 6:1–71, where Peter's confession follows immediately upon the feeding of the five thousand (with, in John, the discourse arising from it), but in Mark 6:32–8:33/Matt. 14:31–16:23 much other matter intervenes.

In the passion-story (starting from the triumphal entry into Jerusalem) the following points of special contact between Luke and John call for mention.

Only in Luke 19:37 and John 12:17f. is the acclamation of the crowd as Jesus enters Jerusalem said to be due to the miracles he had performed.

Only in Luke 22:39 (cf. 21:37) and John 18:2 is it said that Jesus and his disciples used to frequent the Mount of Olives. When Judas and the soldiers come for him there, according to Luke 22:49f., 54, and John 18:8ff., 12 the disciples try to prevent his arrest, but in Mark 14:46ff. and Matt. 26:50f. they try to release him. Only Luke 22:50 and John 18:10 mention that in the skirmish it was the *right* ear of the High Priest's slave which one of the disciples cut off.

In John 18:13–24 (especially v. 19) Annas is somehow said to be High Priest: cf. Luke 3:2; Acts 4:6. In Mark the High Priest is never named; in Matthew he is Caiaphas (Matt. 26:3, 57): but Luke and John both hesitate on the position of Caiaphas (Luke 3:2; Acts 4:6; John 11:49; 18:13f., 24). In Mark 14:53–65/Matt. 26:57–68 Jesus' appearance before the High Priest is a formal trial: in Luke 22:54, 63–71/ John 18:13f., 19–24 it is an informal hearing.

In the trial before Pilate there is an important difference, bearing on the understanding of the reason for Jesus' crucifixion. In Luke 23:2 and John 19:12–15 a charge of sedition is explicitly brought against Jesus by the Jewish authorities. In Mark 15:2, 9, 12/Matt. 27:11 (17, 22) it is implied that Jesus has been charged with claiming to be 'king of the Jews', but no emphasis is laid on what this signified, and in Mark v. 10/Matt. v. 18 the real motive of the accusations against Jesus is said to be 'envy'. Pilate declares Jesus innocent three times in Luke (23:4, 14, 22) and John (18:38; 19:4, 6): in Mark and Matthew he does so only once, and indirectly (Mark 15:14/Matt. 27:23). Only in Luke and John does Pilate take an interest in where Jesus is 'from', though the question is developed in typically different ways in the two gospels (Luke 23:6–12; John 18:33–38; 19:9).

In Luke 23:16 Pilate suggests scourging Jesus, and in John 19:1–12 he carries it out, as a proposed compromise with those who sought his death: in Mark 15:15/Matt. 27:26 the scourging is simply preliminary to execution, which corresponds with Roman practice.

In neither Luke nor John do Jesus' words from the cross include a cry of dereliction (Mark 15:34/Matt. 27:46).

Similarly, there are special connexions between Luke and John in the scenes concerning the resurrection. What the disciples of Emmaus tell Jesus about the events of Easter-morning (Luke 24:23f.) corresponds with the narrative of John 20:1–10, but not with any other of the resurrection-narratives. In Luke 24:26 Jesus tells the Emmaus-disciples that the Christ had to suffer and enter into his glory; in John 12:28ff., it is said that God will glorify the Son of Man when he is lifted up from the earth, which is his death.

Both in Luke 24:36–41a and John 20:19f., Jesus suddenly appears to his gathered disciples in Jerusalem, the phrase 'he stood in the midst' is used, the disciples are filled with joy, and Jesus shows them his hands and feet (Luke) or side (John). Then in Luke 24:47–49/John 20:21–23 Jesus speaks to the disciples about the world-mission, the forgiveness of sins and the gift of the Holy Spirit. There is none of all this in Mark or Matthew.

To return to the examples which stand outside the passion-narrative. The least important for our purpose is the healing at Capernaum, no. 3 in our list taken from J. Schniewind. For though there are special connexions between Luke 7:1–10 and John 4:46–54, such as the part played by intermediaries between Jesus and the petitioner, and Luke's use of the Johannine-sounding expression 'the elders of the Jews', Luke 7:1–10 is much closer to Matt. 8:5–13, and there are also special connexions between the latter and John 4:46–54. In this case we clearly have a complex history of oral transmission, in which the three streams retain a variety of mutual links.

The story about John the Baptist (no. 1 in the list) is a little more interesting. Luke's material in 3:1–20 is basically synoptic, i.e. drawn from Mark and Q. But there are traces of geographical information that recall John (Luke 3:3/John 1:28; 3:22–26), and, more importantly, Luke 3:15 contains a hint of an emphatic Johannine concern, to deny that John the Baptist is the Messiah (John 1:19f., 25f., 30; 3:28–30).

But the most tantalizing set of material in which Luke and John have special contacts is that concerning Martha, Mary and Lazarus. All three names appear in only these two gospels. The characters of the two sisters are perhaps respectively recognizable in Luke 10:38–42 and John 11, the chapter about the raising of their (Johannine!) brother Lazarus. But in John 12:2f. are some interesting details. After Lazarus was raised they gave him a dinner party, and Martha was serving, as she was in Luke 10:40. But Mary anointed Jesus' feet and wiped his feet with her hair: in Luke 10:39 she sat by Jesus' feet and listened to his talk. In Luke the sisters have no brother mentioned, but there is a Lazarus in the parable in Luke 16:19–31, the only character in any parable of Jesus who has a name. This Lucan Lazarus dies and is raised not to a resumed earthly life, like the Johannine Lazarus, but to the banqueting-table of Abraham in heaven (ἐν τοῖς κόλποις αὐτοῦ, Luke 16:23b, cf. 13:28f.) In the two very different settings of John and Luke, 'Lazarus' shares the details that he is raised from death and is entertained at a dinner-party. Then there are the remarkable connexions between this same Martha-Mary-Lazarus-story in John 12:1ff. and, on the one hand, Mark 14:3–9/Matt. 26:6–13 and, on the other hand, still another passage in Luke, 7:36–50. The Lucan form of the anointing-story differs from that in the other three gospels, first as to time and place, for it occurs somewhere in Galilee, relatively early in Jesus' career, rather than at Bethany in association with the passion-story; and second in that the point of the story has to do with the penitence and forgiveness of a sinner, rather than with a spontaneous act of devotion to Jesus, which predicts his death and burial. The three synoptists agree in naming the host as Simon, though in Luke he is described as a Pharisee and in Mark/Matthew as a leper; and in the fact that the woman is not named. But the accounts in Luke and John also share two features over against Mark and Matthew: it is Jesus' feet, not his head, which are anointed; and the woman wipes Jesus' feet with her hair.

These two features common to Luke 7:36–50 and John 12:1–8 have played an important part in the discussion about the nature of the links between these two gospels. J. Schniewind's study of the whole question led him to conclude that the affinities between Luke and John are to be explained by oral tradition rather than literary dependence by John on Luke. However, he did not deny that John 'presupposed' the three synoptic gospels;[19] and in two cases he thought it possible that the form of the story in John was influenced by reminiscence of the Gospel of Luke. These are Luke 5:1–11/John 21:1–19 (to which we shall return later) and Luke 7:36–50/John 12:3–8.[20] With regard to the former example, J. A. Bailey came to the conclusion (much more likely, as we shall see) that the two evangelists were drawing on a common tradition;[21] but for him the anointing-story was decisive proof, on the contrary, that John knew and used the Gospel of Luke.[22] The point here is that Mark 14:3–9 and Luke 7:36–50, with their various resemblances and differences, and despite the remarkable nature of the woman's action in each case, are each tidy and credible stories. But the story in John is difficult, and it is the elements shared with Luke which cause the difficulty. In Luke the woman first wets Jesus' feet with her tears, then wipes the tears away with her hair, then anoints his feet with myrrh. In John there is no mention of tears: the action begins, as in Mark, with the woman (in John, Mary) taking a pound 'of myrrh, very expensive pistic nard', and anointing Jesus with it. But then, in John, she wipes the myrrh off again with her hair. Why should she do that? The only explanation, according to Schniewind and Bailey, is that John has altered the story, which he received essentially in the form as in Mark, under the influence (indirect according to Schniewind, direct according to Bailey) of Luke.

Bailey points out that in Luke the anointing of the *feet* is important, because of the theme of penitence: in John there is no apparent reason for the change from head to feet; and so it is argued that the only explanation for this feature in John is a borrowing from Luke.[23] We would then have to admit that the wiping away of the myrrh in John is a rather clumsy failure to adjust the new to the old form of the story. The matter can however be explained otherwise. If the anointing-story circulated widely in oral tradition, a form in which Jesus' *feet* were anointed may at first have said nothing about the penitence and forgiveness of a sinner, but only have intended to emphasize reverence for Jesus. This would make at least that feature of John's account independent of Luke's. The myrrh may have been understood by John as a liquid, so that the hair-wiping was to remove the excess. Certainly in Mark it is a liquid, for the woman broke the neck of an alabastron and poured out its contents (Mark 14:3).[24] There is no strong reason to look beyond oral tradition to explain where John learned of the hair-wiping, for Luke, too, must have got it from oral tradition.[25]

We may therefore conclude that Bailey's strongest example in favour of the literary dependence of John on Luke is unconvincing. In other cases, Bailey himself agrees with Schniewind that Luke and John have independently used the same or similar oral traditions. It is in fact highly probable that what P. Gardner-Smith argued about the relationship of John to Mark (or to the synoptic gospels in general) also holds true for the special material common to Luke and John: it is independent use of oral tradition which provides the explanation, not literary dependence. And these special contacts are, as we have seen, quite considerable, in matters of small detail as well as in larger narratives. With respect to various individual items that we have considered, it might be objected that there is nothing very significant: in some cases the correspondences between Luke and John are just what one might expect, and it is only accidental that Mark and Matthew have nothing corresponding; in other cases, the alleged resemblances may be judged to be far-fetched. But the list as a whole builds up an impressive picture of streams of oral tradition, emerging in the gospels of Luke and John, which are somehow related.[26]

It is not without importance that the same special relationship with Luke continues on into the later Johannine school, as is shown by more than one example in the epilogue, John ch. 21. Most noteworthy here is the story of the miraculous catch of fish taken by Peter before Jesus calls him to catch men, Luke 5:1–11, and in connexion with the (third) resurrection-appearance of Jesus to his disciples, before Peter is charged to feed Jesus' sheep, John 21:1–14. Since the detailed study of this pair of parallel passages by R. Pesch (1969),[27] it is no longer possible to refer to them in support of 'John's' literary dependence on Luke. We must now regard it as definitely established that what we have here is a case of a highly complicated development, in oral tradition, of the one story into two substantially different forms, which reached Luke and the author of John 21 independently. Within this story in its Johannine form is a detail found also in another part of Luke: according to John 21:12f. and Luke 24:41b–43, Jesus after his resurrection ate broiled fish with his disciples. And then the sequel in John 21:15–17 seems to be a remarkable echo of yet another passage in Luke. At the last supper, according to Luke 22:31f., Jesus said, 'Simon, Simon, look: Satan has asked for all of you so that he may sift you like wheat. But I have prayed for you (singular, Peter only), that your faith may not run out: and when at last you turn, you must strengthen your brothers'. In John 21:15–17 we read, 'Simon, son of John, do you love me more than these people do? . . . Feed my sheep'.

In many of the passages we have considered in this section, the special traditions shared by Luke and John do not have any obvious bias or special interest, and therefore we can surmise little about the channels through which these traditions reached Luke and John. In some cases, however, such a special interest has already emerged: for example, the emphasis that John the Baptist is not the Messiah, and that Jesus was charged by the Jewish authorities before Pilate with sedition.

The special affinities between Luke and John which we have to review in the next two sections are of a different kind, for they suggest not only that Luke and John had common or similar materials available to them but also that the two evangelists had to some extent similar points of view and convictions about the meaning of the gospel-story. For the most part, of course, it remains true that the Gospel of Luke is a 'synoptic' gospel, that for most purposes it is convenient and proper to group it with Mark and Matthew over against John. But the relationships are more subtle than that. There is, for example, to some extent a common historical and especially geographical perspective shared by Luke and John, to which we must now turn.

3 A Common Geographical Perspective

When one reads the Gospel of Luke with a mind conditioned by familiarity with Mark and Matthew, one may have the impression that the mission of Jesus, according to Luke, took place mostly in Galilee. According to Mark and Matthew, the mission was entirely in Galilee and other northern parts until the last week of Jesus' life. According to John, on the other hand, the greater part of it was in Judaea. But in fact the Galilaean section of Luke lasts only from 4:14 to 9:51: then Jesus turns to go to Jerusalem, passing at once into Samaritan territory. Thereafter, Luke presumably means that Jesus is active in Samaria and Judaea, always making his way forward to Jerusalem. The impression that it is otherwise is no doubt due on the one hand to the fact that much of the material in the travel-section (9:51–19:40) is located by Matthew in Galilee (the journey in Matthew lasts only from 20:17 to 21:11), and, on the other hand, that in this section Luke is vague about localities. In fact, despite the long stretch of the journey presumably already achieved, Luke 17:11 seems to suggest that Jesus is still not far from Galilee. Nevertheless, Luke seems to have an editorial interest in showing that Jesus was active in Samaria and Judaea to an extent that one would never suspect from Mark or Matthew.

Not only so, but already in the heavily Galilaean section early in Luke we find some editorial adjustment towards an interest in Judaea. Thus where Mark has in 1:39, 'He went preaching into their synagogues in the whole of Galilee', Luke 4:44 says, 'And he was preaching in the synagogues of Judaea'. And in editing Mark's summary at Mark 3:7ff., Luke (6:17) drops Galilee from the list of places from which people came to hear Jesus, but leaves in Judaea as the first in the list.[28] (In the accusation before Pilate, Luke 23:5, Galilee is mentioned as the beginning-point of Jesus' activity, but there is emphasis on what he has done in Judaea and Jerusalem.)

Then there is the famous journey of Jesus from Galilee to Jerusalem, which in Mark and Matthew takes a chapter or less to tell, but in Luke lasts ten chapters, from 9:51 to 19:40. Many reasons have been proposed for this surprising arrangement of Luke's material. One important one (which we discussed in Chapter Two, section 6) is that Jerusalem is the goal of Jesus' journey, and Luke has a special theological interest in showing that Jesus' whole mission is an approach to the central institutions of Judaism with the authority of the Father to 'visit' them (Luke 19:44) with either blessing or judgement, depending on their response. But another may well be to leave room for the general impression that Jesus was active in preaching in Samaria and Judaea as well as Galilee. The journey-section includes three references to Samaria and Samaritans, who twice appear in a favourable light (Luke 10:33–35; 17:11–19). Mark has no reference to Samaria at all; in Matthew the only one is 10:5, where Jesus, in the mission-instructions to the Twelve, forbids them to enter Samaria. This restriction is not included by Luke in Jesus' instructions either to the Twelve in 9:1–6 or to the Seventy in 10:1–16. In Luke 9:52–56, Jesus, accompanied by his disciples, attempts a mission in Samaria, though it is apparently frustrated by the traditional hostility of the Samaritans towards the Jews. But here we have at least an indication in Luke of the traditions reflected in John 4:1–42 of a Samaritan mission, perhaps an extensive one, carried out by Jesus; and the insult offered to Jesus by Jewish opponents in John 8:48 actually includes calling him a Samaritan.

In the resurrection-story in Mark 16:1–8/Matt. 28:1–8 the disciples are instructed by the angel at the tomb to return to Galilee, where they will meet Jesus. In Luke 24:1–11 this instruction is eliminated, and in v. 49 the risen Jesus himself tells them to stay in Jerusalem until they have received the power of the Holy Spirit, after which they will preach in all the world, beginning from Jerusalem (v. 47f.). And in both Luke 24 and John 20, unlike Mark 16/Matt. 28, Jesus appears to his disciples in Jerusalem and its suburbs. There is a subsequent resurrection-appearance in Galilee in the Johannine epilogue, but not in Luke–Acts.

In Acts Galilee is only mentioned again (as in Luke 24:6) in retrospect, as the place from which Jesus and his disciples originated, except for the solitary mention, in a passing note in Acts 9:31, of the existence of the church in Galilee. Galilee is conspicuously absent from the mission-charge in Acts 1:8, though Samaria is included. In the narratives about missionary enterprise we learn much about Samaria (Acts 8:1, 5–25; 9:31; 15:3) and about Judaea outside Jerusalem (Acts 8:1, 26f., 40; 9:31, 32–43; 11:1, 29; 26:20; in other passages, 15:1; 21:10 and 28:21 'Judaea' may in fact stand for Jerusalem), but, apart from 9:31, nothing about Galilee. This is no doubt partly explained by the actual course of events: Paul's letters generally support the statement of Acts that the disciples, the Twelve and others, moved permanently to Jerusalem to make it the base of their evangelism.

What then lies behind the tradition in Mark 16 and Matt. 28 (and indeed

John 21), that the risen Jesus encountered his disciples only in Galilee? Why do Mark and Matthew leave us with the impression that the disciples had no more to do with Jerusalem than to accompany Jesus thither in the week of his death, and to return from it as soon as the empty tomb was found? To Mark and Matthew Judaea and Jerusalem appear to be foreign territory, at least for the disciples, and essentially for Jesus too. In sharp contrast with this stands the fact that in John 4:43–45 (cf. 54) Judaea is spoken of, in distinction from Galilee, as Jesus' πατρίς, despite the fact that Jesus is several times acknowledged to be a native of Nazareth in Galilee (John 1:45f., 7:41, 52; 18:5, 7; 19:19). Moreover, John 3:22–4:3 speaks of an extended mission of Jesus in the same district of Judaea, and at about the same time, as John the Baptist, quite apart from the many narratives about Jesus' attendance at the festivals in Jerusalem and his sojourns in various parts of Judaea (e.g. 10:40; 11:7–18, 54; 12:1). Luke has no such specific traditions about the residence and activity of Jesus in Judaea, but, as we have seen, his editorial handling of his material reflects the conviction that Jesus was far more active in the south than was indicated by Mark. One might, however, risk the speculation that a tradition of this mission in the south may lie behind the story in Luke 10 of Jesus' appointment of seventy disciples to travel ahead of him to preach the Kingdom of God. The charge to them is given in fuller terms than that to the Twelve in ch. 9, and their appointment comes after Jesus has entered Samaria from Galilee on his way to Jerusalem. Do they perhaps represent a memory that Jesus had other agents, and other spheres of mission, than Galilee and the Galilaean Twelve?

However that may be, we have strong indications in both Luke–Acts and John of a common interest in, and to a lesser extent common information about, the activity of Jesus in the central and southern parts of Palestine, and (explicitly in Acts and implicitly in John) about the establishment and growth of Christian congregations in the same area in the following decades. Beside this we must now set those elements of Luke–Acts and John which hint at a similar theological point of view.

4 A Common Theological Perspective

Between the theologies of Luke–Acts and John there are of course obvious, large and important differences. Behind each of these works lies not only the work of the respective evangelists but also a fairly long and vigorous development in the life of the congregations within which they lived. But the theological affinities are nevertheless sufficiently interesting to be worth examining.

In Chapter Two we explored the importance to Luke of understanding who are the 'people' of God – the question about the relationship of Jews, Gentiles and Christians to God's plans and promises for the world. A similar concern lies in the Gospel of John. On this theme there are a number of important statements in Luke–Acts and John that sound quite similar. In both works, it is said that the failure of the Jews, in the main, to respond positively to Jesus is of a piece with their failure to listen to Moses and the prophets. Thus, in Luke 16:29ff., Abraham tells the rich man in Hades, 'They have Moses and the prophets: let them listen to them . . . if they will not listen to Moses and the prophets, neither will they believe if someone should rise from the dead'. The last clause has an unmistakable Christological reference, which recalls the more explicit Christology of the similar words in John 5:46ff., 'If you believed Moses you would believe me, for he wrote about me. If you do not believe his written words (γράμματα), how will you believe my spoken words (ῥήματα)?'[29] Similarly, the public activity of Jesus in John comes to its end in 12:37–50 with the quotation of Isa. 6:9f., 'He has blinded their eyes and hardened their hearts, so that they may not see with their eyes and understand with their hearts and turn, that I may heal them' (v. 40), commenting on the hesitating response to Jesus of the Jewish leaders (v. 37, 42f.). This has a remarkable parallel in the end of Paul's career in Rome, Acts 28:17–28, where the same passage from Isaiah is quoted, and to the same effect.

In both Luke–Acts and John, the theme of 'Israel' is closely related to Christology. As we have already noted (Chapter One, section 3 (d)), Luke takes great care to set the birth and upbringing of the Messiah within the embrace of orthodox Jewish piety, though the salvation he is to bring also reaches out far beyond Israel, for he is to be 'light for revelation of the Gentiles' (2:30–32). Similarly, the prologue of John announces the theme, to be repeated several times later, that the incarnation brings 'light' for the whole human race (1:4f., 9; 8:12; 9:5; 12:46), yet the narrative from 1:19 onwards immediately establishes the Jewishness of Jesus, 'the King of Israel' (1:49; 12:13). Despite the universal scope set by the prologue and maintained throughout the gospel (cf. 3:16–21; 12:44–50; 17:20–26; etc.), John does not shrink from declaring that 'salvation is from the Jews' (4:22),[30] an assertion with which Luke would certainly have agreed (cf. Acts 3:24f.).

With this Christological perspective we may link the similar attitude taken in Luke–Acts and John to the Gentile mission. More consistently than Mark and Matthew, Luke and John restrict the access of the Gentiles to Jesus until after his death and resurrection. One important reason for Luke's great omission from Mark (Mark 6:46–8:26) is that in this section Jesus travels outside Palestine (and in the course of his travels grants a favour to a Syro-Phoenician woman and feeds what is probably meant as a Gentile multitude). Luke sets the 'Caesarea Philippi'-incident of the very next Marcan pericope at Bethsaida, which he clearly regards as being in Galilee (Luke 9:10–21; cf. John 12:21). Unlike Matt. 8:5–13, Luke 7:1–10 does not let the Gentile centurion come face to face with Jesus. Matthew understands the cases of the Canaanite woman (Matt. 15:21–28) and the centurion of Capernaum as exceptions to Jesus' rule, for the Twelve are in

Matt. 10:5 forbidden to go to the Gentiles: only after the resurrection (Matt. 28:19) is he available to all nations. This theme is stronger in Luke and John: there are no exceptions. However, for both Luke and John the Samaritans are to be grouped with the Jews rather than with the Gentiles (despite John 4:9f., 20), and, as we have noted, the Samaritans indeed have an important place in the mission both of Jesus and of his earliest church according to Luke and John. Acts 8 comes before Acts 10! In Luke 24:47 the Gentile mission is briefly announced, but it cannot begin until the apostles and the whole church are thoroughly convinced, by a further divine revelation, that it is really God's will (Acts 10:1–11:18). In John 12:20–24 some Greeks ask to see Jesus, but they are not allowed access to him: only after he has died will he bear the fruit of the Gentiles (cf. 7:33–36).

Unlike John, Luke lacks any reflection on the significance of Jesus' death as God's deed for the salvation of the world. On the other hand, these two evangelists share the theme that Jesus' death is the means of his entry into his glory. This is foreshadowed in the special Lucan part of the transfiguration-story (Luke 9:31f.) and stated explicitly by the risen Jesus to the Emmaus-disciples (Luke 24:26). Similarly, though with a characteristic Johannine nuance, the death of Jesus is spoken of in John as his 'glorification' (John 7:39; 12:16, 23; 13:31f.). Another point of resemblance in the Christologies of Luke and John is the prominence of Jesus' ascension both in Luke–Acts (see Chapter Five, section 3 (b)) and in John (3:13; 6:62; 20:17); but again a typically Johannine development occurs, in that the concept of 'exaltation' is used to speak simultaneously of Jesus' ascension and of his death (3:14; 8:28; 12:32ff.). In Luke 9:51 we find Jesus' ascension linked with his function of judgement (see Chapter Two, p. 47). This theme occurs with greater prominence and force in John (3:14–18; 8:26–28; 12:31f., cf. 46–48). John 12:31 mentions in this connexion the overthrow of 'the ruler of this world': and this recalls Luke 10:18, where Jesus declares that he has seen Satan fall like lightning from heaven. Only in these two gospels is it said that 'Satan entered into' Judas Iscariot for the betrayal of Jesus (Luke 22:3/John 13:27; cf. John 13:2; 6:70f.). In Luke 22:31f. Jesus prays for the protection of his disciples (especially Peter) from the assault of Satan (on them all): in John 17:15 Jesus prays that God will keep the disciples 'from the evil one'.

With this theme of the ascension, exaltation and glorification of Jesus there is associated, in both Luke–Acts and John, the doctrine of the Holy Spirit (especially Acts 2:33; John 7:39; John perhaps understands the ascension of Jesus, as an event distinct from the crucifixion and resurrection, to have taken place on Easter-day: John 20:17, 22, 27). This doctrine is important common ground for Luke and John. So it is, of course, for all the early Christians: but it is these two, over against Mark and Matthew, who bring the matter strongly into the gospel-story. In both, the Holy Spirit is mentioned as God's great gift to Jesus' disciples. In Luke 11:13, the climax of Jesus' teaching about prayer, following on the teaching of the Lord's Prayer, is that the Father will give (not 'good things', as in Matt. 7:11, but) the Holy Spirit: in John 14:16f., Jesus promises that the Father will give the Holy Spirit to those who keep Jesus' commandments. As to the function of the Holy Spirit, the emphasis on the whole diverges between Luke and John. In Luke–Acts the Holy Spirit is predominantly the agent who empowers evangelism; in John, the main work of the Holy Spirit is to represent the continuing presence and power of Jesus with his disciples and to continue the work of Jesus in the world. But the lines do not diverge completely, for in John 20:21f. is a note reminiscent of the Lucan emphasis: Jesus breathes Holy Spirit into his disciples as he sends them out on a mission corresponding to that on which the Father has sent him. In the synoptics, including Luke, the only promise made by the earthly Jesus about the future function of the Spirit is that he will aid the disciples to make a faithful testimony when they are under arrest in persecution (Mark 13:11/Matt. 10:19f./Luke 12:11f.; cf. 21:14f.). In John this is not said directly, though there is a distant resemblance perhaps in 14:26. But this function is suggested by the name of the Holy Spirit as Paraclete, Advocate, in John 14:16, 26. (In John 16:7ff., the forensic character of the Paraclete takes a new turn, for now he goes on the attack, and expresses Jesus' function as judge.)[30a] But παράκλητος in John must be allowed a wider connotation than this forensic one. The meaning of this word in Koine Greek has shifted from a passive to an active one: the παράκλητος is not only the one who is 'called to one's side', to give assistance: he is also the one who brings παράκλησις, consolation.[31] The idea of 'consolation' has a part in the biblical message of salvation. Isa. 40:1ff. begins with 'Comfort, comfort . . .' because of the new creation, the new exodus, which is coming. This points us to another special link between Luke–Acts and John. In Luke 2:25f., Symeon is 'expecting the παράκλησις of Israel', and he has the Holy Spirit upon him. Acts 9:31, a summary which speaks of the peaceful growth of the church throughout Judaea, Galilee and Samaria, notes that the church 'was filled with the παράκλησις of the Holy Spirit'.

The prominence of the Holy Spirit in both Luke–Acts and John points to another large sphere of agreement, that of eschatology. In Chapter Five we noted that though Luke maintains, and with some vigour, the expectation of a future (and not too long delayed) consummation of the world's history, there is in Luke–Acts another theme, which has not received enough recognition: Luke also wants to emphasize the importance of those parts of the eschatological promises which have already been fulfilled. This takes us a good step in the direction also followed by John. John, too, retains the expectation of the future consummation, though less prominently (5:28f. 6:39f., 44, 54): his chief emphasis is on the 'eschatological' character of the life made available already to those who believe in Jesus (3:15f., 36; 4:14; 5:24; 10:27f.; 17:2f.; etc.), for the eschatological 'hour' is not only coming, but has already arrived (4:23; 5:25; cf. 12:23).

Thus, despite the admittedly substantial differences in their outlooks on many questions, we have been able to discover in Luke–Acts and John a considerable range of theological statements – in Christology, eschatology, pneumatology, ecclesiology[31a] – which *distinctively* characterize these two works within the New Testament. There are special affinities between them, not only in the materials they received from tradition, and in their historical and geographical orientation, but also in certain important aspects of theology.

How is all this to be explained?

5 Jesus' Disciples in Southern Palestine

The three categories of special affinities between Luke-Acts and John, which we have been exploring – common traditions, a similar geographical interest in central and southern Palestine, and a kinship in theology – may well be due to the same cause.

Our beginning-point in reconstructing this cause is the geographical centre of gravity. Mark, the 'Q'-material and Matthew seem to have almost no knowledge of, or interest in, the work of Jesus or the growth of Christian churches in Judaea or Samaria. It seems reasonable to assume that behind these sources (and therefore to a large extent behind Luke as well) there lie the memories of disciples of Jesus living in Galilee. Of course, Jesus himself was a native of Galilee, and there is no doubt that a substantial part of his mission was exercised there, and that he there won a sizeable following. Even John, who seems to claim Jesus as a resident of Judaea (4:43–45), has plenty of material concerning Jesus' work in Galilee. But to these northern traditions there are added in Luke–Acts, and still more strongly in John, what appear to be traditions arising from the memories of Judaean disciples who followed Jesus in Judaea during his lifetime and who formed the core of the Judaean churches after his resurrection. How large a following of Samaritan disciples Jesus may have had during his lifetime is hard to say: but Luke–Acts and John both reflect the vigorous growth of Samaritan churches in the early post-resurrection period. When Acts 2:41 speaks of the baptism of the three thousand people after Peter's Pentecost-sermon, we have no right to assume either that these people were now hearing about Jesus for the first time, or that they were all pilgrims from Galilee (still less, that there is no kind of historical fact behind the report). It is quite likely that among them were a good number of those Judaean disciples who make their existence known through the material of John (e.g. 2:23; 4:1–3; 7:31; 40ff.; 8:30; 9:38; 11:45–48; 12:9–12) and of Luke–Acts. In the Gospel of Luke this is mainly a matter of editorial slanting; though in Jericho, for example, Luke knows of the incident concerning Zacchaeus (19:1–10) as well as that of the the blind man (18:35–43/Mark 10:46–53). It is not clear where Luke locates the various specific incidents recorded elsewhere in the journey-section, such as the visit to Martha and Mary (10:38–42), the Beelzebul-controversy (11:14ff.), the two meals with Pharisees (11:37ff.; 14:1ff.), etc. That Jesus has left Galilee in 9:51f., and that encounters with Pharisees occur so often in this section, seem to suggest that much of it is supposed to be located in Judaea: but this is made awkward by the note that 'he was passing between Samaria and Galilee' as late as 17:11. In Acts, on the other hand, it is impressive how many specific traditions Luke has about both Judaea and Samaria, in contrast with the almost complete silence about Galilee. Luke, then, like John, brings to expression traditions which are best understood as having been developed and preserved among Christian groups in southern Palestine.[32]

If that is so, it will help to explain why Luke–Acts and John have preserved so much common material, even when this common material does not specifically mention southern locations. These were simply traditions which happened to be valued and passed on within a certain area of the church. This is no argument, of course, for locating the final composition of either Luke–Acts or John in this region: in both cases there are good reasons to the contrary. The nature of the similarities we have described not only allows but even to some extent requires that there should have been a rather long period of development of the same traditions along different lines before they found their way into the respective gospels.

But the fact that the common geographical orientation and the common materials are also accompanied by some similarity in the theological point of view of the two evangelists suggests that these southern congregations whose existence we are postulating may well have had, from quite an early date, a different emphasis from the Galilaean congregations in their understanding of the significance of Jesus.[33] This means that, though we may quite legitimately seek to identify and describe the 'Lucan' and the 'Johannine' theology, what we are apparently dealing with in each case is the end-result of a development whose original impulses were rather far removed, both in date and place, from the composition of these two works. It is probably pointless to try to identify, from our surviving materials, individual figures who may have contributed to the early shaping of these traditions and interpretations. As good a candidate as any may be the Philip of Acts 6–8 (according to 21:8, Luke claims to have had some brief personal association with him in the late 50's);[34] but his colleague Stephen may have been remembered as much for a striking but rather untypical point of view as for any lasting impact on the ideas of Judaean and Samaritan Christianity (Acts 8:1). The Johannine Philip, however, is a Galilaean (John 12:21), and so is his friend Nathanael (21:2).

But what has all this to do with the purpose of Luke's work? When Luke in his preface refers to his predecessors, and briefly alludes to his own reason for taking up the same enterprise, it is curious that he does not justify his own undertaking with reference to the additional information he had to offer. This would certainly have been an excellent justification by comparison with his only predecessor clearly known to us, Mark, with respect to the additional material in the Gospel, quite apart from the second volume. But perhaps Luke does not say anything about that, because it is much more than a question of additional information. It is also a matter of a different, or at least additional, perspective on what the story of Jesus means. Despite the substantial differences between the final products, Luke–Acts and John, the comparison between them has helped to identify, and to some extent trace the history of, certain traditions and theological emphases which were important to Luke and *which had not come to adequate expression in the work of his predecessors*.

Whether the readers most directly addressed by Luke belonged to congregations in which these special traditions and perspectives had a long history, we have no means of knowing. What is however very likely is that Luke regarded these special nuances and emphases, ultimately derived from the Christianity distinctive of southern and central Palestine, as having an important significance in providing the reassurance he offers his readers of the ἀσφάλεια of the Christian message.

Notes to Chapter Six

1. J. Blinzler, *Johannes und die Synoptiker*.
2. P. Gardner-Smith, *Saint John and the Synoptic Gospels*.
3. P. Gardner-Smith, op. cit., 92f.
4. D. M. Smith, 'John 12:12ff.'; cited by J. Blinzler, op. cit., 31.
5. J. Blinzler, op. cit., 34ff. See C. K. Barrett, *The Gospel according to St. John*, 34–35; R. H. Lightfoot, *St. John's Gospel*, 26–42; especially 33. Among others who hold the same view is W. G. Kümmel, *Einleitung*, 167f. (ET, 201f.). Blinzler, op. cit., 37, cites an essay of R. Schnackenburg ('Der johanneische Bericht von der Salbung in Bethanien') as supporting the literary dependence of John on Mark, but in his large commentary on John (*Das Johannesevangelium*, 15–32; ET, *The Gospel according to St John*, I, 26–43) Schnackenburg concludes that a direct literary dependence of John on the synoptics is improbable. Similarly R. E. Brown, *The Gospel according to John*, I, XLIV-XLVII. The independence of John from the synoptics was also argued in great detail by C. H. Dodd, *Historical Tradition in the Fourth Gospel*. C. K. Barrett, however, has recently reaffirmed and defended his view that John is dependent on Mark and Luke, in the revised edition of his commentary on John, 1978, 42–46.
6. J. Blinzler, op. cit., 52–57.
7. See J. A. Bailey, *The Traditions Common*, 18, 42–44.
8. The order of events in John's passion-narrative has of course some awkward elements: e.g. the relation of 14:31b to ch. 15–17 and to 18:1, and the relation of 18:12–14 to v. 19 and 24.
9. See above, pages 165–7.
10. Cf. P. Gardner-Smith, op. cit., 25.
11. J. Blinzler, op. cit., 38, with reference to C. K. Barrett, *John*, 34.

12. It has been shown by F. Hahn, 'Die Jüngerberufung Joh 1:35–51', that John has here used a rich stock of oral traditions, which occasionally show a distant connexion with other parts of the synoptic tradition, e.g. Luke 9:57–62/Matt. 8:19–22. See especially 179–182.
13. In Matthew the person healed is consistently called παῖς. In Luke he is three times δοῦλος, but once παῖς. In John he is three times υἱός and once παιδίον, but in v. 51 the MSS are divided between υἱός and παῖς. For the petitioner Matthew uses ἑκατόνταρχος and Luke ἑκατοντάρχης.
14. J. Blinzler, op. cit., 57f., 60.
15. In support of the genuineness of the text here, see C. S. C. Williams, *Alterations to the Text of the Synoptic Gospels and Acts*, 6–8.
16. J. Schniewind, *Die Parallelperikopen bei Lukas und Johannes*.
17. See above, n. 7.
18. *H. Klein*, 'Die lukanisch-johanneische Passionstradition'. See also G. Schneider, *Verleugnung, Verspottung und Verhör Jesu*; and F. Hahn, 'Der Prozeß Jesu nach dem Johannesevangelium', 23–96.
19. J. Schniewind, op. cit., 99.
20. Op. cit., 95.
21. J. A. Bailey, op. cit., 14–17.
22. Op. cit., 1–8. Similarly, W. G. Kümmel, *Einleitung*, 169 (ET, 203).
23. J. A. Bailey, op. cit., 1f.
24. See W. Michaelis, *ThW* IV, 807–809, with n. 3 by G. Bertram: in LXX μύρον is used occasionally instead of ἔλαιον to render שֶׁמֶן.
25. See P. Gardner-Smith, op. cit., 48.
26. H. Klein, 'Passionstradition', speaks of a 'common tradition' behind Luke and John in the passion-narrative, but he interprets this to mean that Luke and John each had a special source for the passion-narrative, and that these special sources were derived from a common ancestor, which itself was derived, not from Mark, but from one of two sources which Mark independently used. See especially 182 and the diagram on 186. Klein's literary arguments for a common source in fixed form seem to me to be too confident (160–164). Although he leaves it open (164) whether the common source was written or oral, he seems in practice to think of it as written.
27. R. Pesch, *Der Reiche Fischfang*.
28. In Luke 5:17 Jesus has an audience of Pharisees and teachers of the Law who have come 'from every village of Galilee and Judaea and Jerusalem'. This, too, seems to be based on Mark 3:7f., for there is no such geographical indication in the corresponding passage, Mark 2:2.
29. Possibly Acts 13:27 points in the same direction: but the wording is difficult and the text perhaps corrupt. Compare E. Haenchen, *Apg*, 394 (ET, 410) with K. Lake and H. J. Cadbury, *Beginnings*, IV, 153.
30. The textual genuineness of this verse has sometimes been doubted. But it has recently been firmly demonstrated by F. Hahn, '"Das Heil kommt von den Juden"' that these words are not only a genuine part of the text but also give expression to a serious and important part of the intention of John.

30a. U. B. Müller, 'Parakletenvorstellung' 31–77, following J. Becker, regards John 15–17 as an insertion into the Gospel, by a later author. In the evangelist's original concept, the Paraclete (14:16, 26) performs a function *within* the church, guaranteeing a continuity of teaching between the earthly Jesus and the special traditions of the Johannine congregation. The later author, however, attributes to the Paraclete (15:26; 16:7–11, 12–15) a function with respect to the world *outside* the church, by which the church is hated and persecuted: he will convict it of sin, especially that of failing to believe in Jesus. Müller also sees a difference in that the Paraclete of ch. 14 will simply *remind* disciples of what Jesus has taught them, whereas in 16:12ff. he will impart *additional* teaching, as if the teaching of Jesus was incomplete. This new teaching, too, must be legitimized, so it is said that the Spirit will not speak on his own authority, but only what he hears, what he receives from Jesus. We do not need here to discuss in detail the much-discussed literary relationship of John 15–17 to the Gospel as a whole. But Müller's emphasis on the difference in the two concepts of the Paraclete seems to me exaggerated. 'He will guide you in all the truth' (16:13) is not remarkably different from 'He will teach all things' (14:26), nor 'He will not speak on his own authority, but . . . take from what is mine and declare it to you' (16:14) from 'He will remind you of all that I told you'. Müller's objection (74) that in 16:7–11 the author of the supplement attributes to the Paraclete a function of judgement that in the Gospel was not part of Jesus' purpose is based on too mechanical an interpretation in view of the Johannine 'dialectic' (cf. C. K. Barrett, *NT Essays*, ch. 4): for over against 3:17 and 12:47 (Jesus' purpose is not to judge) must be set not only the immediate antithesis in each case (3:18; 12:48) but also 9:39 and 5:22–29.

31. See Bauer's lexicon, 1226f. (BAG², 618). Cf. C. K. Barrett, *John*, ²1978, 462: 'The meaning of παράκλητος in John is best arrived at by considering the use of παρακαλεῖν and other cognates in the New Testament. This is twofold. (a) παρακαλεῖν and παράκλησις both refer to prophetic Christian preaching . . . This corresponds to the normal Greek usage in which παρακαλεῖν means 'to exhort'. (b) Both words are used in another sense which seems to have little or no basis in Greek that is independent of the Hebrew Bible; they refer to consolation, and in particular to the consolation to be expected in the messianic age. This usage is common in the Old Testament (e.g. Isa. 40:1) . . .'

31a. As is well known, R. Bultmann firmly rejected 5:28f. and the phrase 'and I will raise him up at the last day' in 6:39f., 44, 54 (together with the whole of 6:51b–58) as insertions by a redactor who attempted to 'correct' the evangelist's unapocalyptic theology in the direction of a more 'orthodox' eschatology: *Johannesevangelium*, 161f., 196f. (ET, 218ff., 261f.). Later commentators have on the whole not been persuaded by Bultmann's view: e.g., R. E. Brown, *John*, I, CXVIIIff. As far as I am aware, the most thorough refutation of Bultmann on this point is that of C. K. Barrett, 'The Dialectical Theology of St John', *NT Essays*, ch. 4. Barrett shows that apparent 'contradictions' in John are to be found on many other topics than those which fall under Bultmann's scissors (eschatology and the Lord's Supper). In all cases, a better interpretation is reached by acknowledging that the evangelist thinks and writes in a 'dialectical' way.

32. J. Schniewind, *Lukas und Johannes*, 3, cites B. Weiß, *Die Quellen der synoptischen Überlieferung*, 172, and idem, *Die Quellen des Lukasevangeliums*, 199, as tracing the common tradition of Luke and John back to Palestine. I was able to consult only the former of these. Here (172–176) Weiß notes that the birth-narratives in Luke 1–2 reflect familiarity with the Judaean countryside and regard Galilee as a distant place. Weiß attributes this material, together with the non-Marcan and non-Q sections of the later part

of Luke, to a written source L, the author of which he locates in Judaea. Weiß also attributes the theme of the journey of the author of L, and thinks the materials in this section are 'so much richer' here than in the previous section, because the author of L lived in the region and had access to 'much richer sources' (176). Weiß makes no mention here of the Johannine traditions or of any connexion between Luke and John. It was against the background of this sort of oversimplified source-criticism that Schniewind pleaded (op. cit., 100) that oral tradition be taken more strongly into account.

33. The argument being proposed here is quite different from that of E. Lohmeyer, who sought to distinguish between the Galilaean congregations and that of Jerusalem in the first century by the specific criterion of Christological titles: in Galilee Jesus was thought of as 'Son of Man' and in Jerusalem as 'Messiah': *Galiläa und Jerusalem*, 92ff. It is also different from that of O. Cullmann, *Der johanneische Kreis* (ET, *The Johannine Circle*). Cullmann argues that Jesus had contact with two distinct groups of disciples: a group from more or less orthodox Judaism, to which Peter and the Twelve belonged, and a group drawn from 'heterodox Judaism', out of which arose both the 'Johannine circle' and the Hellenists of Acts 6–8, and which had a strong element of Samaritan ideas. But he does not explore either the common interest of Luke and John in shifting the geographical centre of Jesus' mission, as well as of the early church, from Galilee towards the south, or the broad range of materials and theological themes common to Luke and John, which are discussed in this chapter.

The discussion about the church-background of the Gospel of John has now been carried further by R. E. Brown, *Community*. Brown is mainly concerned with tracing stages of theological development underlying the Johannine material; he has little discussion about geography, and none about a possible connexion of the traditions underlying John and Luke–Acts.

34. Despite Luke's orientation towards Judaea and Samaria, and the likelihood that the origin of much of his material was in southern Palestinian congregations, it must be noted that his knowledge of the early days of the church in Jerusalem is somewhat hazy. This is especially evident in Acts 1–5: but later, too, it appears that Luke does not know, for example, how James came to be the leader in Jerusalem, or what his relationship to the Apostles was. From Acts 6 onwards, Luke's information becomes more specific, especially with regard to the missionary activities of the Hellenists. This may therefore justify us in identifying the sources of his traditions more particularly with *Hellenistic* congregations of the south.

7. Luke's Purpose in the Church of His Time

1 Some Conclusions about the Character of Luke's Work

In Chapter One, when first raising the question about Luke's purpose, we explored the chief current theories on the subject. But it was also found necessary, as a preliminary step to a serious discussion of Luke's purpose, to consider certain questions of 'introduction' – questions about the work's origin and character. In most cases, we were able to establish quite firm conclusions on these matters. It will now be helpful to reflect whether, and how, those conclusions have been further confirmed or illuminated by the course of our investigations in Chapters Two to Six.

(a) *Luke–Acts is a single work* (Chapter One, section 2 and the end of section 3). Certainly nothing has emerged from our study to weaken this assertion. Theological doctrines flow through consistently from one volume to the other. It is not true, for example, as has been asserted by some, that there is a different concept of eschatology in the two volumes (Chapter Five). Both volumes reveal a concern to shift the geographical centre of interest from Galilee to Judaea and Samaria (Chapter Six, section 3). Not only is the concept of the Twelve Apostles the same, but there is a careful coordination between the two volumes as to the function the Apostles are to fulfil (Chapter Three, section 4). But by far the most powerful confirmation of the unity of the whole work has come from our study of Luke's handling of the theme 'Israel and the Gentiles', for there is a sustained dramatic development of this theme from Luke 1 to Acts 28. The unity of Luke–Acts may indeed be regarded as settled beyond question.

(b) *Luke composed his work about 85–90 AD* (Chapter One, section 3). It is of course not possible to be very precise about the date of composition. But we have found confirmation, especially from Chapter Three, that the period around 85–90 is correct. Paul's great career lies some time in the past, but not so far back as to prevent Luke from seeing Paul as the bridge between the time of the Apostles and that of the author and his readers. Since Luke is not conscious of persecution by the State as a serious problem (Chapter Four), he is likely to have written before the outbreak of the persecution of Domitian reflected in Revelation. On the other hand, his deep concern to explain the institutional rift between Christians and Jews (Chapter Two) is very much at home in the early years of Gamaliel II's presidency of the Rabbinic academy at Jamnia, when from the Jewish side the exclusion of 'Nazarenes' as heretics was formalized.

(c) *Luke's work is addressed to a Christian audience* (Chapter One, section 5). The *shape* of the work (Chapter One, section 4) suggests that Luke–Acts is a book about the Christian church in its relationship on the one hand with the Lord Jesus, on the other hand with Judaism. To say this is not to play down the significance of Jesus – without 'Jesus' there is no meaning to 'church'! – but to observe that it is Luke's distinctive concern, by comparison with Mark, to consider the outcome of the Jesus-story in the church. And it is the Christians themselves to whom such a discussion matters. This has been overwhelmingly confirmed by our study. Luke is deeply involved with the question of the relationship of Jews and Christians, yet not in such a way as to permit the interpretation that he is seeking to placate Jewish opinion or to win it over for the cause of the gospel; on the contrary, he acknowledges that the division between Christians and Jews is now wide and probably permanent, and puts the responsibility for this at the door of the spiritual leaders of Judaism (Chapter Two). Nor is the book addressed to the Roman government, or to non-Christian Gentiles. The fact that Luke–Acts ends with a long section about the imprisonment and trial of Paul blunts the edge of any suggestion that Luke's aim was evangelistic: indeed, at no point in our investigation has anything emerged to make this aim seem likely; on the other hand, we have seen that the Paul-part of Acts makes good sense on the supposition that it is addressed internally to the Christian fellowship (Chapter Three). Nor is Luke–Acts intended, even secondarily, as a political apology, for the elements in the work which bear on the harmonious relation between Christians and the State have also been shown to make best sense as addressed to Christian readers (Chapter Four). Luke–Acts is in every way a book devoted to clarifying the Christian self-understanding. This conclusion is also supported, though less specifically, by the discussions on eschatology (Chapter Five) and on the special affinities with the Gospel of John (Chapter Six).

(d) The conclusion just reaffirmed is further supported by the observation that *Luke–Acts is a 'theological history'* (Chapter One, section 6). Luke–Acts is a 'history' in a quite different way from the other gospels, because of the greatly increased chronological scope of the narrative. It is not to be understood as directly 'kerygmatic' in every part, nor is it written to preserve the memory of events for posterity, but to declare to Luke's contemporaries the nature of their situation and vocation as Christians. This is revealed, as our study has shown, by many aspects of Luke's selection and arrangement of his material. Among the most notable examples are the last half-chapter of the work, Acts 28:14b–31 (Chapter Two section 5) and the whole portrait of Paul (Chapter Three, especially sections 5 and 6).

With respect to the search for Luke's purpose, the product of these conclusions on preliminary questions is that the work Luke–Acts was written for Christians living in about the sixth decade of the church's history, in order to help them understand their life and vocation as Christians.

2 Some Conclusions about Luke's Purpose

In Chapter One, section 7, we reviewed seven current theories about Luke's purpose. The first three envisaged a purpose directed to a readership outside church-circles. These can now be completely set aside. Our remaining discussion can be restricted to the four theories which recognized that Luke was addressing himself to Christian readers: to defend the memory of Paul; to fulfil a theological purpose, such as explaining the delay of the parousia, or combatting Gnosticism; or to 'confirm' the gospel.

(a) The view that Luke's primary purpose was to defend the memory of Paul falls far short of doing justice to the scope and dynamics of the whole work. Moreover, our study revealed nothing to suggest that Luke felt the need to defend Paul in a polemical sense. Rather, Luke *celebrates* Paul, as a great Christian leader of the period between the Apostles and the author's contemporaries. Paul embodies the continuity of the gospel. The content of the gospel remains unchanged: no one has tampered with it or slipped in innovations; so the gospel as preached in Luke's own day is to be accepted as genuine, measured by the preaching of the earliest days (Chapter Three, sections 2 and 5). In addition, Paul embodies the continuity of the witness to the gospel. He worked in fruitful harmony with his predecessors (the Apostles) and his contemporary colleagues in the dissemination of the story of Jesus (Chapter Three, sections 3 and 4). Like them, he had to endure unjustified attacks, both verbal and physical, but came through them all splendidly, by the aid of the Holy Spirit. Thus Paul provided for Christians of Luke's time who were under pressure in their discipleship and mission an inspiring example (Chapter Three, sections 5 and 6). Paul's life is indeed marked by controversy, but this is almost entirely external to the church, being carried on in confrontation with that part of Pharisaic Judaism which rejected the resurrection of the Lord Jesus and its implications (Chapter Two, sections 3–5). But in this respect the Paul-part of Luke's story, though most important, does not stand alone, but continues a theme already developed in the narrative concerning Jesus, the Apostles, Stephen, and indeed the whole church. To define Luke's purpose in terms simply of Paul is to fail to understand the unity and dramatic continuity of Luke–Acts; to express Luke's purpose in terms of 'defence' may be correct, or nearly correct, as we shall see below; but the 'defence', if that is what it is, refers to the whole gospel-story, from Jesus through to the Christians of Luke's time.

(b) It is unquestionably true that Luke's purpose has an important theological dimension. Here the significant consideration is not anti-Gnosticism (see Chapter One, section 7 (f)), but eschatology. We have seen, however, that there is no substance to the idea that Luke was dealing with a crisis caused by the delay of the parousia (Chapter Five, section 3). Luke in fact maintains the expectation that the parousia might come quite soon in his own time, though the theme of the parousia is rather less emphasized than in some earlier stages of Christian thought (Chapter Five, sections 4–7). Rather Luke's emphasis in eschatology is on the need to appreciate the great extent to which God's salvation *has already been fulfilled* in what has happened in the mission of Jesus and its sequel in the gift of the Holy Spirit (Chapter Five, sections 8 and 9). Here is an aspect of Luke's thought where he reveals a point of view like that of John. But this is not an accidental resemblance, for it is due to an extensive history of shared traditions, in consequence of which each evangelist, in his own way, has received, endorsed and brought to expression the understanding of certain groups of early Christians in southern Palestine (Chapter Six). However, as we shall see below, this special understanding of eschatology is by no means merely incidental to Luke's purpose, but lies right at its heart.

(c) The final suggestion introduced in Chapter One was that Luke's chief purpose was to reassure his readers of the significance of the gospel, which they have been inclined to doubt. At that stage we remarked that this suggestion looked promising, especially in the light of our study of the term *ἀσφάλεια,* with which Luke ends his preface. We must now consider in more detail how it looks in the light of the argument in the intervening chapters.

3 The Dominant Themes of Luke–Acts

At the outset of our study we noted that the dominant themes of Luke–Acts have been identified by a number of scholars as 'ecclesiology' and 'eschatology'. This has been borne out by our subsequent discussion, though in important respects the significance of these terms has turned out to be different from what has usually been supposed.

The question of ecclesiology is the question, Who are the Christians? Luke's answer is that the Christians are the heirs of the promises made by God to the Hebrew patriarchs about a coming time of salvation – heirs who have entered into their inheritance. Those promises were made by God to the Hebrew national community, and were in the first instance fulfilled with Israel when God sent Jesus as Jewish messiah and saviour. But he intended, through Israel, to open up salvation to 'all flesh'. God's plan involved salvation for those who accepted it and judgement for those who rejected it. As things have turned out, it is largely Gentiles who have accepted the offered salvation and Judaism which has rejected it. Therefore, surprisingly, Judaism has been judged by God. The substantial exclusion of Judaism from the fulfilment of its own ancestral promises does not however invalidate the promises themselves, or the fulfilment of the promises for those people, mainly Gentiles, who have accepted them.

Now why does Luke emphasize so strongly, to a Christian audience, that if most Jews have no part in God's salvation it is because they have excluded themselves? Presumably he does so because his readers are in danger of thinking the opposite. That is, they are in danger of being persuaded that the division of Judaism and Christianity as distinct institutions might imply that Christians are excluded from the community of salvation. It must have been when Luke was writing, or shortly afterwards, that Gamaliel II inserted into the prayers of the synagogue the twelfth 'Benediction': 'For apostates may there be no hope, and may the Nazarenes and the heretics suddenly perish'.[1] In this situation the question will have arisen with some urgency: Who after all are the 'people of God', and who are the heretics? We may surmise that Jewish propaganda against Christianity, spurred on by the reorganization of Judaism inspired from the Rabbinic academy at Jamnia, was a considerable source of pressure on the faith of Christians. Many Christians will have felt themselves to be in difficulty, because the gospel has been rejected by the leading Jewish authorities and there is an increasingly sharp division between Pharisaic Judaism and a church whose members are predominantly of Gentile origin. The Jews have confidence in their position, which is based on an ancient tradition, with a clearly defined pattern of ethical requirements and a detailed system of interpreting their inherited scriptures. The New Testament itself bears ample testimony to this state of affairs, for example in John 9:28f., 'You are his disciple, but we are disciples of Moses: we know that God spoke to Moses, but as for this man, we do not know where he comes from'; and Acts 28:22, 'What we know about this sect is that it is spoken against everywhere' – everywhere, that is, in the Jewish world, as the context makes clear.[2] The church claims to base its life on the same scriptures and partly on the same traditions: but its own distinctive traditions are of recent origin; the rapid geographical extension of the church, and the large-scale admission of Gentiles, many of whom did not have their roots deep in biblical soil (that is, those who had not been 'God-fearers' in the synagogue), deprived the Christians of the communal and institutional solidity enjoyed by the Jews. If once the charismatic testimony of the Spirit grew dim, the onset of persecution, or even of sustained psychological pressure from the Jews through dispute over the meaning of the scriptures and the credibility of a crucified Messiah, will have shaken many people's confidence in their faith. How could non-Jews hope to find any value in something which has its roots in Judaism, yet seems to be repudiated by the leaders of the Jews?

This problem is not unique to Luke among the New Testament writers. In an earlier form, it also lies behind Paul's Epistle to the Romans. In addition to introducing himself to the Roman Christians so as to prepare a base for future missionary work, and perhaps correcting false reports about his doctrine, Paul intended with this letter to help the Roman Christians deal with a theological difficulty arising from the relationships of Jews and Gentiles in the church and of Christians to their Jewish inheritance. The chief difference between Paul's situation and Luke's is that the breach with Judaism is now wider and deeper: for Luke there is apparently no longer any reason to hope that the Jews as a whole will accept the gospel. In one sense, Paul's image of the olive-tree in which wild olive-branches have been grafted (Rom. 11:17–24) is still valid. Luke acknowledges that the origin of the gospel is in Judaism. But whereas Paul looked for the reinstatement of the pruned olive-branches (Rom. 11:24), Luke would place all the emphasis on the earlier part of Paul's figure: 'they were broken off through unbelief' (v. 20). Whereas Paul presses the Old Testament text into service to prove that the gospel is the true fulfilment of the Old Covenenant, and thus (it is implied) contrary arguments from the synagogue can be refuted, Luke uses a more directly historical argument: far from having any right to excommunicate the Christians, the leaders of Judaism have in repeated instances, and in spite of every opportunity to hear the gospel, excluded themselves from the Kingdom of God.

The importance which Luke assigns to explaining to Christians their historical situation and the nature of their existence as an institution distinct from Judaism is emphasized, as we have seen in Chapter Three, by his picture of Paul. By making Paul's career so prominent in his book, and bringing the book to its conclusion with Paul's imprisonment, Luke shows his fellow-Christians how they are linked with the origins of the gospel-story, both positively and negatively. The positive side of his argument is that Paul continued the witness of the Apostles to Jesus, and handed on to Luke and his contemporaries both the content of the gospel and the charge of witnessing to it; the negative side is that in Paul's time, and despite the character of his extensive mission towards them, the Jews confirmed their decision, already shown in Luke's first volume, to reject Jesus and thereby to reject the offer of God's salvation.

If, then, ecclesiology is a leading concern of Luke's, is it right to speak of his attitude to the church as one of 'early Catholicism'? It has recently been convincingly shown by F. Hahn that the term 'Frühkatholizismus', as applied to Luke by E. Käsemann and others, is confusing as a description and unhelpful as a value-judgement.[3] In view of the historical setting which we have supposed for Luke's work, a tendency towards institutionalism would be entirely natural, and indeed to some extent necessary, to prevent the evaporation of the gospel-message in individualistic mysticism, fanaticism or discouragement. But in fact, for Luke the church as an institution is remarkably free and spontaneous in the impulses of its communal life. Neither the Apostles nor James exercise authoritarian direction of the church in Jerusalem, nor do Paul or others elsewhere. The church is led not by institutional authorities but by the Holy Spirit. By the Spirit the church is consolidated, but also disciplined and purified, and at the same time kept open to the mysterious and always new demands of God's will. And there is no trace of a high sacramentalism. A comparison with 1 Clement and the epistles of Ignatius is enough to recall how much further Luke might have gone in these directions. Luke never gives us the impression that the church exists as a means of salvation in its own right: instead, the function of the church is always to bear witness to Jesus, through whom alone salvation is to be found (e.g. Acts 1:8; 3:12f.; 4:9–12, 29f.; 10:36–44; 13:23–39; 16:30f.; 19:17–20; etc.).

Alongside ecclesiology, in the sense just explained, there stands Luke's second great doctrinal emphasis, eschatology. But these two themes cannot really be considered as distinct from each other in Luke's thought. In his eschatology, too, Luke is explaining to his contemporary fellow-Christians who they are, and what their historical situation is. They are people to whom an enormous privilege has been given. The whole Book of Acts can be thought of as a kind of extended reapplication to Luke's readers of the 'Q'-saying addressed by Jesus to his disciples, Luke 10:23f./Matt. 13:16f.: 'Blessed are the eyes which see what you see: for I tell you that many prophets and kings wished to see what you see and did not see it, and to hear what you hear and did not hear it'. They are the people to whom 'God's salvation has been sent' (Acts 28:28, echoing Luke 3:6 and Acts 2:21). They live in a time of 'fulfilment'. The mission of Jesus was itself the fulfilment of God's promise of universal relief and liberation (Luke 4:18–21), as is already hinted by the extraordinary activity of the Holy Spirit in the circumstances surrounding the birth of Jesus and the beginnings of his activity (fourteen of the eighteen references to the Holy Spirit in the Gospel of Luke early in that volume, between 1:15 and 4:18). For them the Kingdom of God is already a present reality, even though it must also be consummated in the future. The terminology of 'fulfilment' is also applied to Jesus' death, his resurrection, his ascension and especially to the gift of the Holy Spirit. In consequence, the time of the church – the time of Luke and his fellow-Christians – is a time charged with eschatological power; it is a time characterized by the availability of salvation. There remains the ultimate End at the parousia, which may not be far off, but which can be awaited with confidence and hope by Jesus' disciples (Luke 21:28), provided they have meanwhile remained faithful to him (18:8). But the fulfilment already experienced is of such great significance and value that it, rather than the ultimate consummation, is what Luke chiefly emphasizes.

4 The Definition of Luke's Purpose

At an early stage of our discussion (Chapter One, section 4), we observed that Luke's preface gives little immediate indication of the author's purpose. But in the light of our study of the whole work, two words stand out from the preface as evident markers of Luke's intention: they are *πεπληροφορημένα* and *ἀσφάλεια*. It may be that the peculiar force of these two words was more immediately evident to a contemporary than to a modern reader. The subject of the work is those things which 'have been fulfilled among us'; its aim is to allow the readers to perceive the 'reliability' of the message they have heard. It is a work aimed at reassuring the Christian community about the significance of the tradition and faith in which it stands.

The story of Jesus, the Apostles and the growing church is a story of 'fulfilment' in more than one sense. On the one hand, Luke encourages his readers not only to look forward with hope to the consummation of all things at the End, but also to appreciate that 'salvation', the grace and power of God in action, is a *present reality*, in which they already stand because of God's action in sending Jesus to the earth. On the other hand, they are to be reassured that this fulfilment has taken place 'among us', within the Christian community. Luke's emphasis here is by no means to encourage Christian exclusiveness or inward-looking pride. Rather, he writes to reassure the Christians of his day that their faith in Jesus is no aberration, but the authentic goal towards which God's ancient dealings with Israel were driving. The full stream of God's saving action in history has not passed them by, but has flowed straight into their community-life, in Jesus and the Holy Spirit. If there are apostates and heretics who have cut themselves off from participation in the Kingdom of God, it is not the Christians to whom such terms apply. It is Jesus, their Lord, in whom the promises of the ancient scriptures are fulfilled; it is Jesus who sends the Holy Spirit, whose powerful influence the Christians actually experience; and it is Jesus alone through whose name salvation occurs.

With such a message of reassurance, Luke summons his fellow-Christians to worship God with whole-hearted joy, to follow Jesus with unwavering loyalty, and to carry on with zeal, through the power of the Spirit, the charge to be his witnesses to the end of the earth.

Notes to Chapter Seven

1. See G. F. Moore, *Judaism*, I, 292.
2. The existence of this problem in the latter part of the first century is further reflected by the use of *ἀποσυνάγωγος* in John 9:22; 12:42 and 16:2: see W. Schrage, *ThW* 7, 845–850 (ET, *TDNT* 7, 848–852). This consciousness, in both Luke–Acts and John, of a sharp communal separation between Jews and Christians confirms our observation (p. 000) that Luke shares with John a concern about the general refusal of the Jewish people to believe in Jesus. See also C. K. Barrett, *The Gospel of John*, ch. 3 and 4, esp. p. 41, 47–51, 68f.
3. F. Hahn, 'Das Problem des Frühkatholizismus', 350f.

Abbreviations

ASNU	Acta Seminarii Neotestamentici Upsaliensis
BBB	Bonner Biblische Beiträge
BEvTh	Beiträge zur evangelischen Theologie
BGBE	Beiträge zur Geschichte der biblischen Exegese
BHTh	Beiträge zur historischen Theologie
BWANT	Beiträge zur Wissenschaft des Alten und Neuen Testaments
BZ	Biblische Zeitschrift
BZNW	Beihefte zur Zeitschrift für die neutestamentliche Wissenschaft
CBQ	Catholic Biblical Quarterly
EKK	Evangelisch-Katholischer Kommentar
ET	English Translation
EvTh	Evangelische Theologie
ExpT	Expository Times
FRLANT	Forschungen zur Religion und Literatur des Alten und Neuen Testaments
HCNT	Handcommentar zum Neuen Testament
HNT	Handbuch zum Neuen Testament
HThR	Harvard Theological Review
HTS	Harvard Theological Studies
ICC	The International Critical Commentary
JAAR	Journal of the American Academy of Religion
JBL	Journal of Biblical Literature
JBR	Journal of Bible and Religion
JRS	Journal of Roman Studies
JTS	Journal of Theological Studies
Komm z. NT	Kommentar zum Neuen Testament
MTS	Münchener Theologische Studien
NTD	Das Neue Testament Deutsch
NTS	New Testament Studies
SBS	Stuttgarter Bibel-Studien
SBT	Studies in Biblical Theology
SJT	Scottish Journal of Theology
SNT	Studien zum Neuen Testament
SNTSMS	Society for New Testament Studies Monograph Series
SNTU	Studien zum Neuen Testament und seiner Umwelt
ST	Studia Theologica
StANT	Studien zum Alten und Neuen Testament
SBS	Stuttgarter Bibel Studien
StUNT	Studien zur Umwelt des Neuen Testaments
THNT	Theologischer Handkommentar zum Neuen Testament
TLZ	Theologische Literaturzeitung
ThWb	Theologisches Wörterbuch zum Neuen Testament
WdF	Wege der Forschung
WMANT	Wissenschaftliche Monographien zum Alten und Neuen Testament

WUNT	Wissenschaftliche Untersuchungen zum Neuen Testament
ZNW	Zeitschrift für die neutestamentliche Wissenschaft
ZThK	Zeitschrift für Theologie und Kirche

Abbreviations of the Names of Books

The full name of each book is given in the footnote in which it is first mentioned. Publication details are found in the Bibliography. Most abbreviations are self-explanatory, except for the following:

Beginnings	Foakes Jackson, F. J. and Lake, K., *The Beginnings of Christianity*, Volumes I–V, London 1920–1933.
L.S.J.	Liddell, H. G., and Scott, R., *A Greek–English Lexicon*. Revised by H. S. Jones and R. McKenzie, Oxford [9]1940.
M–M	Moulton, J. H., and Milligan, G., *The Vocabulary of the Greek Testament Illustrated from the Papyri and Other Non-literary Sources*, London 1930.
SLA	Keck, L. E., and Martyn, J. L. (edd.), *Studies in Luke–Acts. Essays Presented in Honour of Paul Schubert*, Nashville 1966.

Bibliography

Aland, K. (ed.), *Synopsis Quattuor Evangeliorum*, Stuttgart [10]1978.

Arndt, W. F., and Gingrich, F. W., *A Greek–English Lexicon*, see Bauer, W.

Bailey, J. A., *The Traditions Common to the Gospels of Luke and John*, Leiden 1963 (Suppl. *NT*, 7).

Bammel, E., Barrett, C. K., Davies, W. D. (edd.), *Donum Gentilicium, N.T. Studies in Honour of D. Daube*, Oxford 1978.

Barrett, C. K., *The Gospel according to St. John*, London 1955, [2]1978.

—— *Luke the Historian in Recent Study*, London 1961.

—— *The Signs of an Apostle*, London 1970.

—— *New Testament Essays*, London 1972.

—— *The Gospel of John and Judaism*, London 1975 (ET of *Das Johannesevangelium und das Judentum*, Stuttgart/Berlin 1970).

—— *Donum Gentilicium*, see Bammel, E.

—— Stephen and the Son of Man, *Apophoreta. Festschrift für E. Haenchen*, Berlin/New York 1964 (BZNW, 30), 32–38.

—— Things Sacrificed to Idols, *NTS* 11/1964–1965, 138–153.

—— Shaliah and Apostle, in E. Bammel, C. K. Barrett and W. D. Davies (edd.), *Donum Gentilicium, NT Studies in Honour of D. Daube*, Oxford 1978, 88–102.

Barth, G., see under G. Bornkamm, G. Barth and H. J. Held.

Bartsch, H. W., *Wachet aber zu jeder Zeit! Entwurf einer Auslegung des Lukasevangeliums*, Hamburg-Bergstedt 1963.

—— Zum Problem der Parusieverzögerung bei den Synoptikern *Ev Th* 19/1959, 116–131 (reprinted in his *Entmythologisierende Auslegung*, Hamburg-Bergstedt 1962, 69–80).

Bauer, W., *Griechisch-Deutsches Wörterbuch zu den Schriften des Neuen Testaments und der übrigen urchristlichen Literatur*, Berlin [5]1963, ET, *A Greek–English Lexicon*, edited and translated from the 4th edition by W. F. Arndt and F. W. Gingrich, Chicago/Cambridge 1957. (Second English edition, 1979, revised and augmented by F. W. Gingrich and F. W. Danker from Bauer's 5th edition.)

Benzing, B., Böcher, O., and Mayer, G. (edd.), *Wort und Wirklichkeit. Festschrift für E. L. Rapp*, Meisenheim a. G., I, 1976.

Beutler, J., *Martyria. Traditionsgeschichtliche Untersuchungen zum Zeugnis-Thema bei Johannes*, Frankfurt 1972 (Frankf. Theol. Stud., 10).

Bihler, J., *Die Stephanusgeschichte*, München 1963 (Münch. Theol. Stud., I, Histor. Abtl., 16).

Bihlmeyer, K., see Funk, F. X., Bihlmeyer, K., and Schneemelcher, W.

Billerbeck, P. (Strack, H. L. und), *Kommentar zum Neuen Testament aus Talmud und Midrasch*, Vols. I–IV München 1924, [2]1956.

Black, M., The Christological Use of the Old Testament in the New Testament, *NTS* 18/1971–1972, 1–14.

Blass, F., und Debrunner, A., *Grammatik des neutestamentlichen Griechisch*, bearbeitet von F. Rehkopf, Göttingen [14]1976.

Blinzler, J., *Johannes und die Synoptiker*, Stuttgart 1965 (SBS, 5).

Böcher, O., und Haaker, K. (edd.), *Verborum Veritas. Festschrift für G. Stählin*, Wuppertal 1970.

Boice, J. M., *Witness and Revelation in the Gospel of John*, Grand Rapids 1970.

Bonnard, P., *L'Evangile selon saint Matthieu*, Neuchâtel ²1970 (Commentaire du NT, 1).

Borgen, P., From Paul to Luke. Observations towards Clarification of the Theology of Luke–Acts. *CBQ* 31/1969, 168–182 (ET and revision of Von Paulus zu Lukas, *ST* 20/1966, 140–157).

Bornkamm, G., The Missionary Stance of Paul in 1 Corinthians 9 and in Acts, *SLA*, 194–207.

——, Barth, G., and Held, H. J., *Überlieferung und Auslegung im Matthäusevangelium*, Neukirchen-Vluyn ⁶1970 (WMANT, 1).

—— ET, *Tradition and Interpretation in Matthew*, London 1963.

Bouwman, G., *Das Dritte Evangelium. Einübung in die formgeschichtliche Methode*, Düsseldorf 1968.

Braumann, G., Das Mittel der Zeit. Erwägungen zur Theologie des Lukas-Evangeliums, *ZNW* 54/1963, 117–145.

—— (ed.), *Das Lukas-Evangelium. Die redaktions- und kompositionsgeschichtliche Forschung*, Darmstadt 1974 (WdF, 280).

Brown, R. E., *The Gospel according to John*, Garden City I 1966 (The Anchor Bible, 29).

—— *The Community of the Beloved Disciple*, New York 1979.

Brown, S., *Apostasy and Perseverance in the Theology of Luke*, Rome 1969 (Analecta Biblica, 36).

Browning, W. R. F., *The Gospel according to St. Luke*, London 1960.

Brox, N., *Zeuge und Märtyrer. Untersuchungen zur frühchristlichen Zeugnis-Terminologie*, München 1961 (St ANT, 5).

Bruce, F. F., *The Book of Acts*, London 1954 (New London Commentary).

Bultmann, R., Zur Frage nach den Quellen der Apostelgeschichte, in A. J. B. Higgins (ed.), *New Testament Essays. Studies in Memory of T. W. Manson*, Manchester 1959, 68–80.

—— *Das Johannesevangelium*, Göttingen 1941–¹⁶1959 (Meyer Komm, 2).

—— ET, *The Gospel of John*, Oxford 1971.

—— *Das Urchristentum in Rahmen der antiken Religionen*, Zürich 1949.

—— ET, *Primitive Christianity*, New York 1956.

Burchard, C., *Der Dreizehnte Zeuge. Traditions- und kompositionsgeschichtliche Untersuchungen zu Lukas' Darstellung der Frühzeit des Paulus*, Göttingen 1970 (FRLANT, 103).

—— Paulus in der Apostelgeschichte, *TLZ* 100/1975, 881–895.

Buttrick, D. G. (ed.), *Jesus and Man's Hope*, Pittsburgh 1970.

Cadbury, H. J., *The Style and Literary Method of Luke*, Cambridge, Mass. Part I 1919, Part II 1920 (HTS, 6).

—— The Purpose Expressed in Luke's Preface, *Expositor* 8th Series, 21, June 1921, 431–441.

—— The Knowledge Claimed in Luke's Preface, *Expositor* 8th Series, 24, Dec. 1922, 401–420.

—— In F. J. Foakes Jackson and K. Lake (edd.), *The Beginnings of Christianity* (Part I, Vols. I–V), London 1920–1933.

—— The Tradition, in Vol. I 1922, 209–264.

—— Commentary on the Preface of Luke, in Vol. II 1922, 489–510.

—— The Hellenists, in Vol. V, 1933, 59–74.
—— Lucius of Cyrene, in Vol. V, 1933, 489–495.
—— *The Making of Luke–Acts*, London 1927.
—— *The Book of Acts in History*, London 1955.
—— Acts and Eschatology, in W. D. Davies and D. Daube (edd.), *The Background of the New Testament and its Eschatology*, Cambridge 1956, 300–321.
—— Some Foibles of New Testament Scholarship, *JBR* 26/1958, 215f.
—— Review of H. Conzelmann, *The Theology of St. Luke*, *JBL* 80/1961, 305.
—— Four Features of Lucan Style, *SLA*, 87–102.
Caird, G. B., *Saint Luke*, Harmondsworth 1963 (Pelican Bible Commentaries).
Carley, K. W., *Ezekiel among the Prophets*, London 1975 (SBT II, 31).
Chadwick, H., *The Early Church*, Harmondsworth 1967 (The Pelican History of the Church, I).
Clark, A. C., *The Acts of the Apostles. A Critical Edition with Introduction and Notes on Selected Passages*, Oxford 1933.
Conzelmann, H., *Die Mitte der Zeit. Studien zur Theologie des Lukas*, Tübingen 1954, [5]1964 (BHTh, 17).
—— ET, *The Theology of St. Luke* (translation of 2nd German edition), London/New York 1960.
—— Geschichte, Geschichtsbild und Geschichtsdarstellung bei Lukas, *TLZ* 85/1960, 214–250.
—— *Die Apostelgeschichte*, Tübingen 1963 (HNT, 7).
—— The Address of Paul on the Areopagus, *SLA*, 217–232.
—— Luke's Place in the Development of Early Christianity, ibid., 298–316.
Creed, J. M., *The Gospel According to St. Luke*, London 1930.
Cullmann, O., Immortality of the Soul or Resurrection of the Dead (published as an article in *Harvard Divinity School Bulletin* 21/1955–1956, 5–16, and as a separate monograph, London 1958, and in K. Stendahl (ed.), *Immortality and Resurrection*, New York 1965, 9–35).
—— *Der johanneische Kreis, sein Platz im Spätjudentum, in der Jüngerschaft und im Urchristentum*, Tübingen 1975.
—— ET, *The Johannine Circle . . . A Study in the Origin of the Gospel of John*, London 1976.
Dahl, N. A., The Story of Abraham in Luke–Acts, *SLA*, 139–158.
Daube, D., and Davies, W. D., see Davies, W. D. and Daube, D.
Davies, W. D., Bammel, E., and Barrett, C. K. (edd.), *Donum Gentilicium*, see Bammel, E.
Davies, W. D., and Daube, D. (edd.), *The Background of the New Testament and its Eschatology. Studies in Honour of C. H. Dodd*, Cambridge 1956.
de Halleux, A., and Deschamps, A., see Deschamps, A.
Denaux, A., L'Hypocrisie des Pharisiens et le dessein de Dieu. Analyse de Luc 13: 31–33, in F. Neirynck (ed.), *L'Evangile de Luc. Problèmes littéraires et théologiques. Mémorial Lucien Cerfaux*, Gembloux 1973, 245–285.
Deschamps, A., and de Halleux, A. (edd.), *Mélanges bibliques en hommage au R. P. Béda Rigaux*, Gembloux 1970.
Dibelius, M., *Aufsätze zur Apostelgeschichte* (ed. H. Greeven), Göttingen 1951 (FRLANT, 60).
—— ET, *Studies in the Acts of the Apostles*, London 1956.
Dinkler, E. (ed.), *Zeit und Geschichte. Festschrift für R. Bultmann*, Tübingen 1964.
Dodd, C. H., *The Parables of the Kingdom*, Welwyn [2]1961.

—— *Historical Tradition in the Fourth Gospel*, Cambridge 1963.
—— *More New Testament Studies*, Manchester 1968.
Dömer, M., *Das Heil Gottes. Studien zur Theologie des lukanischen Doppelwerkes*, Köln/Bonn 1978 (BBB, 51).
Dunn, J. D. G., *Baptism in the Holy Spirit*, London 1970 (SBT II, 15).
Dupont, J., *Les sources du Livre des Actes*, Bruges 1960.
—— ET, *The Sources of Acts*, London 1964.
—— Le Salut des gentils et la signification théologique du Livre des Acts, *NTS* 6/1959–1960 (reprinted in his *Études sur les Acts des Apôtres*, Paris 1967 (Lectio Divina 45), 393–419).
—— Die individuelle Eschatologie im Lukasevangelium und in der Apostelgeschichte, in *Orientierung an Jesus. Festschrift für J. Schmidt*, Freiburg 1973, 37–47.
Easton, B. S., *The Purpose of Acts*, London 1936 (reprinted in *Early Christianity, the Purpose of Acts and Other Papers* (F. C. Grant, ed.), Greenwich, Conn. 1954).
Egelkraut, H. J., *Jesus' Mission to Jerusalem: a redaction-critical study of the Travel Narrative in the Gospel of Luke, Lk. 9:51–19:48*, Frankfurt/M. 1976 (Europäische Hochschulschriften 23/80).
Ellis, E. E., Present and Future Eschatology in Luke, *NTS* 12/1965–1966, 27–41.
— Die Funktion der Eschatologie im Lukasevangelium, *ZThK* 66/1969, 387–402; reprinted in G. Braumann (ed.), *Das Lukas-Evangelium: Die redaktions- und kompositionsgeschichtliche Forschung*. Darmstadt 1974 (WdF, 180), 378–397. (Cited according to the latter.)
—— ET, *Eschatology in Luke*, Philadelphia 1972 (Facet Books, Biblical Series 30).
—— *The Gospel of Luke*, London [2]1974 (The Century Bible, new edition based on the RSV).
Eltester, W. (ed.), *Neutestamentliche Studien für R. Bultmann*, Berlin 1954.
—— Israel im lukanischen Werk und die Nazarethperikope, in idem (ed.), *Jesus in Nazareth*, Berlin/New York 1972 (BZNW, 40), 76–147.
Epp, E. J., *The Theological Tendency of Codex Bezae Cantabrigiensis in Acts*, Cambridge 1966 (SNTSMS, 3).
Ernst, J., *Das Evangelium nach Lukas*, Regensburg 1977 (Regensburger Neues Testament, 3).
—— *Herr der Geschichte. Perspektiven der lukanischen Eschatologie*. Stuttgart 1978 (SBS, 88).
Feuillet, A., La Connaissance naturelle de Dieu par les Hommes, *Lumière et Vie*, 14/1954, 63–80.
Flender, H., *Heil und Geschichte in der Theologie des Lukas*, München 1965 (BEvTh, 41).
—— ET, *St. Luke: Theologian of Redemptive History*, London 1967.
Foakes Jackson, F. J., and Lake, K. (edd.), *The Beginnings of Christianity, Part I: The Acts of the Apostles*, Vols. I–V, London 1920–1933.
Francis, Fred O., Eschatology and History in Luke–Acts, *JAAR* 37/1969, 49–63.
Franklin, E., The Ascension and the Eschatology of Luke–Acts, *SJT* 23/1970, 191–200.
—— *Christ the Lord. A Study in the Purpose and Theology of Luke–Acts*, London 1975.
Frend, W. H. C., *Martyrdom and Persecution in the Early Church. A Study of a Conflict from the Maccabees to Donatus*, Oxford 1965.

Friedrich, G., Lukas 9:51 und die Entrückungschristologie des Lukas, in his *Auf das Wort kommt es an*. Gesammelte Aufsätze. Zum 70. Geburtstag herausgegeben von J. H. Friedrich, Göttingen 1978, 26–55. (Originally in *Orientierung an Jesus. Festschrift für J. Schmid*, 1973, 48–77.)

Fuchs, A. (ed.), *Jesus in der Verkündigung der Kirche*, Linz 1976 (SNTU).

Fuller, R. H., *The Mission and Achievement of Jesus*, London 1954 (SBT, 12).

Funk, F. X., Bihlmeyer, K., and Schneemelcher, W., *Die Apostolischen Väter*, 1. Teil, Tübingen [2]1956.

Gardner-Smith, P., *Saint John and the Synoptic Gospels*, Cambridge 1938.

Gärtner, B., *The Areopagus Speech and Natural Revelation*, Uppsala 1955 (ASNU, XXI).

Gasque, W., *A History of the Criticism of the Acts of the Apostles*, Tübingen 1975 (BGBE, 17).

Geiger, R., *Die lukanischen Endzeitreden. Studien zur Eschatologie des Lukas-Evangeliums*, Bern/Frankfurt am Main 1973 (Europäische Hochschulschriften 23/16).

Glöckner, R., *Die Verkündigung des Heils beim Evangelisten Lukas*, Mainz 1975.

Glover, T. R. (translator), Tertullian's *Apology*, Loeb edition, London/Cambridge, Mass. 1931.

Gnilka, J., *Die Verstockung Israels: Is. 6:9–10 in der Theologie der Synoptiker*, München 1961.

—— (ed.), *Neues Testament und Kirche. Festschrift für R. Schnackenburg*, Freiburg/Basel/Wien 1974.

Goodenough, E. R., The Perspective of Acts, *SLA*, 51–59.

Gräßer, E., *Das Problem der Parusieverzögerung in den synoptischen Evangelien und in der Apostelgeschichte*, Berlin/New York [3]1977 (BZNW, 22).

—— Acta-Forschung seit 1960, *ThR* 41/1976, 141–194, 259–290; 42/1977, 1–68.

—— Die Parusieerwartung in der Apostelgeschichte. (Lecture given at the Biblical Colloquium at Louvain, 17.8.1977, unpublished.)

Grelot, P., La quatrième demande du 'Pater' et son arrière-plan sémitique, NTS 25/1978–1979, 299–314.

Greßmann, H., Vom reichen Mann und armen Lazarus, *Abhandlungen der preu. Akad. der Wissensch.* no. 7, Berlin 1918.

Grundmann, W., *Das Evangelium nach Lukas*, Berlin [3]1966 (THNT).

Güttgemanns, E., *Offene Fragen zur Formgeschichte des Evangeliums*, München 1970 (BEvTh, 54).

Haaker, K., see O. Böcher.

Haenchen, E., *Die Apostelgeschichte*, Göttingen 1956, [7]1977 (Meyer Komm, 3).

—— ET, *The Acts of the Apostles: A Commentary*, Oxford 1971 (translated from the 5th German edition 1965).

—— Judentum und Christentum in der Apostelgeschichte, *ZNW* 54/1963, 155–187 (also in *Die Bibel und Wir*, Gesammelte Aufsätze, II, Tübingen 1968, 338–374).

—— Das 'Wir' in der Apostelgeschichte und das Itinerar, in his *Gott und Mensch: Gesammelte Aufsatze*, Tübingen 1965, 227–264 (originally in *ZThK* 58/1961, 329–366, English translation in *Journal for Theology and the Church*, 1/1965, New York).

—— The Book of Acts as Source Material for the History of Early Christianity, *SLA*, 258–278.

Hahn, F., *Das Verständnis der Mission im Neuen Testament*, Neukirchen-Vluyn [2]1965 (WMANT, 13).

—— ET, *Mission in the New Testament*, London 1965 (SBT, 47).

—— *Der urchristliche Gottesdienst*, Stuttgart 1970 (SBS, 41).

—— Das Gleichnis von der Einladung zum Festmahl, in *Verborum Veritas. Festschrift für Gustav Stählin*, Wuppertal 1970, 51–82.

—— *Der Prozeß Jesu nach dem Johannesevangelium*, Zürich/Köln/Neukirchen 1970 (EKK Vorarbeiten, 2), 23–96.

—— Die Jüngerberufung Joh 1:35–51, in J. Gnilka (ed.), *Neues Testament und Kirche. Festschrift für R. Schnackenburg*, Freiburg/Basel/Wien 1974, 172–190.

—— Die Himmelfahrt Jesu. Ein Gespräch mit Gerhard Lohfink, *Biblica* 55/1974, 418–426.

—— Die Rede von der Parusie des Menchensohnes, Markus 13, in R. Pesch und R. Schnackenburg (edd.), *Jesus und der Menschensohn. Festschrift für A. Vögtle*, Freiburg/Basel/Wien 1976, 240–266.

—— Das Heil kommt von den Juden. Erwägungen zu Joh 4:22b, in B. Benzing, O. Böcher, and G. Mayer (edd.), *Wort und Wirklichkeit. Festschrift für E. L. Rapp*, Meisenheim a.G., I, 1976, 67–84.

—— Das Problem des Frühkatholizismus, *EvTh* 38/1978, 340–357.

—— Das Problem altchristologischer Überlieferungen in der Apostelgeschichte unter besonderer Berücksichtigung von Act 3:19–21. (Lecture given at the Biblical Colloquium at Louvain, 18.8.1977, unpublished.)

Hawkins, J. C., *Horae Synopticae. Contributions to the Study of the Synoptic Problem*, [2]1909.

Heard, R. G., The Old Gospel Prologues, *JTS* new series 6/1955, 1–16.

Held, H. J., see under G. Bornkamm, G. Barth and H. J. Held.

Hengel, M., *Judentum und Hellenismus. Studien zu ihrer Begegnung unter besonderer Berücksichtigung Palästinas bis zur Mitte des 2.Jh.s vor Christus*, Tübingen [2]1973 (WUNT, 10).

—— ET, *Judaism and Hellenism*, 2 vols, London 1974.

Hicks, R. D. (translator), Diogenes Laertius, London/Cambridge, Mass., Loeb edition, I, 1925.

Hiers, R. J., Why Will They Not Say 'Lo here!' or 'There!'?, *JAAR* 35/1967, 379–384.

—— The Problem of the Delay of the Parousia in Luke–Acts, *NTS* 20/1973–1974, 145–155.

Higgins, A. J. B. (ed.), *New Testament Studies in Memory of T. W. Manson*, Manchester 1959.

Hill, D., *The Gospel of Matthew*, London 1972 (The New Century Bible).

Holtz, T., *Untersuchungen über die alttestamentlichen Zitate bei Lukas*, Berlin 1968 (Texte und Untersuchungen, 104).

Holtzmann, H. J., *Die Apostelgeschichte*, Tübingen und Leipzig [3]1901 (HCNT, 1.2).

Hooker, M. D., Adam in Romans 1, *NTS* 6/1959–1960, 297–306.

Jastrow, M., *Dictionary of the Targumim, the Talmud Babli and Jerushalmi and the Midrashic Literature*, I, New York 1950 (=1903).

Jeremias, J., *Jerusalem zur Zeit Jesu*, Göttingen [3]1962.

—— ET, *Jerusalem in the Time of Jesus*, London 1967.

—— *Das Vaterunser im Lichte der neueren Forschung*, Stuttgart, [4]1967 (Calwer

Hefte, 50) (=*Abba. Studien zur neutestamentlichen Theologie*, Göttingen 1966, 152–171).

—— ET, in *The Prayers of Jesus*, London 1967.

—— *Die Gleichnisse Jesu*, Göttingen [8]1970.

—— ET, *The Parables of Jesus*, London [3]1972.

Jervell, J., *Luke and the People of God. A new Look at Luke–Acts*, Minneapolis 1972 (consisting of 7 essays separately published between 1962 and 1971 and 3 previously unpublished essays).

Kaestli, J.-D., *L'Eschatologie dans l'Oeuvre de Luc*, Genève 1969.

Käsemann, Ernst, Das Problem des historischen Jesus, *ZThK* 51/1954, 125–153, reprinted in *Exegetische Versuche und Besinnungen*, Göttingen, I [4]1965.

—— ET, *Essays on New Testament Themes*, London 1964.

—— *An die Römer*, Tübingen [3]1974 (HNT, 8a).

Keck, L. E., and Martyn, J. L. (edd.), *Studies in Luke–Acts. Essays Presented in Honour of Paul Schubert*, Nashville 1966.

Kilpatrick, G. D., On *γραμματεύς* and *νομικός*, JTS new series 1/1950, 56–60.

—— The Gentile Mission in Mark and Mark 13:9–11, in D. E. Nineham (ed.), *Studies in the Gospels in Memory of R. H. Lightfoot*, Oxford 1955, 145–158.

—— Mark 13:9–10, *JTS* new series 9/1958, 81–86.

—— *Λαοί* at Luke 2:31 and Acts 4:25, 27, *JTS* new series 16/1965, 127.

—— 'Kyrios' in the Gospels, in *L'Evangile, Hier et Aujourd'hui, Mélanges offerts au Prof. F.-J. Leenhardt*, Genève 1968, 60–70.

—— The Gentiles and the Strata of Luke, in O. Böcher and K. Haaker (edd.), *Verborum Veritas, Festschrift für G. Stählin*, Wuppertal 1970, 83–88.

—— Luke – Not a Gentile Gospel, unpublished.

Klein, G., *Die Zwölf Apostel. Ursprung und Gehalt einer Idee*, Göttingen 1961 (FRLANT, 77).

—— Die Prüfung der Zeit (Lukas 12:54–56), *ZThK* 61/1964, 373–390.

—— Lukas 1:1–4 als theologisches Programm, in E. Dinkler (ed.), *Zeit und Geschichte. Festschrift für R. Bultmann*, Tübingen 1964, 193–216.

Klein, H., Die lukanisch-johanneische Passionstradition, *ZNW* 67/1976, 155–186.

Klein, R. (ed.), *Das frühe Christentum im römischen Staat*, Darmstadt 1971 (WdF, 267).

Klijn, A. F. J., In Search of the Original Text of Acts, *SLA*, 103–110.

Klostermann, E., *Das Lukas-Evangelium*, Tübingen [2]1929 (HNT, 5).

Knox, W. L., *The Acts of the Apostles*, Cambridge 1948.

Kränkl, E., *Jesus der Knecht Gottes*, Regensburg 1972 (Münchener Universitäts-Schriften, Biblische Untersuchungen, 8).

Kuhn, H. W., *Enderwartung und gegenwärtiges Heil. Untersuchungen zu den Gemeindeliedern von Qumran*, Göttingen 1966 (SUNT, 4).

Kümmel, W. G., *Verheißung und Erfüllung*, Zurich [3]1956.

—— ET, *Promise and Fulfilment*, London 1957 (SBT, 23).

—— Lukas in der Anklage der heutigen Theologie, *ZNW* 63/1972, 149–165 (reprinted in G. Braumann (ed.), *Das Lukas-Evangelium. Die redaktions- und kompositionsgeschichtliche Forschung*, Darmstadt 1974 (WdF, 280), 416–436 (cited according to the latter); originally published in French in *Ephemerides Theol. Lovanienses* 46/1970, 265–281).

—— *Einleitung in Das Neue Testament*, Heidelberg [18]1973.

—— ET, *Introduction to the New Testament*, London [2]1975.

Lake, K., and Foakes Jackson, F. J., see Foakes Jackson, F. J.

Leaney, A. R. C., *The Gospel according to St. Luke*, London 1958 (Black's New Testament Commentaries).

Lévy, J., *Wörterbuch über die Talmudim und Midraschim*, Berlin/Wien I ²1924.

Liddell, H. G., and Scott, R., *A Greek–English Lexicon*, revised by H. S. Jones and R. McKenzie, Oxford ⁹1940.

Lightfoot, J. B., *Commentary on the Epistles to the Colossians and Philemon*, London 1875.

Lightfoot, R. H., *St. John's Gospel: A Commentary*, Oxford 1957.

Lindemann, A., *Paulus im ältesten Christentum*, Tübingen 1979.

Lohfink, G., *Paulus vor Jerusalem. Arbeitsweisen der neuren Bibelwissenschaft, dargestellt an den Texten, Apg. 9:1–9; 22:3–21; 26:9–18*, Stuttgart 1965 (SBS, 4).

—— *Die Himmelfahrt Jesu. Untersuchungen zu den Himmelfahrts und Erhöhungstexten bei Lukas*, München 1971 (StANT, 26).

—— *Die Sammlung Israels: eine Untersuchung zur lukanischen Ekklesiologie*, München 1975 (StANT, 39).

Lohmeyer, E., *Galiläa und Jerusalem*, Göttingen 1936 (FRLANT, 52).

Lohse, E., Lukas als Theologe der Heilgeschichte, *EvTh* 14/1954, 256–275.

—— *Πεντηκοστή*, ThW 6/1959, 44–53.

—— *Umwelt des Neuen Testaments*, Göttingen ²1974 (Grundrisse zum NT, NTD Ergänzungsreihe, 1).

Löning, K., *Die Saulustradition in der Apostelgeschichte*, Munster 1973 (NT Abhandlungen, neue Folge, 9).

Lührmann, D., *Das Offenbarungsverständnis bei Paulus und in den paulinischen Gemeinden*, Neukirchen-Vluyn 1965 (WMANT, 16).

Maddox, R., The Function of the Son of Man according to the Synoptic Gospels, *NTS* 15/1968–1969, 45–74.

Manson, W., *The Gospel of Luke*, London 1930 (the Moffatt New Testament Commentary).

Marshall, I. H., *Luke: Historian and Theologian*, Exeter 1970.

—— *The Gospel of Luke*, Exeter 1978 (The New International Greek Text Commentary).

Mattill, A. J., Naherwartung, Fernerwartung and the Purpose of Luke–Acts. Weymouth Reconsidered, *CBQ* 34/1972, 276–293.

McCown, C. C., Palestine, Geography of, in *Interpreter's Dictionary of the Bible*, Vol. 3, Nashville/New York 1962, 626–639.

Meinertz, M., 'Dieses Geschlecht' im Neuen Testament, *BZ* 1/1957, 283–289.

Merk, O., Das Reich Gottes in den lukanischen Schriften, in *Jesus und Paulus, Festschrift für W. G. Kümmel zum 70. Geburtstag*, Göttingen 1975, 201–220.

Metzger, B. M., *A Textual Commentary on the Greek New Testament*, London/New York 1971.

Michaelis, W., *μύρον, μυρίζω, ThW* 4, 1942, 807–809.

Michel, H.-J., *Die Abschiedsrede des Paulus an die Kirche, Apg. 20:17–38. Motivgeschichte und theologische Bedeutung*, München 1973 (StANT, 35).

Milligan, G., see Moulton, J. H.

Minear, P. S., Luke's Use of the Birth Stories, *SLA*, 111–130.

—— Dear Theo. The Kerygmatic Intention and Claim of the Book of Acts, *Interpretation* 27/1973, 148f.

Moore, C. H. (translator), Tacitus' *Histories*, Loeb edition, London/Cambridge, Mass. 1931.

Moore, G. F., *Judaism in the First Centuries of the Christian Era: the Age of the Tannaim*, Vols. I–III, Cambridge, Mass. 1927–1930.

Morgenthaler, R., *Statistik des neutestamentlichen Wortschatzes*, Zürich/Frankfurt 1958.

Moulton, J. H., and Milligan, G., *The Vocabulary of the Greek Testament Illustrated from the Papyri and Other Non-literary Sources*, London 1930.

Müller, U. B., Die Parakletenvorstellung im Johannesevangelium, *ZThK* 71/1974, 31–77.

Nauck, W., Die Tradition und Komposition der Areopagrede, *ZThK* 53/1956, 11–52.

Neirynck, F. (ed.), *L'Evangile de Luc. Problèmes littéraires et théologiques. Mémorial Lucien Cerfaux*, Gembloux 1973.

Nellessen, E., *Zeugnis für Jesus und das Wort. Exegetische Untersuchungen zum lukanischen Zeugnisbegriff*, Köln 1976 (BBB, 43).

Nickelsburg, G. W. E., *Resurrection, Immortality and Eternal Life in Intertestamental Judaism*, Cambridge, Mass. 1972 (HTS, 26).

Nineham, D. E. (ed.), *Studies in the Gospels in Memory of R. H. Lightfoot*, Oxford 1955.

Noack, B., *Das Gottesreich bei Lukas*, Uppsala 1948 (Symbolae Biblicae Upsalienses, 10).

Nock, A. D., The Book of Acts, in his *Essays on Religion and the Ancient World*, 1972, II, 821–832 (originally in *Gnomon* 25/1953: a review of M. Dibelius, *Aufsätze zur Apostelgeschichte*, ed. by H. Greeven, Göttingen 1951 (FRLANT, 60)).

—— Religious Developments from the Close of the Republic to the Death of Nero, ch. 15 in S. A. Cook, F. E. Adcock, and M. P. Charlesworth (edd.), *The Cambridge Ancient History* X, 1934, 465–511.

Norden, E., *Agnostos Theos. Untersuchungen zur Formen-Geschichte religiöser Rede*, Berlin 1913, Darmstadt 1971.

Oliver, H. H., The Lucan Birth Stories and the Purpose of Luke–Acts, *NTS* 10/1963–1964, 202–226.

O'Neill, J. C., *The Theology of Acts in its Historical Setting*, London [2]1970.

Ott, W., *Gebet und Heil. Die Bedeutung der Gebetsparänese in der lukanischen Theologie*, München 1965 (StANT, 12).

Painter, J., *John: Witness and Theologian*, London 1975.

Perrin, N., *Jesus and the Language of the Kingdom. Symbol and Metaphor in New Testament Interpretation*, Philadelphia 1976.

—— *What is Redaction Criticism?*, Philadelphia/London 1970.

Pesch, R., *Die Vision des Stephanus*, Stuttgart 1966 (SBS, 12).

—— *Naherwartungen. Tradition und Redaktion in Mk 13*, Düsseldorf 1968.

—— *Der Reiche Fischfang Lk 5:1–11/Joh 21:1–14*, Düsseldorf 1969.

——, und Schnackenburg, R. (edd.), *Jesus und der Menschensohn. Festschrift für A. Vögtle*, Freiburg/Basel/Wien 1976.

—— *Das Markusevangelium*, Freiburg/Basel/Wien 1977 (Herders Theol. Komm., 2).

Peterson, E., ἀπάντησις, ThW 1/1933, 380.

Polag, A., *Die Christologie der Logienquelle*, Neukirchen-Vluyn 1977 (WMANT, 45).

Plummer, A., *The Gospel According to S. Luke*, Edinburgh [5]1922 (ICC).

Plümacher, E., *Lukas als hellenistischer Schriftsteller. Studien zur Apostelgeschichte*, Göttingen 1972 (StUNT, 9).

—— Lukas als griechischer Historiker, in A. Pauly and G. Wissowa, *Realencyclopädie der classischen Altertumswissenschaft*, Stuttgart Suppl. 14, 1974.

Rackham, R. B., *The Acts of the Apostles*, London 1901.

Radl, W., *Paulus und Jesus im lukanischen Doppelwerk. Untersuchungen zu Parallelmotiven im Lukasevangelium und in der Apostelgeschichte*, Bern/Frankfurt a.M. 1975 (Europ. Hochschulschr. 23/49).

Rengstorf, K. H., *Das Evangelium nach Lukas*, Göttingen 1962 (NTD, 3).

Rese, M., *Alttestamentliche Motive in der Christologie des Lukas*, Gütersloh 1969 (SNT, 1).

Rigaux, B., Die Zwölf Apostel, *Concilium* 4/1968, 238–242.

Roberts, C. H., The Kingdom of Heaven (Luke 17:21), *HTR* 41/1948, 1–8.

Robinson, W. C. Jr., *Der Weg des Herrn. Studien zur Geschichte und Eschatologie im Lukas-Evangelium. Ein Gespräch mit Hans Conzelmann*, Hamburg-Bergstedt 1964 (Wissenschaftliche Beiträge zur Kirchlich-Evangelischen Lehre, 36).

Rohde, J., *Die redaktionsgeschichtliche Methode. Einführung und Sichtung des Forschungsstandes*, Hamburg 1966.

—— ET with additions, *Rediscovering the Teaching of the Evangelists*, London 1968.

Ropes, J. H., St. Luke's Preface, ἀσφάλεια and παρακολουθεῖν *JTS* 25/1924, 70f.

Russell, H. G., Which was Written First, Luke or Acts?, *HTR* 48/1955, 167–174.

Rüstow, A., ENTOC YMWN ECTIN: Zur Deutung von Lukas 17:20–21, *ZNW* 51/1960, 197–224.

Scharlemann, M. H., *Stephen: A Singular Saint*, Rome 1968 (Analecta Biblica, 34).

Scheele, P.-W., and Schneider, G. (edd.), *Christuszeugnis der Kirche. Festschrift für F. Hengsbach*, Essen 1970.

Schmid, J., see Wickenhauser, A.

Schneemelcher, W., see Funk, F. X.

Schnackenburg, R., Der johanneische Bericht von der Salbung in Bethanien, *Münch. Theol. Zeitschrift* 1/1950, 48–52.

—— Der eschatologische Abschnitt Lk 17:20–37, in A. Deschamps and A. de Halleux (edd.), *Mélanges bibliques en hommage au R. P. Béda Rigaux*, Gembloux 1970, 213–234.

—— *Das Johannesevangelium*, I, Freiburg/Basel/Wien 1972 (Herders Theol. Komm., 4).

—— ET, *The Gospel according to St. John*, I, New York/London 1968.

Schneider, G., *Verleugnung, Verspottung und Verhör Jesu nach Lukas 22:54–71. Studien zur lukanischen Darstellung der Passion*, München 1969 (StANT, 22).

—— Die Zwölf Apostel als 'Zeugen'. Wesen, Ursprung and Funktion einer lukanischen Konzeption, in Scheele, P. W., and G. Schneider (edd.), *Christuszeugnis in der Kirche*, Essen 1970, 39–65.

—— *Parusiegleichnisse im Lukas-Evangelium*, Stuttgart 1975 (SBS, 74).

—— *Das Evangelium nach Lukas*, Gütersloh 1977 (2 vols: Ökumenischer Taschenbuch-Kommentar zum NT, 3/1 and 3/2).

—— Der Zweck des lukanischen Doppelwerkes, *BZ* 21/1977.

Schniewind, J., *Die Parallelperikopen bei Lukas und Johannes*, Leipzig 1914 (reprint Darmstadt 1970).

Schrage, W., *Die Christen und der Staat nach dem Neuen Testament*, Gütersloh 1971. – συναγωγή, etc., *ThW* 7/1964, 798–850.

Schramm, T., *Der Markus-Stoff bei Lukas*, Cambridge 1971 (SNTSMS, 14).

Schubert, P., The Structure and Significance of Luke 24, in W. Eltester (ed.), *Neutestamentliche Studien für R. Bultmann*, Berlin 1954, 165–186.

Schürmann, H., *Das Lukasevangelium*, I, Freiburg/Basel/Wien 1969 (Herders Theol. Komm. z. NT).

Schütz, F., *Der leidende Christus. Die angefochtene Gemeinde und das Christuskerygma der lukanischen Schriften*, Stuttgart 1969 (BWANT V/9).

Schweizer, E., *Das Evangelium nach Markus*, Göttingen 1967 (NTD, 2).

—— ET, *The Good News According to Mark*, London 1971.

—— *Das Evangelium nach Matthäus*, Göttingen 1973 (NTD, 1).

—— ET, *The Good News according to Matthew*, London 1976.

—— Concerning the Speeches in Acts, *SLA*, 208–216.

Sherwin-White, A. N., *Roman Society and Roman Law in the New Testament*, Oxford 1963.

Simon, M., *St. Stephen and the Hellenists in the Primitive Church*, London 1958.

Smith, D. M., John 12:12ff. and the Question of John's use of the Synoptics, *JBL* 82/1962, 58–64.

Stählin, G., *Die Apostelgeschichte*, Göttingen 1962 (NTD, 5).

Stendahl, K., Matthew, in M. Black and H. H. Rowley (edd.), *Peake's Commentary on the Bible*, New Edition, London 1962, 769–798.

—— (ed.), *Immortality and Resurrection*, New York 1965.

—— *The School of St. Matthew and its use of the Old Testament*, Lund/Philadelphia [2]1967.

—— *Paul among Jews and Gentiles and Other Essays*, Philadelphia/London 1976–1977.

Stolle, V., *Der Zeuge als Angeklagter. Untersuchungen zum Paulusbild des Lukas*, Stuttgart 1973 (BWANT, 102).

Strack, H. L., see Billerbeck, P.

Talbert, C. H., *Luke and the Gnostics*, Nashville 1966.

—— An Anti-Gnostic Tendency in Lucan Christology, NTS 14/1967–1968, 259–271.

—— *Literary Patterns, Theological Themes and the Genre of Luke–Acts*, Missoula 1974.

—— The Redaction Critical Quest for Luke the Theologian, in D. G. Buttrick (ed.), *Jesus and Man's Hope*, Pittsburgh 1970, 171–222.

—— *What is a Gospel?*, Nashville 1977.

Thackeray, H. St. J. (translator), Josephus' *The Jewish War*, Loeb edition, London/Cambridge, Mass. 1928.

Thompson, G. H. P., *The Gospel According to Luke*, Oxford 1972 (The New Clarendon Bible).

Trocmé, E., *Le 'Livre des Actes' et l'Histoire*, Paris 1957.

Trompf, G. W., *The Idea of Historical Recurrence in Western Thought*, Berkeley/Los Angeles/London 1979.

Turlington, H. E., Review of *Die Mitte der Zeit* of H. Conzelmann, *JBL* 76/1957, 321.

van der Minde, H.-J., *Schrift und Tradition bei Paulus. Ihre Bedeutung und Funktion im Römerbrief*, München 1976 (Paderborner Theol. Studien, 3).

van Unnik, W. C., Luke–Acts, a Storm Centre in Contemporary Scholarship, *SLA*, 15–32.

—— The 'Book of Acts' the Confirmation of the Gospel, in *Sparsa Collecta* Part I, Leiden 1973, 340–373 (originally in *NT* 4/1960, 26–59).

—— Éléments artisques dans l'évangile de Luc, in F. Neirynck (ed.), *L'Évangile de Luc, Problèmes littéraires et théologiques, Mémorial Lucien Cerfaux*, Gembloux 1973, 129–140.

Vielhauer, P., Zum Paulinismus der Apostelgeschichte, *EvTh* 10/1950–1951, 1–15.

—— ET, On the Paulinism of Acts, *SLA*, 33–50.

Vince, C. A., and Vince, J. H. (translators), Demosthenes, Loeb edition, London/Cambridge, Mass., II 1926.

Weder, H., *Die Gleichnisse Jesu als Metaphern*, Göttingen 1978 (FRLANT, 120).

Wegenast, K., *Das Verständnis der Tradition bei Paulus und in den Deuteropaulinen*, Neukirchen-Vluyn 1962 (WMANT, 8).

Weiβ, B., *Die Quellen der synoptischen Überlieferung*, Leipzig 1908.

—— *Die Quellen des Lukasevangeliums*, Stuttgart/Berlin 1907.

Wikenhauser, A., and Schmid, J., *Einleitung in das Neuen Testament*, Freiburg/Basel/Wien [2]1973.

Wilckens, U., Interpreting Luke–Acts in a Period of Existentialist Theology, *SLA*, 60–83.

—— *Die Missionsreden der Apostelgeschichte*, Neukirchen-Vluyn [3]1974 (WMANT, 5).

—— *Der Brief an die Römer*, vol. 1 (Röm. 1–5), Zürich/Neukirchen-Vluyn 1978 (EKK, VI/1).

Williams, C. S. C., *Alterations to the Text of the Synoptic Gospels and Acts*, Oxford 1951.

—— The Date of Luke–Acts, *ExpT* 64/1952–1953, 283ff.

—— *A Commentary on the Acts of the Apostles*, London [2]1964 (Black's New Testament Commentaries).

Wilson, S. G., Lukan Eschatology, *NTS* 16/1969–1970, 330–347.

—— *The Gentiles and the Gentile Mission in Luke–Acts*, Cambridge 1973 (SNTSMS, 23).

Wlosok, A., Die Rechtsgrundlagen der Christenverfolgungen der ersten zwei Jahrhunderte, in R. Klein (ed.), *Das Frühe Christentum im römischen Staat*, Darmstadt 1971 (WdF, 267), 275–301 (originally in *Gymnasium* 66/1959, 14–32).

—— *Rom und die Christen. Zur Auseinandersetzung zwischen Christentum und römischem Staat*, Stuttgart 1970.

Zahn, T., *Das Evangelium des Lukas*, Leipzig/Erlangen [3,4]1920 (Komm. z. NT, 3).

Zingg, P., *Das Wachsen der Kirche. Beiträge zur Frage der lukanischen Redaktion und Theologie*, Freiburg (Schweiz)/Göttingen 1974 (Orbis Biblicus et Orientalis, 3).

Zmijewski, J., *Die Eschatologiereden des Lukas-Evangeliums. Eine traditions- und redaktionsgeschichtliche Untersuchung zu Lk. 21:5–36 und Lk. 17:20–37*, Bonn 1972 (BBB, 40).

—— Die Eschatologiereden Lk. 21 und Lk. 17. Uberlegungen zum Verständnis und zur Einordnung der lukanischen Eschatologie, *Bibel und Leben* 14/1973, 30–40.

Index of Biblical Passages

Old Testament

New Testament

Mark (contd.)

Luke

Luke (contd.)

Luke (contd.)

Acts (contd.)

Acts (contd.)

Index of Passages from Ancient Writers

Index of Authors

1/58 = Chapter 1, footnote number 58,
212 = page 212 of the text.